THE MAYA ROAD

The Maya Road

Jim Conrad

BRADT PUBLICATIONS, UK
HUNTER PUBLISHING, USA

First published in 1992 by Bradt Publications, 41 Nortoft Rd, Chalfont St Peter, Bucks SL9 0LA, England. Distributed in the USA by Hunter Publishing Inc., 300 Raritan Center Parkway, CN94, Edison, NJ 08810.

British Library Cataloguing-in-Publication data

A catalogue record for this book is available from the British Library

Front cover photo: Temple of the warriors, Chichén Itzá, by Jim Conrad, and waterfall (Belize) by Alex Bradbury
Illustrations by Jim Conrad
Maps by Patti Taylor
Typeset from the author's disc by Patti Taylor, London NW10 3BX
Printed by Guernsey Press

ACKNOWLEDGEMENTS

The author thanks Joseph R. Quiroz and Brian L. Houseal of The Nature Conservancy for background information on conservation programs in the Ruta Maya area. Joann Andrews, President of the Yucatán Chapter of PRONATURA, provided much-appreciated encouragement and advice. Thanks to Dr. Sigrid Liede for the best proofreading a native German-speaker could provide.

From none of the establishments or people mentioned in this book were courtesies requested or received, except from the Micklers at Maya Mountain Lodge in San Ignacio, Belize, who generously gave me some meals, a bed, and the use of their scrub board and clothes-drying line, for which many thanks.

PREFACE

At first, just lying on the beach in sunshine and wind can be enough. After long months of humdrum and grind, the spirit and body simply may need to unwind, decompress, ignore reality... Sun, wind, sand... good.

However, eventually regular tourist life becomes boring; what earlier was soothing and romantic grows monotonous and superficial. The time comes when the traveler must raise his or her head off the beach towel, gaze inland and wonder what lies beyond the wall of seaside hotels.

What if... What if, in the exotic-looking stores and restaurants a few blocks off the tourist strip, you could actually *talk* with these interesting people in their own fast-paced, softly ebbing and flowing, musical language?

What if somehow you could wander deep into the countryside, completely away from the tourist zone's high-priced, artificial environment, and among your host country's average folk, in small towns, villages and the countryside, follow your own itinerary? Arrange your meals and lodging according to your own special tastes, and not according to arrangements set down in a pre-packaged, mass-produced, tourist plan?

And what if you knew enough about this country's natural history that you could walk into any of its forests — even those with wild orchids on tree branches, and toucans and parrots chattering high in the trees — and begin understanding why things there are as they are, and thus feel at home in the jungle?

What if, as you traveled across the landscape, you could relate to the changes in vegetation, geology, climate, the indigenous language being spoken around you, the vestiges of historical events... in such a way that on an aesthetic level the differences were like variations upon a melodic theme, occurring in a vast, lovely symphony brimming with wondrous tone textures and combinations?

What if eventually you should return to your home having changed so much that many things that once were alien and fearsome to you now evoked feelings of admiration and, sometimes, even love... ?

These are the expectations of eco-tourism...

TABLE OF CONTENTS

PART ONE
Chapter 1: ECO-TOURISM ON THE RUTA MAYA   1
What is Eco-Tourism? 1, The Word Itself 1, Two Ways to Discover
Sugar-Cane Stems 1, Putting Eco-Tourism Theory into Practice 3,
Specimen Ruta Maya Experiences 8, Miscellaneous Traveler's Tidbits
11, Prices 11, Maps 11, Traveling Cheaply 12

Chapter 2: TRANSPORT ALONG THE RUTA MAYA   13
Automobiles 13, Trains 15, Buses 16, Miscellaneous Bus-Riding Facts
16, More On-the-Road Hints 21, Not More than Three Items 21,
Backpacks 21, The Makeshift Sleeping Bag 22, Clothing 23, Packing
Odds and Ends 25

Chapter 3: FOOD   27
Alternative Eating Styles 27, Cooking Gear 27, Fancy Eating 27, Maya-
Road Soul Food 28, *Mercados* and *Comedores* 29, More Special Hints
for On-the Road Eating 31

Chapter 4: WHERE SHALL WE SLEEP TONIGHT?   33
Camping 33, At the Ruins Themselves 33, In Isolated Areas 33,
Camping in Small Villages 35

Chapter 5: HEALTH AND SAFETY   37
Health 37, Diarrhea 37, Cholera 38, Amoebic Dysentery 38, Malaria 39,
Rabies 40, Hepatitis A 41, Heat Stroke 42, Sunburn 42, Bee Stings 42,
Bots 43, Ticks 43, Chiggers 44, Snakes 44, Scorpions 45, Tarantulas
46, Intestinal Worms 46, Ear Fungus 46, The Problem of Robbery 48

Chapter 6: TRAVELING WITH GOALS   51
Become an Amateur Mayanist 51, Add Bird-Species to Your Life List
52, Improve Your Spanish 54, Get a Handle on Tropical Ecology 55,
Help Us Keep this Book Updated 57

Chapter 7: THE MAYA LANDSCAPE   59
Continental Drift Sets the Stage 59, Ancient Climates 61, The General
Setting 62, The Southern Uplands 62, The Northern Lowlands 62

Chapter 8: PEOPLE OF THE RUTA MAYA   65
The Maya and European Settlers 65, The Maya are not Extinct 65, A
General Outline of Postconquest History 70, History like a Spicy Soup
70, Dividing Up the Indians 70, Man and Nature along the Ruta Maya
72, Languages of the Ruta Maya 74

Chapter 9: FUNDAMENTALS OF MAYA ARCHEOLOGY   **77**
The Prehistoric Development of Maya Civilization 77, Ice-Age Precursors 77, "Archaic" Cultures 78, The Preclassic Period 80, The Classic Period 81, The Postclassic Period 83, Maya Architecture 85

Chapter 10: MAYA ART   **87**

PART TWO: RUTA MAYA DESTINATIONS   **91**

Chapter 12: THE YUCATÁN PENINSULA   **93**
The Setting 93, Geography 93, Biology 94, The People 96, Places to Visit 99, Campeche State 99, Xpuhil 99, Becan 100, Chicaná 102, Hormiguero 102, Río Bec 104, Calakmul 105, Escárcega 106, The Road between Escárcega and Campeche 106, Edzna 107, Hopelchén 110, Dzibalchén 110, Hochob 111, Dzibilnocac 112, Nohcacab 113, Tabasqueño 113, Tahcob 113, Xtacumbilxunan Cave (Bolonchén Cave) 113, Yucatán State 115, Sayil, Xlapak and Labná 115, Kabáh 118, Uxmal 119, Mérida 120, Celestún 122, Río Lagartos 124, Chichén Itzá 127, Balankanche Cave 130, Quintana Roo State 131, Punta Laguna 132, Cancún 132, Playa del Carmen 133, Cozumel Island 134, San Gervasio 138, Xcaret 139, Xelha 139, Tulum 140, Sian Ka'an 142, Cobá 143, Chetumal 145, Crossing to Belize 147, Kohunlich 147

Chapter 13: BELIZE   **151**
The Setting 151, Geography 151, Biology 152, The People 153, Places to Visit 155, Santa Elena: Border Town 155, Corozal 156, Santa Rita 157, Cerros 158, Orange Walk 159, Cuello 159, Nohmul 161, Lamanai 161, Crooked Tree Wildlife Sanctuary 163, Altun Ha 164, Belize City 169, The Barrier Reef/Caye Scene 169, The Community Baboon Sanctuary 170, The Belize Zoo 174, Guanacaste Park 174, San Ignacio 178, Cahal Pech 180, Caracol 180, Xunntunich 181, Benque Viejo: Crossing Point 182

Chapter 14: GUATEMALA   **183**
Northern Guatemala (Petén) 183, The Setting 183, Geography 183, Biology 183, The People 184, Places to Visit 185, Melchor de Mencos: Border Town 185, Naranjo 187, Yaxhá, Topoxte and Nakum 191, Flores 196, Santa Elena 198, The Sayaxché Area 199, Dos Pilas 200, Aguateca 200, Altar de Sacrificios 201, Yaxchilán 201, Seibal (El Ceibal) 201, Tikal 203, Uaxactún 204, The Gringo Perdido and Family 205, Poptún's Finca Ixobel 206, Upland Guatemala and Copán 209,

The Setting 209, Geography 209, Biology 210, The People 211, Places to Visit 214, Río Dulce (El Relleno) 214, Quiriguá 214, Copán in Honduras 217, The "Mario Dary Rivera" Quetzal Reserve 221, Kaminaljuyú 225, Iximché 227, Zaculeu 229, The Crossing between Guatemala and Chiapas 229

Chapter 15: CHIAPAS 231
The Setting 231, Geography 231, Biology 231, The People 232, Places to Visit 236, The Southern Highlands 235, Ciudad Cuahutémoc: Border Town 235, Lagunas de Montebello National Park 235, Chinkultic 237, San Cristóbal de Las Casas 237, The Tzotzil Highlands 241, Zinacantán 243, San Juan Chamula 244, Mitontic 245, Chenalhó 245, Chalchihuitán 245, Amatenango del Valle 245, Grutas de San Cristóbal 245, Ocosingo 246, Toniná 247, The Cascades of Agua Azul 248, Misol-Ha 249, Palenque 249, The Northern Lowlands 255, Bonampak 255, Lacanhá 258, Yaxchilán 260

BIBLIOGRAPHY 263

LIST OF BOXES

A truck is a lorry 2
Don't give gifts; interact like a friendly neighbor 4
Spanish words creeping into everyday English 5
Bicycling Mexico 14
Miscellaneous helpful remarks for the back-country traveler 22
Tortillas 28
Four starchy staples 30
The guanacaste tree 34
Miscellaneous useful Spanish sentences 55
How plants succeed in the humid forest and rain forest 56
Leaf-cutter ants 58
How the weather may have affected Maya history 60
Tropical ecology: miscellaneous considerations 63
Why did classic Maya society collapse? 66
Books written by the Maya 72
Maya language groups 73
Famous names 75
Maya agricultural systems 79
Rethinking the Maya 82
Notes on some special trees 95
How do you pronounce "Xpuhil"? 96
The Río Bec, Chenes and Puuc architectural styles 108
Birds you might see around Uxmal and nearby ruins 119
Gulf-coast turtles 125
The Itzá and Mayapán 128
Bacalar and the Cruzob Cult 146
Belize: a different history, a different language 152
Acorn woodpeckers 167
Are there really baboons in Belize? 171
Road conditions in the Petén district 188
On the art of navigating braided trails 190
Handling army checkpoints 194
Chicleros 195
Tayasal 197
Is all jade green? 209
Aid for Highland Indians 213
Guatemala's sweetgum trees 217
Lichens 222
Upland Guatemala's language schools 223
Lago Atitlán's flightless grebe 225
Pedro de Alvarado 228
A visit to Reserva Ecológica Pronatura 240
THe mushroom eaters at Maya Bell 252

PART ONE

Before You Go

What is the Ruta Maya?

In this book the Ruta Maya follows the same 2,400-km (1,500-mile) route described in the article "La Ruta Maya," by Wilbur E. Garrett, in the October, 1989 issue of *National Geographic* magazine. It is a figure-eight route drawn so that travelers can visit as many of the region's major Maya ruins as possible, using already-existing roads.

"La Ruta Maya" is also a regional *plan* developed around the idea of providing jobs and income to people in the Ruta Maya region by increasing environmentally oriented tourism in a sustainable, nondestructive way.

Other maps and publications define the Ruta Maya differently. This is neither surprising nor grounds for contention. Not only does diversity lie at the heart of eco-tourism, but as new highways are built and new discoveries come to light, the viability of the Ruta Maya concept will depend upon its ability to evolve appropriately with the times.

The Ruta Maya's most prominent features are its emphasis on the Maya region's archaeology, present-day cultures and ecology, and its absolute respect for diversity and sustainability.

Note: This book is titled *The Maya Road* to make its subject instantly recognizable by English-speaker readers. In the text I use the Spanish *Ruta Maya* which is the term you will hear in the region itself.

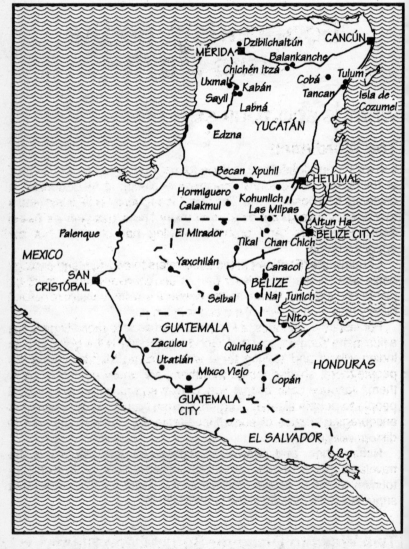

Mayan ruins along La Ruta Maya

Chapter 1

Eco-tourism on the Ruta Maya

WHAT IS ECO-TOURISM?

The Word Itself

If there's a good definition for "eco-tourism," I haven't seen it. In fact, at this stage of the tourist industry's evolution, if "eco-tourism" is anything, it's a loaded term. The term "eco-tourism" is *in*. If last year a tour agency was known as Sam's Luxury Tours, this year it's called Sam's Eco-Tours. And probably nothing has changed but the agency's name.

Certainly the "Eco" part of the word refers to ecology, and ecology deals with nature, so at least part of eco-tourism's focus must be plants and animals. However, the average traveler considers natural history only as one slice of the eco-tourism pie.

For instance, Jacques, a French Canadian who recently gave me a ride in the Yucatán, said that "Good eco-tourism is like going into an Indian village and staying for a while. Making friends among the people there, sharing things with them, and really getting to know them." Jacques believes that eco-tourism embraces an unequivocal people-to-people element. I agree, though I question the wisdom of encouraging hordes of superfluous folks like Jacques and me to disrupt village life.

Nature, then, and people... Good eco-tourism requires of the traveler a special sensitivity to these two ingredients. However, eco-tourism seems to be even more than this. Here are two stories that suggest what's missing in the final definition:

Two Ways to Discover Sugar-Cane Stems

Along much of the Ruta Maya people walk around chewing segments

A Truck is a Lorry

Though this book is published in England, readers schooled in "British English" will soon realize that the writing is "American English." Author Jim Conrad was raised on a tobacco farm in the southeastern US state of Kentucky; he just can't refrain from calling a lorry a truck, and from removing the u from colour.

In case you learned your English someplace other than in the US, here's a brief list of English/American equivalents.

AMERICAN	BRITISH
apartment	flat
bathroom	lavatory
can tin	
candy	sweets
corn	maize
crackers	biscuits
gas(oline)	petrol
grain	corn
hood (of car)	bonnet
kerosene	paraffin
line (at bank)	queue
lumber	timber
molasses	treacle
round-trip	return
one-way	single
sidewalk	pavement
terminal	terminus
vacation	holiday
RV (recreational vehicle)	motor home

of sugar-cane stem. With a machete or knife the hard, fibrous rind of a sugar-cane stem is peeled off, and then the stem's sweet, juicy, pulpy pith is chewed in big bites. Once the pith is sucked dry, it is spat out. Of course, though a good stem is delicious, chewing cane habitually ruins the teeth. Anyway, during my most recent trip along the Ruta Maya, twice I watched travelers discovering sugar-cane-chewing for themselves.

The first instance was at the shelter beside Belize's Altun Ha. A group of US visitors on an agency-organized day-trip had just finished inspecting the ruin. As they prepared to enter their van for a quick drive and flight back to their hotel on Ambergris Cay, the tour leader reminded everyone that part of their package included "a little surprise." The surprise was that each person would get to learn about eating sugar-cane stems.

On cue a local Creole man approached the group, explained that he brought the advertised surprise, and with a machete began carving his sugar-cane stems into manageable segments, stripping off the bark and distributing the canes. Well, carrying off the "little surprise" was so methodical, so lacking in spontaneity — and everyone was so hot, sweaty and dog-tired after clambering about the ruins — that no one seemed interested in learning about cane-chewing. Moreover, the Creole man, who was clearly well educated, gave the impression that he was embarrassed to be seen making his living cutting sugar-cane segments for tourists. In short, the whole sugar-cane experience fell flat.

In contrast, a few weeks later in San Cristóbal de las Casas I noticed a German couple animatedly discussing something that caused them to laugh, shrug their shoulders and scratch their heads. Finally the pair crossed the street and approached an old man carrying long, cylindrical objects that looked like purple-stemmed bamboo. In very hesitant Spanish the woman asked, "¿Qué es eso?" — "What's that?" "Caña," replied the old man, with a big smile and raised eyebrows.

Together the travelers searched in their Spanish/German dictionary for the word caña; finding it, they exclaimed, "Ach, so!" and laughed, and asked how much a segment cost. As they dug into their pockets, the old man made a show of neatly shaving off the hard rind; he even pantomimed how to take big bites, chew the pulp and swallow the juice, and finally spit the dry pulp into the gutter. In short, this cane-eating experience was definitely a pleasant, memorable one.

Putting Eco-Tourism Theory into Practice

Once you step off the bus or out of the plane, feel the heat, breathe the heavy, humid air and see the gorgeously different world around you... how does eco-tourism theory translate into on-the-ground reality?

Of course, each of us develops his or her own traveling strategies and demeanor; doing so is part of the fun of traveling and lies at the heart of eco-tourism's challenge. However, here are some miscellaneous thoughts on the matter, mostly for those for whom traveling independently may be a new experience.

Relating to people along the Ruta Maya anywhere other than in the English-speaking parts of Belize absolutely requires that you involve yourself with the Spanish language. If you can't speak it, then at least you should be able to show people that you're vigorously trying to learn it. On page 55 the basics of learning Spanish are discussed.

During the years before I became fluent in Spanish I developed

Don't Give Gifts; Interact like a Friendly Neighbor

If you set up a tent beneath someone's orange tree in an isolated village probably that night you'll be visited by multitudinous kids and, even without being asked to do so, *señoras* may bring you bananas, tortillas smeared with bean paste, and cups of coffee. This wonderful hospitality presents the visitor with a dilemma.

The natural tendency is to want to reciprocate the generosity by giving out little presents — ballpoint pens, postcards, and other knickknacks — and certainly the locals will be happy to receive these. Unfortunately, experience shows that such gift-bestowing visitors sour things for future visitors. Once the gift-giving custom is established, in the future hordes of kids will expect such presents from all visitors. Later visitors won't enjoy a moment's peace; sometimes kids who don't get what they want may even pilfer. What once was a pleasant give-and-take can become a tense stand-off between mutually disappointed parties.

Instead of handing out trinkets, bring along a frisbee, a ball, or string with which to make cats-cradles, and play with people. If you have any artistic talent at all, carry a sketch book; you can draw your house and family, and invite the kids to draw theirs. If you carry fieldguides for bird identification, bring them out; especially country people enjoy finding the birds they know, for instance, telling you their local names, and maybe mimicking their calls. If you *must* give presents, give only to the adults, and present them with something practical in exchange for their services.

some rather deep-rooted and unfortunate opinions — prejudices — about Latins and their culture. Because of my inability to communicate with people around me, quite a few of my early "people-to-people" experiences were actually full-grown conflicts. Latin culture was something I *endured* so that I could enjoy good birding, a fascinating landscape, and decent weather during the northern winter! However, nowadays I can't think of Latin America without visualizing the faces of some of my best friends and remembering many experiences that have been critical for my own personal growth. Without a whole catalogue of episodes made possible by my Spanish, right now I'd feel much less self-confident and I'd certainly be a less interesting person.

It's very hard to properly eco-tour without allotting yourself adequate traveling time and flexibility. If a sugar-cane-discovering experience avails itself, you should have the time to gravitate to a shady spot in the Zócalo, sit for half an hour or so, chew and spit, talk with your friend, and "do it right." It's even better if, upon deciding that you like

Spanish Words Creeping into Everyday English

campesino = farmer or peasant

cenote = a sinkhole — in limestone areas the result of collapsed underground passageways (caves)

colectivo = a van or microbus operated along an established route, usually in or near a town

colonia = small settlement or village

comedor = eatery — one level less formal and less expensive than a cheap restaurant

cumbe = a van or microbus

Don = If you wish to be respectful to a mature man, especially an older one, whose name is Fernando Fulano, but you don't want to be so formal as to appear unfriendly, you may call him Don Fernando

Doña = the feminine equivalent to "Don"

finca = ranch or farm

frijoles = beans, usually black ones; sometimes they come in the form of a refried paste good for smearing onto tortillas; other times you get a bowl of watery, entire beans

gringo = foreigner

huipil = the attractive, traditional loose blouse worn by Indian women

ladino = anyone who has adopted Western clothing, customs and ideas, regardless of whether he is racially Indian or *mestizo*

mercado = marketplace — the kind with goods, especially fruits and vegetables, heaped in stalls; stores with canned foods are *supermercados* or *tiendas de abarrotes*

mestizo = people of mixed Indian and European stock

milpa = cornfield; frequently used as an adjective describing slash-and-burn agriculture resulting in cornfields that are abandoned after two or three years

refresco = soda-drink, such as Coke, Pepsi or the like

Señor = Mr, sir, man/ *Señora* = Mrs, madam, woman/ *Señorita* = young, unmarried woman or girl

tamale = form a tortilla into a kind of envelope, stuff the envelope with a small quantity of chicken meat, refried beans or some other goodie, neatly wrap the whole thing inside well-tied cornshucks or banana leaves, thoroughly steam the creation, and you have a tamale...

tortilla = flat, round, thin, white "bread" made of corn (or wheat if they're store-bought); the epitome of Latin "soul food," especially when smeared with bean paste and eaten with fresh, green chili

tortillaría = where tortillas are born; it's worth visiting one just to see the ancient, rumbling, gesticulating, dinosaur-like machine begetting the tortillas

San Cristóbal much better than you thought you would, you're able to stay a few extra days.

Of course, many travelers just don't have much time. This brings up the question of whether it's better, if you only have limited time, to cover a lot of territory and see things superficially, or to visit only a small number of places, but settle in while you're there. In my opinion, real eco-tourism requires choosing the latter option. We benefit from eco-tourism's different traveling philosophy *only* when, with sensitivity, respect and intelligence, we interact with the world around us. If we're trying to meet schedules and we feel as if we're being dragged along by a mass of indifferent humanity it's just human nature for "sensitivity, respect and intelligence" to get kicked out the window!

Once you're off the main tourist routes you need a special understanding of the host country's customs, traditions, attitudes, and the general ways that things get done — for your own safety and convenience. For example, an experienced traveler would not plan to take the bus from Flores to Guatemala City, intending to catch a jet home the very next day. Buses traveling roads like the Petén's frequently break down, or get mind-bogglingly mired in mud holes, or simply don't run because of *fiestas*, strikes, sick drivers or the unavailability of gasoline. Before entering a foreign culture the traveler should read books and talk to others who have traveled there before.

Pre-travel homework also sensitizes us to our host-region's biology and landscape. For example, because of the giant cacti it's hard to miss the fact that Guatemala's Motagua Valley harbors a unique vegetation. However, it takes someone who's done some background study to get a bang out of spotting Cozumel Island's endemic Cozumel vireo. We need to know beforehand that on the whole earth the Cozumel Vireo is found *only* on Cozumel Island. This means that we should know enough about birds in general to recognize that this species's extremely limited distribution is something special. Moreover, if we're familiar with other species of vireo, we can recognize what's special about our bird's appearance, behavior and habitat preference. The Ruta Maya is incredibly rich in rare, unique and otherwise interesting things; however, their rareness, uniqueness and interesting nature only become apparent after background research. Without background information, the Cozumel vireo is just a mousey-looking little bird.

At the risk of sounding patronizing, it should be emphasized that when we enter another culture, usually it's our responsibility to change to accommodate the culture, and not the other away around. For instance, at Latin banks, sometimes we stand in line for an hour or more for services that back home would be handled in a minute. Check-cashing travelers often become so frustrated that they make scenes. This does no one any good.

As a general rule, when things fall apart at banks, bus stations, restaurants, etc., unless someone is obviously trying to rip us off or is endangering us — and away from tourist zones this seldom happens — when frustration strikes we should just take deep breaths and accept what's happening as a kind of character-building yoga. Pull out a paperback and re-define the lost-time experience as quality reading time.

Here is eco-tourism's inescapable paradox: If eco-tourism at a rarely visited destination becomes popular, a touristic infrastructure develops, and eventually crowds of visitors diminish the thing they've come to see. Despite recognizing that this process has happened again and again, and will continue to happen, I make no apologies for publicizing isolated, rarely visited locations in this book. That's because all through the Ruta Maya region attractions are being destroyed at a phenomenal rate. Ruins are being looted, swamps are being drained, sprawling rural slums are appearing along pristine rivers, very steep mountain slopes are succumbing to slash-and-burn and immense acreages of lowland rainforest are being converted to weedy cow pastures... If something isn't done *quickly*, everything lovely along the Ruta Maya soon will be profoundly damaged or destroyed. This is not hyperbole; you'll see for yourself.

Thus, along the Ruta Maya, the decision is *not* between keeping something wonderful and unvisited, or diminishing a destination's charm by encouraging eco-tourism; it *is* between doing nothing at all as everything lovely is destroyed, and at least trying to save it through the eco-tourism route.

Time and again it's become apparent that simply declaring natural areas to be reserves and biospheres is not enough; biosphere boundaries mean nothing to a man needing money that selling a baby monkey can bring. But if the man's friends and neighbors tell him that those monkeys need to be left alone because *gringos* leave hard cash in the community when they come to see them, then that's a powerful deterrent working on behalf of the monkey, the entire ecosystem, and the local human community.

Finally, enjoying the full potential of eco-tourism requires of the traveler a certain *spark*, a kind of being alive, an *élan* that can hardly be described. Someplace in the *Tao Te Ching* it's written that "That which can be explained as the Tao, is not the Tao." With such a light stroke I'll allude to that evasive essence that enables certain people to blossom on the open road.

SPECIMEN RUTA MAYA EXPERIENCES

To give you an idea of what traveling along the Ruta Maya is like, here are some miscellaneous memories from my most recent trip.

Chachalacas

Camped near Campeche's isolated ruins of Hormiguero, one morning I'm startled awake by the raucous calls of several nearby chachalacas — large, very loud birds looking like brown, streamlined wild turkeys; they're frequently hunted for food. Chachalacas make two kinds of call. One is squeaky and high-pitched, reminiscent of the humorous kind of voice a Sesame-Street character might use, and it seems to be yelling "Knock-it-off, knock-it-off!" Another voice, obstreperously gruff and low-pitched, replies, "Keep-it-up, keep it up!"

Gringo pobre, gringo viejo...

In Poptún, Guatemala, one morning I'm buying a kilo of tortillas from a Mopán Indian woman. She and her friends standing nearby watching the transaction are surprised that a foreigner is buying tortillas instead of eating in a restaurant. As I stand there, a young woman next to me, dressed in colorful and richly decorated traditional clothing, whispers to her companions, "Gringo pobre, gringo viejo," which sets everyone around us laughing, because it means "Poor, old gringo." When she realizes that I heard her, and that I understood her Spanish, she is highly embarrassed. "Oh, *señor*, I mean nothing by saying that," she gushes. "It's just that your buying our cheap tortillas reminds me of a wonderful movie from your country called "Gringo Pobre, Gringo Viejo!"

Army Ants

After pegging my tent in the forest near the ruins of Quintana Roo's Kohunlich I hear a strange rustling on the forest floor around me. Peering through my tent's "windows" covered with mosquito netting, I see battalions of army ants swarming toward me. The army, consisting of several ever-advancing ant-streams — each stream several ants wide — flows over and around my tent; as they accumulate beneath my flaps I thump the nylon, sending them scurrying. After about 15 minutes, all is calm again, with no sign of any ant.

The Miracle of Language

On the Guatemalan/Honduran border near the ruin of Copán, I spot an elderly tourist with a very distressed look on her face; I ask if she needs help. "I need a bathroom in the worst way," she grimaces, "but I can't find one." Within 30 seconds, speaking to those around us in Spanish, I locate the bathroom, pay for use of the key, and set the grateful lady on her way. I can hardly imagine a better example of the advantages of speaking at least a little of the language of the country you're visiting!

Resplendent Quetzal

At Guatemala's quetzal reserve, we are eight foreigners — three from the US, two Canadians, two Germans and a Frenchman — each going our own way. Then someone spots a male quetzal landing in a tree in plain view. We all cluster together in the best viewing spot, oohing and ahing, and simply becoming breathless when the wind unfurls the bird's 90cm-long (three-foot), intensely emerald-green tail feathers. In these moments all nine of us are made into brothers and sisters, and we are *all* resplendent!

Five Banana Peelings

Waiting for a city bus on a busy Guatemala City street, I manage to eat five bananas; then find myself holding the peelings with nowhere to throw them. I look everywhere and walk around the corner, but of course there are no trash-cans. Suddenly, as I'm about to yield to the urge to throw them into the street with other trash, the door behind me opens, a little girl with huge eyes and a trash-can rushes up to me, I drop the peelings into the can, and the little girl rushes back inside, having never said a word.

Those Primitive Lacandón Indians

On the gravel road leading to the mud trail to the ruin of Chiapas's Bonampak, a sputtering pickup truck eases past me and coughs to a standstill ten meters down the road. Barefoot, with long, black hair, and wearing the traditional flowing, white gown, a Lacandón Indian jumps from the truck's cab, props open the hood, fiddles with the engine, jumps back into the truck, starts it back up, and pulls away.

Chol Time

On a bus parked in heavy sunshine somewhere between Palenque and Bonampak, while the driver nonchalantly eats his lunch as we passengers wait for him, mostly sleeping in the awful heat, I half-listen to two Chol-Maya Indians squatting in the bus's shade below my window. Embedded in the stream of Chol words being spoken suddenly I hear the Spanish phrase, "*hora y media...* ," meaning "hour and a half." In my sleep-trance suddenly the insight dawns that in the Chol language of course no words exist for chopping up time the way we foreigners do. For an instant I glimpse the world in which the Chol language evolved, where nature was untamed and a concept of time existed insisting that time was not a linear thing, but rather something cyclical, causing time's passage to be mere illusion; since all events are destined to be repeated, in the end all will be as always it has been. This flash of insight jolts me into a full awakening. But, now I've lost it. I'm just hot and sweaty, stuck in a stifling bus, while outside my window two men, wearing straw hats and rubber boots, gossip within a ramshackle bus's meager shade.

MISCELLANEOUS TRAVELER'S TIDBITS

Prices

All prices in this book are quoted in U.S. dollars. The main reason is that prices given in local currencies, mostly because of inflation, quickly become out of date. Also keep in mind that most locations covered in this book are in rapidly evolving "frontier" areas where prices are especially vulnerable to fluctuation. Newly paved roads can swiftly bring down the prices of canned goods in stores; floods washing out bridges can cause the prices of gasoline and bus tickets to jump; political problems can cause boat-motor replacement parts to soar sky high, taking the costs of river trips with them.

Maps

The main inspiration for this book was the article, "La Ruta Maya," by Wilbur E. Garrett, appearing in the October, 1989 issue of *National Geographic* magazine. Accompanying distribution of that issue was a 51 X 69cm (20 x 27 inch) map called the "Land of the Maya A Traveler's Map." That map locates all the archeological sites described in this book. In usual *National Geographic* fashion the map provides much more than mere map data; it locates the main centers of each Maya language group, the locations of National Parks and biotopes, gives brief descriptions of major sites, etc. Frequently in this book reference is made to it.

The most up-to-date and detailed maps of the area I have seen are the *Traveller's Reference Map of Yucatán Peninsula* and *Guatemala and El Salvador*, both published in North America by International Travel Map Productions, P. O. Box 2290, Vancouver, B.C., V6B 3W5, Canada; in Europe they are distributed by Bradt Publications. These maps cover the entire Ruta Maya area; the Yucatán one includes plans of Chichén Itzá, Palenque, Uxmal, Tikal, Tulum and Cancún, and the Guatemala one has insets of Tikal, Quiriguá, and Zaculen (Huehuetenango), along with an enlargement of the Guatemala City area.

If you use these maps keep in mind that all the red lines do not signify passable roads; here, even Guatemala's quagmire-trail from Melchor de Mencos to Naranjo is designated as a "seasonal road, track, etc."! Several trails and ruins I've never heard of are located on this map. Moreover, some trails are shown that I know to be overgrown and no longer passable. This map pushes detail to the limit and for the serious back-country Ruta Maya traveler is simply a must.

Traveling Cheaply

Some guidebooks are aimed at that breed of traveler who wanders foreign lands with the goal of spending as little money as possible. Though this guide shares some traits with those books (We extol camping, visiting relatively cheaper out-of-the-way places, shopping in *mercados* where fresh food is not only better tasting and safer but also less expensive...) this book is not of the spend-as-little-as-you-can genre.

Consider the situation in Cancún. There, approximately 80% of money spent by vacationers ends up in the pockets of people other than local Mexicans. A goal of eco-tourism is to funnel money to local people — local guides and local artisans, the lady in a rustic *comedor* who prepares fried eggs, black beans, rice and tortillas in front of us... instead of to far-way administrators of international hotels and restaurants.

This makes sense because, in the end, local people have more to say about whether their local attractions remain intact than do far-away administrators. When in Xpuhil we hire Checo Riou and some of his crew to guide us to Río Bec and Hormiguero, we're saying very clearly to everyone in Xpuhil that the forests and ruins in that area are valuable as they are, and therefore should be protected from illegal logging, uncontrolled settling, and tomb-looting. Money talks, and the more money we eco-tourists spend in out-of-the-way places, the more likely the things we care for will survive.

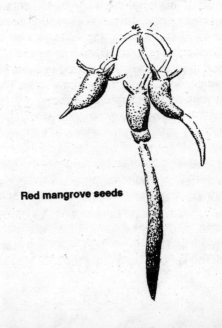

Red mangrove seeds

Chapter 2

Transport along the Ruta Maya

AUTOMOBILES

For motorized travel along the Ruta Maya, nothing beats bus travel, in my opinion. However, if your Spanish isn't up to par, you just don't like buses, or you're simply a car-oriented person, a car may be your favorite option. Before I learned how to master the bus system, I drove my own car several times in this area without disastrous consequences. However...

Other guidebooks tell you the difference between *Nova* and *Extra*, and how to buy insurance at the border, so I'll tell you about the time I was on a six-lane super-highway entering Mexico City. As I approached town, contrary to what I expected, traffic began thinning out. When finally I was the only car on the highway I became suspicious enough to slow down to a crawl. This was fortunate, for as I crossed the peak of a hill, right there not 200 meters away, the six lanes simply ended at a modest barricade. There hadn't been a single sign announcing the highway's end!

Open, unmarked manholes, monstrous breaks in the pavement in the middle of busy streets and roads, cows and burros bolting from roadside bushes, other vehicles on the road without brake lights or any lights at all, police/army checkpoints in the most unlikely places... "Stay alert" is an understatement. "Don't drive at high speeds," and "Don't drive at night," more than mere common sense, are survival tactics.

Sometimes mere vigilance isn't enough. For instance, once I barely made it into a town because my engine was coughing and sputtering, apparently from dirty gas purchased earlier. At a service station I asked for an additive that would clean out the carburetor; the fellow started to pour something into the tank he said would work. But I asked to see the can first; it was brake fluid. My car used unleaded

Bicycling Mexico

The Ruta Maya can be biked! Moreover, much of the route in the Yucatán Peninsula and Chiapas is covered in the excellent guide *Bicycling Mexico*, by Ericka Weisbroth and Eric Ellman. In Europe and the US this book is distributed by the same people who market the *Maya Road*, so if you found this one you should be able to find that one.

Bicycling Mexico provides detailed descriptions of eight trips in the Ruta Maya area — four in the Yucatán Peninsula and four in Chiapas. These trips take in most of the Mexican ruins mentioned in this book. Because the Yucatán's landscape is fairly level, roads there are the best in Mexico, and because on most roads in the Yucatán traffic is light, the authors consider the peninsula to be bikeable even by less experienced cyclists. On the other hand, they don't hide the fact that biking in Chiapas can be tough. Not only are the roads there frequently difficult to manage, but much of Chiapas is mountainous. One trip, from San Cristóbal to Tuxtla, is entitled "Cycling for the Non-Pedaler," because 47 of the 83 kilometers traveled are downhill. If Chiapas is bikeable, I'd say that Belize and Guatemala also are, though I personally would hesitate to try the Petén's gravel roads.

So few places in Mexico rent bikes that the authors advise bringing your own. However, bringing your own bike can present problems. The authors tell this story:

A fellow on the US East Coast bought a new bike, boxed it up and transported it unassembled to El Paso. But when he tried to get the boxed bike across the border he was refused entry; customs said it looked too much like something he planned to sell. So the biker went back onto US soil, assembled his little beauty, muddied it up, and rode across the border with no problems. The authors also suggest that sometimes a US$5.00 "tip" can help; if that doesn't work, wait for the border guard shift to change.

Mexico is well equipped with repair shops, and mechanics do good jobs patching things together in unorthodox ways. To write their book Ericka and Eric rode mountain bikes because they were more versatile. However, they report meeting people successfully using every kind of bike from single-speeders to many-speeders to recumbents. One fellow from India was going around the world on a one-speed!

Bikes must be boxed when shipped by air. The authors say that in Mexico it's hard to find a proper box when you want to fly your bike out of the country. In Mexico City they say you can find boxes at the "Benotto" Bicycle Factory at Calz. de Tlalpan, no. 744. Bikes can be transported on bus, train and ferry without being boxed.

gas but this station didn't sell that. "Do any other stations in this town carry unleaded?" I asked my brake-fluid friend. "No, we're the only station within 50 kilometers," he replied. After buying half a tank of leaded gas, as I left town I passed a brand new station selling unleaded gas.

Taking a vehicle across borders also makes us a little more vulnerable to "border surprises." A while back I saw a Canadian standing next to his big RV at a Mexican customs station on the Texas border. He wanted to spend the winter at an RV campground near Guadalajara, and now he was distraught. "The customs man says that either I pay a US$350 tax on my RV's electricity generator, or I have to leave it here!" the man explained. "Before I came down here I read all the regulations but I never read anything about this!" I suggested that he try another crossing station, or wait until the customs shift changed. Or maybe offer $10 or so to the agent to take a second look at the law, and maybe there'd be some kind of loophole.

One way to avoid border-crossing surprises is to rent a car. At all the main airports you'll find car-rental agencies well represented. Be sure before you leave an agency's garage that you have a spare tire and equipment with which to change a tire; also test the lights, and stop and start the engine several times. Drive around the block and test the horn and brakes. If you do rent a car you should carry with you a screwdriver set, an adjustable wrench, pliers, and a pocket knife. If you know absolutely nothing about simple car repair (change tires, replace jogged-loose radiator hoses, scrape battery terminals...), and especially if you plan to drive in out-of-the-way places, you should take along someone who does know these things.

TRAINS

The last time I took a train in Chiapas it chugged into the station exactly 12 hours late; the time before that my train didn't come at all; the time before that, it only arrived four hours late, but for two hours during the trip I had to stand beside a stinking toilet, and while standing there I was told that on the same route the day before the engineer had become drunk, speeded up, and lost the train's entire first-class section somewhere in Oaxaca.

Nonetheless, the first several times we northerners ride Latin trains, the experience is usually so colorful and interesting, and our fellow passengers are so *friendly*, that afterwards we're glad to have had the experience. However, my opinion is that riding trains in the Ruta Maya area is so hit-and-miss that I'd be misleading you by advising you about schedules, connections and procedures.

BUSES

Though in some places along the Ruta Maya roads are a bit bumpy or, rarely, even impassable, busing infrastructure throughout the region is fairly good to downright excellent. For those of us from the car-oriented US where most medium-sized and small towns are not even served by buses and where sometimes it's cheaper to fly than to take a bus, bus service along the Ruta Maya is a tremendous bargain.

First-class buses along the Ruta Maya usually run on time. Even rickety buses plying back-country roads are surprisingly punctual. Perhaps even more important than being on time is the fact that the bus driver and his ticket-taking helper, as well as the baggage handlers at terminals, usually behave in a very professional manner. Here's an often-seen second-class-bus example:

A bus approaches a *campesino* standing along the road beside a big sack of beans; the bus stops and by the time the rider is aboard the bus-driver's helper has jumped outside, literally run with the sack of beans to the back of the bus, and as the bus surges forward, the helper already has stored the bag and is running to leap back into the moving bus. In Guatemala, the helper may be atop the vehicle tying down the bag, and once the bag is secure, with the bus moving at full speed, he may slide over the side of the bus and swing into the open door.

Miscellaneous Bus-Riding Facts

A first-class ticket from Nuevo Laredo, on the Texas/Mexico border, to Poza Rica, Veracruz — a 7½-hour trip of about 900km (600 miles) — costs approximately US$12.75.

● In many towns, especially smaller ones, no specific building serves as a bus terminal. *El terminal* may consist of nothing more than a gravel area next to the municipal market, or an unmarked parking area on a street where buses habitually park, load and unload passengers.

● In Mexico, distinctions are usually made between first-class and second-class buses, though sometimes the differences are hardly apparent to outsiders. In general, first-class buses cost a little more than second-class ones, are less likely to stop along the road for anyone who flags them down (and thus travel faster), and in them you're more likely to have a seat number assigned, which ensures that you won't be standing. The cost differential between first-class buses and perpetually stopping, wondrously full second-class ones is so small that it's best to go first class if time is a factor, even if you're on a shoestring budget. On the other hand, second-class bus rides often provide very memorable and colorful experiences, and are true to the spirit of eco-tourism. In the Ruta Maya, only in Mexico are distinctions habitually made between first- and second-class tickets although major routes in Guatemala (eg from Guatemala City to Flores or Puerto Barrios) may have first class buses.

• In larger towns, first-class and second-class terminals are frequently in different places. For example, you may arrive at the first-class ADO terminal in Villa-hermosa, heading for Palenque, only to find that for the rest of the day no tickets are available. Don't despair; just ask where the second-class terminal is, walk a few blocks, and there you'll find a variety of bus lines offering service either all the way to Palenque, or to an intermediate destination, where you'll be able to take another bus that will carry you closer.

• Departure times on bus-company schedule-boards usually are noted in the European system. Thus 6am is shown as 600 or 0600, and 6pm is 1800.

• To catch a bus from alongside the road, wave your arm up and down or simply hold your arm at about 11 o'clock, with your hand open. Keep signing for the bus to stop until you're absolutely sure the driver intends to do so, for often when a bus draws close enough for the potential passenger along the road to read what's printed in the destination window above the windshield, the passenger changes his or her mind, stops motioning, and the driver interprets this as meaning that the person no longer wants the bus to stop.

• Many buses, instead of originating at the terminal in which you're buying your ticket, are only passing through — you'll get a ticket on these buses only if a seat is available. Buses just passing through are said to be traveling *de paso*. If your bus is coming *de paso* and it's a first-class bus, you must wait until it is announced before you can attempt to buy a ticket. First-class buses arriving *de paso* are sometimes full (especially on weekends and holidays) and then you just have to wait for another one; on second-class buses they can always squeeze in one more passenger.

• When you pay for your ticket it's possible that you'll be asked to pay a little more than what's posted. If you bring this to the agent's attention, inevitably he'll mention taxes, service charges, or maybe that the posted prices are simply out of date. In view of the crush of humanity desperately trying to get tickets, unless the price is outrageously higher, it's probably just best to let it slide.

● The ticket agent may write your bus's number on your ticket; later you can look for this number painted next to your bus's entrance door. Instead of giving you the bus's number, the agent may provide the gate number or bay number in which the bus is parked. And it's quite possible that the agent won't know any of this information, and you'll just have to figure it out for yourself.

● When your ticket is handed over, confirm that the date (*fecha*) and time (*hora*) are correct. The price you paid is the *valor*, and your seat number is given in the box marked *asiento*.

● When you find your bus, if you have a backpack, instead of getting into line to enter the bus, go stand beside the baggage bay (In Guatemala and Belize stand behind the bus, making sure that the attendant sees you). Eventually the attendant should tag your bag and give you a baggage check. On first class buses don't worry about others getting on the bus before you; if you have a seat number, you're guaranteed a seat. On second-class buses, having to wait outside to store your baggage is a problem unless you have a friend who can enter before you, and claim two seats.

● Inside the bus, seat numbers usually appear in little windows on the side of the baggage rack over the passengers' heads. Inside the windows you may see something like "VENT 18 PAS 19." This means that the window seat is #18 (VEN for *ventana* means "window"), and the aisle seat is #19 (PAS for *pasillo* means "aisle"). If you were issued no seat number, you can sit (or stand) wherever you wish.

● In Mexico, backpacks and other large parcels are stored in the bays below the passengers, between the front and rear wheels. In Belize, usually the rear door is opened and backpacks are stored inside the bus, behind the last seats; in Guatemala, most of the time backpacks end up atop the bus, where the attendants are almost always conscientious about strapping them to railings so they don't fall off. In Guatemala, if you see other passengers riding atop the bus with your backpack, you should go on top yourself to make sure your bag is not robbed. In general, just keep valuables out of your backpack whenever you must be separated from it.

● In Guatemala, but not in Mexico and Belize, most bus lines expect you to give your ticket back as you leave the bus; the attendant may even come during the trip to punch it or just look at it.

In Belize the buses are usually long, yellow US-style "school buses." Since Belize has as many *topes*, or speed bumps, as Mexico, if you don't like to be bounced around, you should sit toward the bus's front. When the bus's rear wheels hit a bump, everyone sitting behind the rear axle instantly learns the true meaning of "the catapult effect."

● In old buses, sometimes the curved metal sheets forming the ceilings do not exactly meet because their rivets have been jarred loose. This causes a delicate situation for tall *gringos*, for if a scalp is moving toward a low-hanging sheet, it'll probably leave a patch of skin and hair there. Moreover, those ceiling lights can bruise what isn't scraped away. Hats help.

● Bus trips in the Ruta Maya are fairly informal, laid-back affairs; during the trip, *groove* with the bus driver's mariachi music being played on the tapedeck mounted above the windshield next to the decal of the Virgin of Guadalupe and beneath the red-bangled curtain, and when vendors at intermediate stops stream onto the bus or gather outside windows selling not only *refrescos*, but also plastic bags of peeled oranges, roasted peanuts, hot tamales wrapped in corn shucks, local sweetbreads... *enjoy* (taking precautions mentioned later with regard to diarrhea)!

● Here are some phrases that come in handy when buying bus tickets:

"*Un boleto para el autobús que sale a las nueve para Mérida, por favor.* "A ticket for the bus that leaves at 9:00 for Mérida, please."

"*Qué es el número de mi autobús?*" "What's my bus's number?"

"*¿Es este el autobús que sale a las nueve para Mérida?*" "Is this the bus that leaves for Mérida at nine o'clock?"

"*Si usted oye el anuncio para Mérida, ¿puede usted avisarme?*" "If you hear the announcement for Mérida, will you please let me know?"

"*¿Sabe usted cual autobús va a Mérida?*" "Do you know which bus goes to Mérida?"

"*¿Ya ha llegado el autobús para Mérida?*" — "Has the bus for Mérida arrived yet?"

MORE ON-THE-ROAD HINTS

Not More than Three Items

It's not possible to maintain an agreeable on-the-road demeanor and to feel free and unencumbered if you're enslaved to great bulks of luggage; also, nothing ruins a trip more than losing one or more of your belongings. My most effective rule for avoiding these disasters is this: I never carry more than three items.

Over the years I've discovered that travel disasters — robberies, forgetting things, breaking handles — occur at specific times, especially at those moments of confusion such as when you're buying a ticket or trying to find the right bus; at these critical moments my mind, which I assume to be fairly average in these matters, simply cannot cope with keeping track of more than three items. The three items are: a backpack carrying the great bulk of my belongings; a food-bag; and, the bag holding what I don't want stolen from my backpack, exclusive of money and documents, which are in bags strapped to my body. In practice, usually the third bag holds my camera equipment.

Backpacks

My backpack tends to be larger than most because I travel with a tent, bedding and usually a goodly number of books — especially field guides for the identification of plants and animals. Nowadays most backpacks come with interior frames. Metal exterior frames are vulnerable to breakage during transit and are hard to handle in tight situations. Padded belts that snap together in front are a must for heavy packs destined for long hikes because they distribute much of the weight away from shoulder muscles, onto the hips and rump.

Some backpacks without lots of compartments are like big bags into which everything can be dumped. The advantage of these is that large, irregularly shaped objects can be packed (tripods, bowls, etc.), with other items fitted around them. My backpack is divided into two compartments, with the one below accessible from a zippered flap opening from the back, and the top attainable by lifting a large top-flap that ties down. Into the top goes all clothing and "miscellaneous" items; into the bottom go camera equipment, books, batteries and other heavy items. Because of weight-distribution dynamics, heavy items need to go as low as possible in backpacks. My tent and bedroll ties beneath the backpack.

Side pockets hold toiletry items and, during long walks, inside a waterproof bag, my documents and money. (On long hikes, if money or documents are kept on the body, they become soaked with sweat.) Also in these side pockets I carry canteens. I try to keep two canteens

Miscellaneous Helpful Remarks for the Back-Country Traveler

• All along the Ruta Maya, never assume that any bathroom will be equipped with toilet paper.

• It should be considered a general impossibility, for more than a few hours, to carry ripe bananas in a soft bag without smashing them into a brown, slimy mush.

• Along trails, hikers should stand aside for horses and not make sudden moves, or the horse might bolt.

• Don't sit on logs without first checking for snakes. Sometimes snakes rest beneath a log's loose bark or just under the log, right behind the sitter's heels.

• Away from tourist areas, especially when changing money at banks, avoid accumulating large bills. Buses, *mercado* salespeople, and even small-town restaurants and hotels usually don't have change. "*Si es posible, hágame el favor de darme el dinero en billetes pequeños, por favor — no más grande que ___.*" — "If possible, please give me the money in small bills not larger than __."

• If you plan to snorkel or dive, and have a mustache or beard, use vaseline to plaster down your facial hair, so air won't escape beneath the mask.

• When driving behind a truck you can't see around, if the left rear-light blinks, that means "It's safe to pass."

• In Mexico, on Sundays, the ruins are free. On the other hand, at the entrance to many Mexican ruins stands a sign saying, "For commercial photography, movie camera and/or use of a tripod, a permit is required from 'La dirección de asuntos jurídicos del I.N.A.H.' Córdoba No. 45, México 7 D.F." Happily, camcorder-toting tourists need not go to Mexico City for a permit. Simply pay the ruin's custodian or ticket office an extra US$5.00 for each tripod and an extra US$8.00 for each camcorder. This rule is in effect even for tiny ruins without much to photograph.

full of pure water in reserve, as well as a large bottle in my food bag. You sweat a lot on the trails and in most back-country places it's hard to find adequate clean water — even clean enough to put purification tablets in.

The Makeshift Sleeping Bag

On the Ruta Maya my personal preference is to travel without a sleeping bag — though sometimes I do wish for one. Especially because carrying ample water and several field guides make my bag heavy, I consider all sleeping bags too heavy and bulky; besides, most of the time along the Ruta Maya it's warm enough to get by with a simple lightweight blanket. However, during the northern winter, cold snaps do occur throughout the Ruta Maya and if you're in a hammock on the beach at Playa del Carmen or even in a tent at tropical Tikal, if you're sleeping in summer clothing and a light blanket you can become desperately cold; sometimes the temperature drops to 8° C. (45° F.) or colder!

On those occasional cold nights when my light blanket is not enough, here is how I construct a "makeshift sleeping bag": I add layers of regular clothing, including wooly socks kept dry just for sleeping, a hooded pullover, and a one-piece jumpsuit that covers me from neck to ankles. Then atop my thin blanket, which is wrapped around me cocoon-like three times, I spread a lightweight poncho made of PVC. This thin layer of PVC does an amazing job trapping warm air beneath it.

Nor do I carry a sleeping mat or an inflatable cushion to fit beneath the hips; they simply are too bulky and weigh too much. However, I know people who say they can't sleep on ground without them.

Clothing

I carry two ponchos. One is old and a little holey, and it gets spread beneath the tent to keep the tent's floor from becoming perforated. The other is the one that on cold nights goes atop my makeshift sleeping bag, and which is my main protection against rain and cold wind. PVC ponchos are preferable to fancy Goretex models because all along the Ruta Maya spines abound, and snagging anything made of Goretex is like scratching fine silverware. Goretex costs an arm and a leg, but my made-in-China, 132 x 203cm (80 x 52 inch) PVC poncho cost US$1.99.

My one-piece jumpsuit also gets lots of use. I don't really understand the dynamics of heat exchange in the human body, but I do know that having my body's midsection well protected from wind seems to provide more protection than I'd expect.

Hats also work mystical heat-retaining wonders. Years ago I settled on traveling with berets because they store easily, don't have brims that snag on things, and because on trains and buses they can be pulled over the eyes during night-trips. However, a while back I got into trouble with a Guatemalan soldier who said that only guerrillas wear berets. He confiscated mine and since then I've been wearing sock-tops and baseball caps, which aren't nearly as travel-worthy.

This brings up an important point. Not only should you avoid wearing berets, but *anything* that even remotely suggests a military affiliation. By no means wear clothes ornamented with camouflage patterns. Khaki is wonderful, but soldiers like it, and therefore khaki is to be avoided.

Camping books always seem to insist that travelers in the tropics should wear white shirts of 100% cotton, because such shirts are cool, they dry quickly, and their whiteness reflects the sun's radiant energy. That's all perfectly true, but a problem with 100%-cotton fabric is that it's too delicate. If for a couple of days you wear a 100%-cotton shirt down a typically spiny-palm-rich rain-forest trail, 100% cotton will disintegrate on your back. Moreover, though the whiteness certainly reflects radiant energy, it also shows every speck of dirt and mildew.

My favorite jungle-walking shirts are plaid ones made of 65% polyester, with only 35% cotton. The polyester is so strong that though the shirts are only a single, very slender thread thick, they're tougher than cotton shirts and nearly as cool. Since they're plaid instead of white, filth and mildew don't show up so badly. In hot weather, heavy polyester is stinkingly awful but when the material is exceedingly thin, it's OK.

For trousers I like brown (not military-like khaki) or gray ones, with lots of pockets. Bluejeans are hot and show filth; after a couple of days of trail walking, they acquire a disgusting sheen. If you have lots of pockets, in one pocket you can carry a bird guide, in another you can keep peanuts to nibble on, in another you can keep an extra camera lens, etc.

In tropical heat shorts are an option for easy walks. However, if you're hiking muddy, weedy trails like the one to Nakum, or narrow paths between structures scattered in the woods at such places as Kohunlich, trousers are necessary. Mainly protection is needed from spines on plant stems. In the tropics, even seemingly innocuous scratches, if not adequately cared for, can become seriously infected. Shorts also leave your legs exposed to insects and ticks.

Hiking boots should provide good ankle and arch support. Some people swear by "jungle boots," but I find them too heavy. Though it's true that boots with canvas upper parts tend to rot and fall apart, they also dry easily. Gortex and nylon upper parts also are nice, but it's a shame the way they get shredded in the thorn-rich Ruta Maya area. Soles should be soft enough not to slip on wet rocks, and they shouldn't be so deeply chinked that they collect loads of mud. Many schools of footwear-thought exist and probably the only thing they all agree on is the need for good ankle and arch support.

Concerning all other clothing articles, such as underwear, I'm sure you'll have your own preferences. Some people insist that on long hot hikes it's much cooler to omit underwear altogether (keeping a dry set for evenings). I tried that once and came up with a painful below-the-belt equivalent to "jogger's tit." Women fare better, however. Remember that in more humid areas it's often hard to dry washed or sweat-saturated clothing, and after a day or so moist clothing begins to mildew.

Finally, at the end of a day, if it's a bit chilly, it's nothing less than wonderful to sleep in a clean pair of fluffy, dry socks and other sleeping wear. In my backpack, in their own little plastic bag, I always keep one pair of hand-knitted wool socks and some 100% polypropylene longjohns, which never are allowed to become dirty or sweaty. Even the thickest socks, if the least bit sweaty, lose an incredible amount of their capacity to insulate.

Packing Odds and Ends

Whenever I've taken a towel into the Ruta Maya area, it's been more trouble than it was worth. Any cloth that doesn't dry completely and quickly becomes contaminated with stinking mildew, and when you're on the move towel-drying can be an awkward task. Instead of a towel I carry several bandannas — large, usually red or blue handkerchiefs of the type that movie-cowboys wear. After bathing, one bandanna can take the body from being wet to simply moist ("dry" would be too much of a luxury), and the bandanna — a single layer of cotton threads — dries quickly. If it doesn't completely dry before camp is broken, it can be tied to the backpack. Hilary Bradt also uses bandannas to strain the ingredients of on-the-road ginger beer, to make cream cheese from curdled milk, and to collect unusual insects.

Finally, two items I always carry with me are binoculars and a small hand lens, or magnifying glass. Binoculars needn't weigh too much. My little 9 x 25 Nikon Travelite II's weigh only 300g (11oz). Unfortunately, such small glasses have very narrow fields of vision so that unless you're well practised it's hard to spot what you're aiming at; it's like shooting from the hip. If you are unpractised using small binoculars then it's best just to lug along big, heavy ones; nothing is more frustrating that trying to spot a quetzal or howler monkey, and seeing only blurry leaves.

Not only will a hand lens provide an endless source of fascination for kids, but also it'll open up to you all kinds of new vistas — orchid flowers' complex anatomies, crystal faces in minerals, insect mouthparts, sori on fern fronds... If you buy a hand lens in a jewellery shop it can cost you dearly. Sometimes you can purchase them in university bookstores. In the US I buy mine in toy-store detective kits. That way I get a badge and false moustache, to boot.

Chapter 3

Food

ALTERNATIVE EATING STYLES

Cooking Gear

Many travelers planning to do a little camping automatically shove into their pack some kind of stove. If you simply can't get going without a hot cup of coffee or a hot breakfast, then I suppose you have to do it, but I find that because of the weight and bulk of cooking paraphernalia, I'm happier to reserve all my hot meals for restaurants. If I awaken in a tent, I'm simply content with pouring some water into a cup with powdered milk, and then eating whatever happens to be around, whether it's peanuts, animal crackers, tortillas, fruit or something else. In isolated places hot meals are a luxury, not a necessity. Comes the crack of dawn I'd rather be birding or breaking camp than wrestling with cooking.

Fancy Eating

At the tourist-information booth in Mérida, maybe you'll discover that Mérida is "the gastronomical capital of the Yucatán." If you patronize Mérida's restaurants certainly you'll learn about *huevos motuleños*, (a breakfast of layers of black beans, ham, and fried eggs on crisp tortillas, topped with a spicy red sauce); there's also *pavo en relleno negro* (turkey in black sauce), *cochinita pibíl* (pork cooked in a tangy vinegar-laced sauce), *longaniza* (the local sausage), and plenty more. What could be more fun than sampling such exotic dishes? Eat them all! However, fancy eating is the domain of traditional guidebooks, not this one, so where food is concerned, in this book I'll focus on what most other guidebooks neglect — what's available locally to carry you through those times when you're not being fancy.

Tortillas

Among the Ruta Maya's Spanish speakers, no food is more ubiquitous, easy to obtain and generally inexpensive than the tortilla. In the poorest areas, calories from tortillas keep people alive; tortillas are the Latin staff of life.

Traditionally, tortillas are made this way: Uncooked grains of corn are put into a large pot of water and lime. Frequently this is done in the afternoon; a fire is set beneath the pot, the water boils, and overnight the lime softens the corn kernels, the kernels soak up water, and the next morning the grains are about twice their original size, and soft.

Originally stone mortars and pestles were used to grind the softened kernels into a paste, but nowadays even poor folks have metal grinders; as the handle is turned, softened grains are poured into the grinder's funnel, and paste that comes out is called *masa*. The *masa* is then patted into flat, thin, circular discs, which are baked atop sheets of metal.

Though in Guatemala most tortillas continue to be made by hand (the best-tasting kind), in most of the Ruta Maya they're made by large, clattering, dragon-like machines in buildings called *tortillarías*; the machines form and bake the tortillas in one quick operation. These businesses can be found on any mid-morning, in almost any town, big or small, just by walking down the street listening for the roar made by gas burners quick-baking the tortillas, and the metallic clanking sound made by the machine, and by sniffing for the wholesome odor of baking *masa*.

In Mexico, one kilo of machine-made tortillas contains about fifty tortillas; in Belize, one pound of tortillas numbers about 35. In both countries one tortilla costs about 1¢ US. In Guatemala, tortillas generally are sold one at a time and each costs about 4¢ (but they're bigger).

And here's the main thing I want to say: At least once in your life you should try eating a fresh, hot tortilla wrapped around one of those little, thin-skinned, sweet bananas... !

Maya-Road Soul Food

The diets of all the major indigenous American civilizations, from Aztec to Maya to Inca, were based on the triad of corn (maize), beans and squash. Apparently this precise combination is no accident. Both corn and beans are equipped with incomplete assemblages of amino acids; but when eaten together their arrays of amino acids complement one another so that inside the body they combine to form a complete protein. Squash adds vitamins and minerals.

Probably no great culture could ever develop with its members eating just corn, or just beans or just squash. One wonders how many civilizations languished simply because the amino acids in their staple foods were not complementary... In the vicinity of Belize where African-rooted Creole Caribbean culture takes more pleasure in rice and beans than in corn and beans, the protein-makes-for-success theory is supported because rice and beans *also* carry complementary amino acids!

All through the Spanish-speaking portion of the Ruta Maya the quintessential soul-food meal is tortillas, black beans and scrambled eggs — *tortillas, frijoles y huevos revueltos*. Usually scrambled eggs are seasoned with sautéed onions, tomatoes and chili pepper. For my taste, eggs without these exact ingredients are inadequately seasoned. However, if you can't stand chili, you can ask for eggs "*sin chili*" — without chili pepper. By the way, in Mexico such eggs are sometimes referred to as *huevos a la bandera* — "flag eggs" — because the red, white and green Mexican flag is the color of tomatoes, onions and chili peppers.

Of course, if you buy prepared food from roadside peddlers, or find a local *señora* to provide your eggs, beans and tortilla meal, or if you eat in a really "rustic" *comedor* or restaurant, you do need to worry about hygiene. Don't buy food that isn't scalding hot, or cannot be peeled, shucked or somehow have its germ-carrying surface completely removed. It would be an education for you, at least once during your trip, to sit and watch what food peddlers do with their hands before handing their customers food... Piping-hot *elotes* — sweet corn skewered on wooden sticks — are OK if you're handed them by the stick. Fruits with even tiny punctures in their rinds or husks constitute invitations to diarrhea.

Mercados and *Comedores*

In nearly every town there's a *mercado* where fruits, vegetables, nuts and other items are sold in open stalls; here you can buy rainbows of foods to add diversity to a basic corn-and-beans or rice-and-beans diet. Foremost among *mercado* fruits, for me, are the bananas. In Latin America you'll find a remarkable diversity of bananas, from short, thin-peeled sweet ones to long, thick-peeled pulpy ones. Sometimes in *mercados* you'll spot special seasonal fruits. Frequently these are from the forest, — such as the chicle tree's *chicozapote*, and the *mamey*, which sweetly melts in the mouth — both surely favorites of the ancient Maya.

Comedores deserve special attention because they constitute yet another secret to colorful and nutritious eating. A *comedor* is an eating place a level lower than a full-fledged restaurant. Frequently it amounts to a *señora* renting an open-sided stall in the *mercado* or along a busy street, where she fixes meals that are simpler, less likely to be equipped with eating utensils, and cheaper than those found in

Four Starchy Staples

At a market if you see what looks like a pan of more or less cylindrical gobs of white potato, probably you're seeing the boiled tuberous roots of *yuca*, *Manihot esculenta*, a member of the spurge family. It's a "poorman's staple" through much of the tropical world. *Yuca* has nothing to do with the yucca of the US Southwest. Sometimes *yuca* is called manioc; cassava and tapioca come from it. The *yuca* plant itself is similar in appearance to the unrelated marijuana plant. A serving of this excellent starchy food, with a dash of optional hot sauce, costs only about 5¢ US. Unfortunately, people selling *yuca* generally use their fingers, which probably are less than sterile.

Another starchy staple is the *elote* — sweetcorn boiled and sold in its original shuck, or roasted shuckless over a fire. When you peel back the shuck of a boiled *elote* that's still steaming hot, you can be sure that it's safe to eat. Sometimes *elotes* are offered with mayonnaise or butter (which may be less sterile). *Elotes* roasted over a fire usually are hygienically served on a wooden stick. The roasted ear may be drenched with lemon juice, then sprinkled with salt and chili powder.

Common sweet potatoes — about 15cm (six inches) long, reddish or orangish and tapering at both ends — are frequently sold boiled and ready to eat. Sometimes they're baked in wood fires, sold with ashes still sticking to their skin, and somewhat scorched. Though such potatoes look risky, if the skin is removed the sweet flesh is safe and delicious. If you want a sweet potato ready to eat, be sure that what you buy already is cooked. It should be soft to the touch. If you're offered sweet potatoes you can ask "*¿Son cocidas?*" — "Are they cooked?"

If you see a baseball-sized, egg-shaped, light-green fruit with low, blunt, softish prickly skin, that's a kind of squash, and one of the most important foods for Native Americans all through the American tropics. In Mexico it's called *chayote* but in Guatemala it's referred to as *huisquil*. Cooked, it's an excellent ready-to-eat food; just peel off the leathery skin. The flesh tastes more like white potato than what we Temperate Zoners call squash. I like to eat the big seed, too. In the *mercado* they're usually displayed raw and uncooked, but if they're offered from a *señora*'s basket they'll be cooked and edible as is. By the way, the *huisquil* vine, frequently planted in cornfields, can grow 15 meters (50 feet) per year and produce 50 to 100 fruits! Its flowers and tender buds can be eaten and its tuberous roots can be cooked as potatoes. An infusion of its leaves is said to lower the blood pressure, and to combat arteriosclerosis.

restaurants. Though probably the *señora* will have to run out looking for eggs, most any comedor will provide you with the standard Ruta-Maya soul-food meal of *frijoles, tortillas y huevos*. If with your meal you receive no knife, fork or spoon, you're expected to scoop up the beans and eggs with half of a tortilla, then eat the tortilla along with its load. Just watch how your companions at the table do it.

More Special Hints for On-The-Road Eating

On long walks or stays in isolated areas, two foods are especially fine companions because they are so lightweight and do not putrefy after a couple of days of heat and humidity. One of these is roasted peanuts, a fine source of protein. Bags of peanuts frequently are available in *mercados* at reasonable prices.

Mexican animal cracker *Galleta hippopotomi*

The other special food — and as a health-conscious vegetarian I'm fairly embarrassed to recommend it, though it has brought me through many long stays in wild places — is something available in almost any Mexican canned-food kind of supermarket (but not in Belize and Guatemala). It's incredibly cheap, surprisingly tasty, not vulnerable to going stale, and is nothing less than... animal crackers. I'm talking about small, sweetish (not salty) crackers made of white flower and sugar, and shaped like giraffes, hippopotamuses, bears... Usually they sell for less than a dollar a kilo. Why in Mexico they're so cheap, ubiquitous and good-tasting, I don't know. Sometimes when the stomach is upset and revolting at all food, a few Mexican animal crackers will stay down when nothing else will. Ask for "*animalitos — las galletas dulces...* "

By the way, tortillas kept more than a couple of days in a plastic bag will sour; kept in a knotted bandanna they become stale and remarkably hard.

Sometimes when you're in isolated places for extended periods you worry about getting enough protein. Usually even small stores in isolated places are equipped with condensed milk, (*leche evaporada*, and powdered milk, (*leche en polvo*). You can get used to them; in fact, I've actually developed a fondness for them. More than once I've survived for several weeks at a time eating nothing but animal crackers, powdered milk and vitamin pills. My energy level and health stayed remarkably stable! Just for the sake of comparison, here is some nutritional data gleaned from the US Government Printing Office's "Home and Garden Bulletin No. 72":

food	amount	grams of protein
potato	1 baked, peeled	4
banana	1 banana	1
apple	1 raw	trace
powdered and evaporated milk	1 glass	8
shelled peanuts	1 cup	37
corn (maize)	1 cup (an ear)	2
egg	1 egg	6
chicken	6.2oz/176g	42

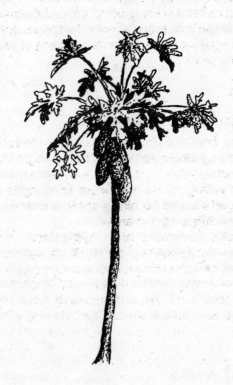

Papaya
Carica papaya

Chapter 4

Where Shall We Sleep Tonight?

Plenty of clean, comfortable and eminently pleasant hotels, lodges and pensions are found all along the Ruta Maya — even in places off the usual tourist routes. However, pointing travelers toward nice hotels is the domain of traditional guidebooks. I focus on options available when evening approaches and, for one reason or another, a "nice hotel" isn't in the picture.

CAMPING

At the Ruins Themselves

At most Mexican and Guatemalan ruins along the Ruta Maya camping is allowed in the parking area or elsewhere *outside* the ruin proper; usually this is not so in Belize, though Altun Ha is a notable exception. At the time of writing, at no ruin where camping is permitted are campers charged a fee for pitching a tent in or near the parking area, or even for spending a night in an RV.

However, with custodians and night-guards at ruins, tips — *gratificaciones* — are always appropriate. At some of the more isolated ruins you feel as though the custodian is permitting you access to his almost-personal domain; sometimes, as with Sr Ignacio Ek Dzul, who at Kohunlich took over the custodianship from his father who discovered the ruin, that's almost true. Here *gratificaciones* feel obligatory.

In Isolated Areas

Sometimes at the end of a day of traveling between the more isolated ruins you can find yourself near neither a ruin nor a town with a hotel. In such areas it's seldom hard to find a good camping spot. Deeply shaded forest floors are usually rather open and park-like.

However, most forests along the Ruta Maya are secondary (cut over) and therefore somewhat scrubby; in arid northern Yucatán even mature forests are scrubby, dense and spiny. Tent-pitching sites are usually accessible in such forests by following abandoned timber roads and footpaths made by local people.

During my many years of camping in Latin America's isolated areas I've never had any trouble at all. That's because I always follow some very strict, self-imposed rules. I wait until dusk to put up my tent, don't make camp within a kilometer of anyone's habitation or field, and I assiduously abide by the rules of parks and reservations. I pitch my tent as far off the path or trail as possible — without wandering so far

The Guanacaste Tree

At many crossroads and parks throughout Latin America stand one or more immense guanacaste trees, *Enterolobium cyclocarpum*, a member of the bean family. During the dry season, when usually it loses its leaves, it looks rather similar to another favorite tree-giant, the ceiba. However, though guanacaste trunks are smooth and gray like the ceiba's, they're not as straight, cylindrical and massive. The guanacaste's twice-pinnate leaves are similar to acacia leaves. Sawdust from the guanacaste causes allergies in some people, and is poisonous to fish.

The guanacaste's heavy, black fruits are flat, ear-like pods, not long, straight pods, as is typical in the bean family. Cattle relish eating these pods and the seeds can be toasted for human food. In fact, during years when beans and corn are scarce, the seeds make a nutritious emergency food. The tree's wood maintains its integrity in water, so guanacaste trunks traditionally have been used in the construction of boats and water troughs. However, none of its attributes are appreciated quite as much as the cool shade that pools beneath its widely spreading canopy.

away that when I break camp the next morning I can't find my way back! I don't make campfires.

I don't mind following these rules because I know that in an isolated area if I'm discovered by someone who is superstitious and fearful, drunk, involved in tomb-looting or drug-running, or desperately in need of a little cash, I can find myself in a heap of trouble. Besides following these camp-making rules, I also know to keep hands and feet out of places I can't see, and to use a tent that zips up so that not even an ant can enter.

For security reasons, I do not camp in isolated, unprotected areas that are immediately recognizable as perfect spots for camping. I never camp alone on isolated beaches, for instance, because everyone knows that campers like to pitch their tents next to the ocean; if a robber is looking for someone to hit, the beach will be the first place he looks.

Along the whole Ruta Maya, the best non-beach camping site I saw was right beside the ruin of Hormiguero. Breaking from deeply shaded forest, the trail ends beneath a widely spreading tree, with the main pyramid not 15 meters away. A much-used campfire area lies equipped with a circle of stones; seeing the spot, anyone visualizes himself or herself lying in the tent at night, dreamily gazing through the tent's "window" at the pyramid's monumental monster-mouth-entrance glowing other-worldly in the moonlight.

However, during my visit I camped in the forest where I could see nothing, and no one could see me. I knew that earlier that day as I had hiked through a village on my way there, everyone who saw me could figure out exactly where I was going, and that most of them knew about Hormiguero's "perfect camping spot." I didn't like the idea of a whole village knowing precisely where they could find me that night. Next time I visit Hormiguero, I hope it's with a group large enough that we can all sleep next to the pyramid feeling secure.

Taking all these precautions becomes worthwhile when in the night our sleep is accompanied by shimmering cricket sounds and the calls of pauraques, and when the next morning we awaken in a natural fantasyland, with chachalacas calling and, in the distance, howler monkeys roaring.

Camping in Small Villages

If you're really uncomfortable with camping in the forest, but you don't want to give up seeing the more isolated ruins, then it's almost always possible to find a nearby village where someone will rent you a tent-spot beneath a tree in their front yard. People are generally delighted not only to get a little extra cash, but also to meet foreign visitors; and you can be sure that you'll be vigorously protected and made to feel at home. For example, at the entrance to the Hormiguero road, in the village of Ejido Eugenio Echeverria Castellot Nº 2, I'm sure that someone will be happy to let you pitch a tent in one of the several grassy areas.

Chapter 5

Health and Safety

HEALTH

Diarrhea

We all know about the stomach cramps and diarrhea that seem almost inevitable when traveling in exotic places. Along the Ruta Maya travelers refer to the problem as *las turistas* or "Montezuma's revenge"; doctors call it gastroenteritis. The problem is mostly caused by a species of bacteria we all have in our intestines, called *Escherischia coli*. Usually our bodies' defenses keep this germ under control. Problems arise when we eat food contaminated by strains of *E. coli* different from the strain our bodies are equipped to handle. People who travel the Ruta Maya for several years usually develop a resistance to the region's various *E. coli* strains, thus acquiring the gift of being able to "eat with impunity."

Good anti-diarrheal "corks" are Lomotil and charcoal tablets (charcoal can be scraped off charred campfire-wood). If you find yourself without Lomotil or charcoal, don't worry, for Latin American towns are full of little *farmacías*. For regular cases of gastroenteritis, the best treatment is rest and lots of fluids. In especially bad cases, water and electrolytes (salts) lost from the body need to be replaced to prevent dehydration. A simple rehydration solution consists of four level teaspoons of sugar and a quarter teaspoon of salt for each half liter (pint) of liquid. No solid food should be eaten until symptoms subside.

Diarrhea is hard for newcomers to avoid. I'm fairly sure I've contracted cases from dust being blown down a street! However, here are some tips:

Avoid eating prepared items that aren't steamy hot. Don't eat fruit from which you yourself, with clean fingers, have not removed the peeling, husk or rind. Don't eat salads in restaurants and don't drink fluids with ice in them. (I've seen chunks of ice "made from purified water" pushed across perfectly filthy restaurant floors). Watermelons with tiny cracks and bruises are bad. Lukewarm stews are deadly.

Sometimes diarrhea is not caused by bacterium but by spicy foods — especially those laced with chili pepper.

Cholera

Cholera is always acquired by swallowing food or water contaminated with a bacterium — in this case a comma-shaped creature called *Vibrio cholerae*. Until fairly recently cholera wasn't a big problem in the Ruta Maya area. However, at this writing the disease is establishing a toe-hold here and I expect it to become a more serious problem as time passes. Often we hear of large numbers of people dying of cholera so *V. cholerae* has a nasty reputation. However, cholera is not really a deadly disease if simple treatment is provided.

If cholera becomes much more prevalent in the Ruta Maya area than it is now, then certainly before going there you should be inoculated. Cholera shots last for only about six months; moreover, they don't give 100% protection. In a cholera area you should drink nothing but bottled or well-boiled beverages, and you should avoid foods such as salads that may have been prepared by a sick restaurant employee. Don't eat shellfish, because they seem able to harbor the vibrio bacterium. I'd stay away from all foods that once spent their lives in possibly contaminated waters.

Cholera symptoms appear within one and five days after infection and consist mainly of diarrhea and vomiting. Of course, this sounds like the usual, relatively tame case of gastroenteritis and, in fact, the treatment for cholera is essentially the same as for very bad cases of Montezuma's revenge, as outlined above. In general, cholera produces more fluid loss through diarrhea so the rehydration salt/sugar liquid described on page 37 should be taken. If this doesn't seem to do the job, intravenous infusion may be necessary. Antibiotics such as tetracycline hydrochloride can shorten the period of diarrhea.

Amoebic dysentery

If diarrhea is recurrent and eventually the watery discharge becomes flecked with blood, you may well have amoebas, known to doctors as amoebiasis. Amoebas are free-ranging, one-celled animals that are tremendously more complex than any mere bacterium or virus; in Latin they're known as *Entamoeba histolytica*. Amoebas are acquired by drinking water or eating food contaminated with amoeba cysts.

Amoebic dysentery can be very dangerous if left untreated,

possibly causing abscesses in the liver or even in the brain. If you suspect amoebas, go immediately to the doctor. Tropical doctors are familiar with this problem and are accustomed to handling it; if you wait for your temperate-zone doctor to take charge you may be leaving yourself open to misdiagnosis and mistreatment. Once accurately diagnosed, treatment is easy and effective, using drugs such as metronidazole or iodoquinol. In bad cases it may become necessary to drain a liver abscess.

Malaria

Throughout the Ruta Maya area, contracting malaria is a real possibility; it's the single most important disease-hazard for travelers in warm climates. When I read how awful and how common this disease is, sometimes I begin wondering whether I should continue traveling in the tropics. However, I've been jaunting through malaria-infested areas for quarter of a century without acquiring the disease.

The parasites that cause malaria are single-celled organisms called plasmodia, belonging to the genus *Plasmodium*; they're transmitted to humans via the *Anopheles* mosquito. One quirky characteristic of *Anopheles* mosquitoes is that when they bite you, they rear forward and hike their hind legs up, as if really enjoying themselves. In some parts of the Ruta Maya, malaria is a worse problem than it was several years ago. This is largely because the *Anopheles* mosquito has evolved strains resistant to insecticides used to control it (mostly the environment-degrading DDT, banned in the US but still produced there in large quantities and exported); also, the malaria plasmodium itself has evolved strains resistant to the drugs used to combat it.

Travelers entering hot malaria spots generally visit their doctors a couple of weeks before leaving, get a prescription, immediately begin taking their antimalarial prophylaxis, continue the treatment during the trip, and maintain dosage until a little after coming back. For many years chloroquine has been the main drug. However, in some areas the malaria plasmodium has become resistant to chloroquine, so you may need to take something else.

Up to date information on malaria prophylaxis can be obtained free in North America by phoning the Center for Disease Control in Atlanta, Georgia at (404) 332-4559. They'll also tell you about any other outbreaks of any kind of disease in the area you're visiting. In Britain phone the Malaria Reference Laboratory at 071 636 7921 for a tape recording of advice on avoiding malaria in Central America.

The antimalarial drug scene is also messy because drugs don't really prevent malaria — they just control the symptoms. Malaria symptoms include fever alternating with chills, and headaches. Remembering the combination of alternating chills and fever is important; frequently I acquire bugs causing periods of recurrent fever, and always I suspect malaria. Happily, however, chills never develop, and that puts my mind at ease. The time between the mosquito bite and the appearance of symptoms is usually only a week or two, but if you've been taking antimalarial drugs it can take as long as a year.

To diagnose malaria properly, blood smears must be examined in a laboratory; the parasites are clearly visible under a microscope. If you suspect you have malaria while still abroad, you should visit a *local* doctor or clinic because of their familiarity with the specific strain of plasmodium in their area, and the medicines currently considered most effective. Of course, when you return home, you also can visit your own doctor, who certainly will be grateful for any information you can provide with regard to the plasmodium strain and what antimalarial drugs currently are being used.

The cornerstone of my strategy for avoiding malaria has been one piece of knowledge: The *Anopheles* mosquito is active at dawn and dusk. At these times I either make sure that I'm well covered with repellent, or I'm inside my mosquito net or mosquito-proof tent. If I'm in a hotel where doors or windows are left open, I string a net above my bed. And I have a *big* net — one that my feet won't

Anopheles
(malaria-carrying mosquito)

stick from under, and one inside which I can roll around, without my butt pressing against the net's wall, inviting an *Anopheles* blood-meal. The only traveler I know who has contracted malaria acquired it at dusk when he'd had too much to drink, and fell into bed without closing his window. By the way along the Spanish-speaking part of the Ruta Maya malaria is referred to as *paludismo*.

Rabies

All mammals, not just dogs, are vectors for this disease; they carry the rabies virus in their saliva. Along the Ruta Maya vampire bats are prime carriers. However, if you sleep in buildings without open windows and doors, in closed tents, or mosquito nets, vampires shouldn't be a problem. If you're bitten by a dog or other mammal, immediately begin gathering information. Ask the dog's owner if the animal has been acting strangely. Find out from local doctors if rabies is prevalent in the area; you may be a candidate for postexposure immunization. No longer are these shots painful ones into the abdomen; they are simple injections into the arm spaced over a three month period.

If you decide you need shots but you want to have them in your own country, you may do this if you are returning soon, for the rabies virus's migration along the nerves toward the brain is a slow one. If bitten on the face, dramatic and usually fatal symptoms appear as soon as two weeks after the bite, but if the bite was to a foot it may take months.

Vampire bat
Desmodus rotundus

Probably it is a good idea for the back-country traveler to be immunized for rabies (as well as tetanus), before leaving. Even if you are immunized and you are bitten, especially if the bite is severe or the wound is dirty and deep, you should seek medical attention.

Hepatitis A

While among traditional tourists hepatitis A usually is not an important disease, for those traveling in areas with low standards of hygiene the situation is sometimes bad. There is now an effective vaccine against hepatitis A. It is called Havrix, and two shots taken two weeks apart provide protection for a year. If you anticipate eating and drinking in places where you suspect hygiene standards are low, you are advised to have the shots.

Some years ago while staying in a Chol Indian village in Chiapas I contracted hepatitis A, and regard it as by far the most serious health problem I've ever had. Hepatitis A, I am disgusted to say, is spread by virus in feces from infected people — feces that finds its way into drinking water and onto food. Though among the Chol I certainly tried to maintain the highest standards of hygiene, obviously my efforts were not good enough.

My symptoms developed two weeks after leaving the village. Quite suddenly I found myself utterly exhausted and with a high fever. During upcoming days the whites of my eyes developed yellow splotches and my skin and urine turned as orange as carrots. My feces turned ashy or clay-colored. During the two months following the disease's onset, I seemed to age physically by at least ten years. Before going take gamma globulin shots — also called immune globulin or immune serum globulin. Globulin shots don't immunize; they just bolster the body's natural resistance.

Heat stroke

If soon upon arriving in the Ruta Maya area you strap on a heavy backpack and start marching through the awful heat and humidity to an isolated ruin, you're a good candidate for heat stroke; and it can kill you if not handled properly. Heat stroke is preceded by fatigue, weakness, faintness and profuse sweating. When the stroke hits, sweating diminishes or completely stops, the skin becomes hot, dry and flushed, breathing is shallow, and the pulse beats rapidly and weakly.

Treatment consists of cooling the body. Ideally the naked patient is placed beneath a sheet that is continually drenched with water while a fan blows on it. Not having such equipment on the road, do the best you can. Of course, to prevent heat stroke, just take your time, listen to what your body is telling you, rest regularly, and drink all the water you can spare.

Sunburn

Overexposure to sunlight not only can cause skin cancer, but it ages skin prematurely, causing it to become yellowish and wrinkled. Some tanning preparations don't contain a sunscreen, and thus are of no protection against sunburn. Make sure your sunscreen contains either PABA (para-aminobenzoic acid) to absorb ultraviolet rays, or else the white paste called titanium dioxide, which reflects the sun's rays. Be especially careful of your nose. Of course, having your face or just your nose splotched with white titanium dioxide looks ridiculous. In small towns, if you use it, you'll have to balance for yourself the desirability of protecting your skin with that of maintaining credibility as a sober and respectable visitor. In many areas I suspect it's best to smear on the PABA extra thick instead of resorting to titanium dioxide. Many compounds are rated with protective factors. Factors over 10 really do work, and don't show on the skin.

Bee stings

Bee stings deserve special mention because over much of the Ruta Maya, especially in the Petén and Chiapas, beekeeping is an important industry. It's typical to be following a trail into a woods hoping to find a nice picnic or camping spot, and come face to face with a dozen or so multicolored hives. I've never had problems with them, or even met anyone who had, but the potential for disaster seems to be there. Bees often leave their stinger, with pulsating venom-sac attached, stuck in the wound. Therefore, when you're stung, the first thing is to see if the stinger is there and, if so, scrape it off. Use fingernails or a knife blade; do not grasp with the fingers or use tweezers because if you squeeze the sac you can inject more venom. Stings in the mouth or throat are dangerous because swelling can obstruct breathing; if this happens to you, suck an ice cube if possible and seek medical attention. Regular stings should be washed with soap and water, a cold compress applied, and analgesics should be taken to ease the pain. Anyone known to be hypersensitive to bee or wasp venom should carry an emergency kit for self-injecting epinephrine.

Bots

Once, either during a mule-train trip to El Mirador or else on a hike to Nakum before the trail was established, I returned home with some "chigger bites" that didn't heal. In fact, they got worse, itched badly, and at night my red bumps seemed to be inhabited by something moving around inside them. I'd become infected with several flesh-eating grubs of the botfly, *Dermatobia hominis*. I got rid of the things by painting their breathing holes with several layers of fingernail polish (thus smothering them); then, after enlarging their hole with a razor, I just squeezed them out!

Ticks

If you're in an area with cattle or other large mammals, when you undress in the evening you may find small, flat ticks sticking to your skin, sucking your blood. Some ticks (seed ticks) are so tiny you hardly see them; others, at least when laden with blood, are bean-size. If a tick seems to have attached itself fairly recently, just pull it off. If it's full of blood, that means that its head is probably deeply buried, and if you pull on the tick's body, the head may come off, remaining embedded in a spot that might become infected.

Tick

To avoid collecting ticks, tuck your trouser legs inside your socks and use repellent around the legs. At night, always conduct tick-checks, being especially vigilant in the crotch area, around the midsection's belt area, under armpits, and at the base of the scalp. One way of ridding yourself of unattached seed ticks swarming over your body (sometimes brushing against the wrong bush bestows legions of them on you) is to wrap your fingers in masking tape with the sticky side out, and work over your whole body.

Chiggers

Chiggers are such tiny mites that they're almost invisible. They burrow under the skin causing red bumps about 1cm across (half an inch), which itch intensely. They're especially easy to gather when you walk through tall grass in moist areas; I got bad cases of them walking to Naranjo and Nakum. Try to stay on trails, even if they are muddy. Use repellent on your legs.

At US$5.00 a bottle (price includes shipping), a fellow in Oklahoma sells something called RELIEF, which is not a repellent, but which does kill chiggers in their bumps (as well as stuck-on ticks). He's John Biever, 3374 E. 25th, Apt. 22-C, Tulsa, OK 74114. A little dab of this stuff will do you.

Especially in hot, humid areas, scratched chigger bites can become infected. Over the years I've actually developed something of a resistance to chiggers. They still bore into me, but they don't itch nearly as much as they used to.

Snakes

Despite years of jungle-wandering I've not been bitten by a poisonous snake. One reason is that these cold-blooded critters just don't find the deeply shaded forest very attractive; also, snakes often are nocturnal. Moreover, nothing seems to delight back-country folks more than killing a snake, no matter how harmless and beneficial to local ecology it is. Unless you specifically go looking for them, you just don't see many snakes.

Along the Ruta Maya, the two poisonous snakes most likely to be encountered are the coral snake and the *barba amarilla* (yellow-beard), also called *fer-de-lance* (iron rod). Several snakes look very much like coral snakes, which are adorned with alternating red, yellow and black bands. To determine whether a banded red, yellow and black snake is a real coral snake or a look-alike mimic, just remember the little rhyme "Red on yellow, will kill a fellow." That is, the red band must be surrounded by yellow bands, so that it looks like the red band lies atop a broader yellow band beneath it. Coral snakes are found in a variety of habitats, from sunny, weedy roadsides to beneath rotting logs. Instead of injecting venom through long fangs, coral snakes chew on their victim.

The *barba amarilla*, in contrast, stabs with two long fangs. Being a pit viper like the US rattlesnake, it bears a pit between its eye and nostril; this pit contains a heat-sensing organ enabling the snake to locate warm-blooded mammals in total darkness. *Barba amarillas* are especially common around small settlements where rats and mice abound.

If you're bitten by a poisonous snake under any condition less than ideal — "ideal" being able to positively identify the snake and having the appropriate antivenin on hand — what you're supposed to do is something of an unsettled issue.

In earlier days it was comforting to know that you could tie a tourniquet between the bite and the heart, cut Xs over the fang punctures, suck out the blood, and you'd survive. But then someone pointed out that tourniquets sometimes cause gangrene, and when you release the tourniquet to keep from having gangrene, the dammed-up venom surges toward the heart, causing more problems than if you'd not used the tourniquet. Finally someone else pointed out that most people seem to do more damage razor-cutting nerves around bites than the bites themselves cause.

Personally, I carry a small snakebite kit with a razor in it, and a suction bulb. If ever I get bitten by a pit-viper in a fatty part of the body, I won't hesitate to cut Xs and suck out the blood with my bulb. If the bite is in a muscular area, as on the calf of my leg, I'll cut shallowly and longitudinally in the direction the muscles run, trying to avoid cutting across muscle tissue. If I get bitten on bony, nerve-filled hands or feet, I'll just suck with my little bulb, and hope for the best.

However, I doubt I'll ever have to do any of this. I follow a very simple rule that always has worked: In snaky areas I don't put hands and feet where I can't see what's near them. I also bear in mind that even poisonous snakes only inject their venom 50% of the time.

Scorpions

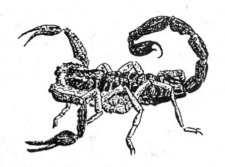

Scorpion

Shake out your shoes before you put them on. Actually, scorpions, unless you're especially sensitive to their venom, are no big deal. In the homes of most country folks in the Ruta Maya area you can probably find several scorpions creeping around; kids get stung by them all the time. Scorpions are regarded with about the same awe that we northerners have for wasps. After being stung, you hurt intensely for a brief period of time; then you forget about the problem.

Tarantulas

These are harmless, unless you really harass one causing it to bite. The bite produces mild pain and swelling. The hairs that come off handled tarantulas can irritate sensitive skin. Just leave tarantulas alone. They don't deserve their bad press.

Intestinal worms

If you spend much time along the Ruta Maya, you should probably just assume you have contracted intestinal worms. Each time I end a long trip, before I leave the area I visit a local *farmacía*, ask for some worm medicine, and once I've been back home for about a month — after all the eggs and cysts have had time to become full-fledged worms — I give myself a good de-worming. Sometimes it's astonishing to see what comes out.

Pinworms, *Enterobius vermicularis*, are about 10mm long (⅓ inch), white, and cause tickling or itching in the anal region, especially at night; common roundworms, *Ascaris lumbricoides*, look like earthworms up to 40cm long (15 inches). Both of these are acquired by eating food contaminated with worm eggs. Hookworms, *Necator americanus* and *Ancylostoma duodenale*, are about 1.25cm long (half an inch) and enter the body through the feet (so you get them by going barefoot).

Worms drain a person's energy and the big ones can perforate the intestinal wall. Sometimes after ridding yourself of a population it's as if somebody turns on the lights because now *you* benefit from your food's nutrition, not your worms! If you take your worm problem to a northern doctor he or she will need a stool sample and later you'll get a prescription, and that will cost quite a bit both in terms of time and money; but if you walk into a *farmacía* on the Ruta Maya and say, "*Necesito algo para mis lombrices — mis gusanos intestinales*," you'll get a package of anthelmintic drugs for about US$1.50. Buy two packages and repeat the treatment about a month after the first de-worming. Your medicine should have the anthelmintic drug called mebendazole in it. My last package of something called Zentel contained albendazol instead of mebendazole, but my gray-haired and therefore well-informed pharmacist said that it functioned the same way. Anyway, it worked.

Ear fungus

After a few weeks in hot, humid territory — especially if you're taking swims and getting your ears wet, or even sweating a lot — you may develop an ear fungus, which makes itself known when your ear-holes start itching. You'll know you have a bad case if you find black, scaly skin or black goo around your ear holes; fungi reproduce with spores, so black spores are responsible for the blackness. Bad cases of ear fungus can cause hearing loss.

However, taking care of the problem is not a problem. Once again, if you bring this simple problem to a northern doctor, the ultimate cost may be substantial. But you can walk into any Ruta Maya pharmacy, tell them you have an ear fungus (*Tengo un hongo en mi oido...*), and you'll be supplied with an inexpensive ointment or, more expensively but not necessarily better, drops to put into your ear. If your ears don't begin itching until you're back home, then in any drugstore, without a prescription, you can buy "jock-itch ointment," which serves the purpose beautifully. Carefully, without making contact with the eardrum, swab the ointment in the ears twice a day. Do this for about six weeks, even if the itching ends after only a few days; though the process of ridding one's ears of fungus is simple, it does take some time.

THE PROBLEM OF ROBBERY

It's awkward to talk about this subject because people along the Ruta Maya are by nature so cordial, so unselfish and so full of congenial hospitality that it's simply unpleasant to suggest that any of them might be capable of wrongdoing. However, eco-tourism teaches that we are all brothers and sisters of the same family, and we all know that every family has its black sheep. Moreover, in certain places along the Ruta Maya living conditions are so wretched that you can hardly blame anyone from being tempted to rob a relatively rich *gringo*.

Besides not camping on beaches and other isolated "perfect" spots, the main way to keep from being robbed is simply *always* to keep your guard up. Here are some specific, common-sense suggestions:

- Don't flash your money anywhere.
- Keep your documents and larger bank notes in a chest-pouch or some other secret, close-to-the-body holder; don't keep all your valuables in one place.
- When carried in your trousers, your money is safest in a zipped or buttoned front pocket.
- Be especially careful about going out to drink with new-found friends; sometimes robbers befriend lonely visitors, get them tipsy, take them on a walk, and then beat and rob them.
- In Guatemala, rooftop baggage on buses is very susceptible to being robbed by passengers riding on top, and to disappearing from the top at intermediate stops, especially at night. If your fellow passengers start riding on top, where the baggage is stored, you should either go ride with them so that you can watch your equipment, or bring your valuables down with you (probably impossible), or simply take your baggage and leave the bus. Padlocks on zippers offer a little protection. Anyone planning a lot of bus travel in Guatemala would do well to make or buy a lockable bag constructed of something like tough nylon mesh, to cover the entire backpack. Of course, even this is little defense against a determined thief.
- Don't drive at night and in more isolated areas where the roads are bad, such as Guatemala's Petén region, don't ride buses at night.
- It's best not to travel alone.
- For those of us habitually traveling in isolated areas, a can of mace —the chemical used by police, which temporarily blinds and disables an attacker — may not be a bad idea. On my last trip I met a man who'd been unwisely driving his car at night. As he was attempting to unclog a carburetor jet a band of drunks appeared brandishing machetes. The man's inability to speak good Spanish seemed to enrage the drunks. One man raised his machete, about to take a swipe, but was stopped instantly when the tourist squirted some mace in his face; he'd been carrying a can on his belt. One squirt knocked

the attacker down and disoriented the rest long enough for the tourist to escape. Two main problems with mace are that in Europe it's not commonly available and, more seriously, having it handy, there may be too much temptation to use it unwisely. Certainly it should be used only as a last resort, and then only if you're absolutely sure that your action will do more than just make your assailant angry. I've seen angry drunks display almost supernatural resilience.

Regular tourists who look like tourists and do touristy things in well established touristic zones seldom have theft problems amounting to more than occasional pilferage. But those who roam far afield and sail through the best and worst of a culture's *real life* must be extra careful. No place in the world is entirely free of danger, and the Ruta Maya is no exception.

Sweetgum
Liquidambar styraciflua
(see page 216)

Chapter 6

Traveling with Goals

Traveling is more fun with goals. If in a restaurant some travelers ask how your trip is going and you say something like, "Well, I'm collecting rubbings from Maya stelae... " or, "I'm trying to add species to my life list of identified birds... " or, "I'm collecting Maya fairy tales for possible publication in a book... ", you'll be surprised at how lively the conversation becomes.

More important, there's simply some kind of mysterious tourist-law that when you're traveling with a specific goal (even a fruity one) all kinds of interesting doors open up to you. Serendipity becomes a friend and a plethora of interesting situations blossom. Who cares if you really fulfil these goals? The magic comes from simply having them! Here are some suggestions for the Ruta Maya:

Become an Amateur Mayanist

At the major ruins, day after day tourist buses disgorge hordes of travelers snapping pictures right and left and oohing and ahing as the guides explain what's what. But when I talk to these people it becomes clear that hardly any of the information has been assimilated into a larger, coherent body of knowledge or understanding.

"At Chichén Itzá you see Toltec influences"; "Kaminaljuyú was a major Preclassic site"; "Tayasal was the last Maya stronghold to fall to the Spanish... " But, what does all this *mean*? How do these bits of knowledge interrelate and what's so special about the facts in the first place? Without feeling the buzz that comes from interconnecting bits of information, snippets of history are more like two-dimensional stamps pasted in an album than hard-won jewels of evidence revealing a civilization's temper, dreams, weaknesses... attributes that cause the ancient Maya to be people with whom we can relate.

Books, lectures, museums and guides at the ruins themselves help us develop the background information we need. (Be careful about ruin-guides who angle for better tips by embellishing their interpretations with theories about ancient astronauts!) At all the major ruins in Mexico and at Tikal you'll find pamphlets and books filled with information in both Spanish and English. This book's bibliography lists a number of excellent sources; probably Michael Coe's *The Maya* is the most accessible general-background book available (though a bit out of date). Most books overwhelm the beginner with details, so the reader must read and reread, and search for information in various sources; gradually, with perseverance, information coalesces into understanding.

And then someday at Uxmal you just stand in the heavy sunlight looking at long noses on the corners of the Palace of the Governor and you muse that to the ancients those noses weren't ridiculous at all, but rather awe-inspiring, for they belonged to the sky-serpent, and you wonder at the psychology of a people who would populate their sky with long-nosed serpents, and during this meditation you find yourself having grown a little...

Or, consider picture-taking. For traditional travelers the prime motive behind taking all those ruin-pictures is later to say to oneself and friends, "I was there." In contrast, the eco-tourist with the goal of seriously understanding Maya archeology automatically becomes less self-oriented. The amateur Mayanist at a ruin, with camera in hand, asks the more creative question, "Later, how shall I use this picture to remind myself, and to express to others, what is most meaningful or beautiful about this thing? Once this question is formulated, magic happens.

Back at the Palace of the Governor beholding curled noses, you decide that your picture must portray more than a simple curled nose; it must somehow capture the turbulent spirit of those people who revered long-nosed serpents. You decide to take your picture of a mask from below, with ragged rain-clouds boiling up in the background, thus artistically accentuating the unsettling natures of the people you're analyzing. You work on this picture adjusting the angle, waiting for the background clouds to express the proper mood, using a tripod for good depth of field... and in the end you create something far more relevant than a tourist's snapshot, and you yourself for a while have been a seeker transfixed by the Maya sky-serpent. Now you carry within yourself certain ties with the ancient Maya, for in your own way you have come to grips with the long-nosed sky serpent.

Add Bird-Species to Your Life List

It's appropriate to ask, "Why birds?" and "Why lists?" For the first question, the short answer is that accessible field guides exist to help us identify the Ruta Maya's birds, (mainly, *A Field Guide to Mexican Birds* by Peterson and Chalif, Houghton Mifflin, Boston, 1973) but for other classes of organism, good field-guides don't yet exist. To address why making lists of birds is fun requires a little more space.

I agree that for some birders, adding species to a life list seems to become more important than going out and watching birds. I feel uncomfortable when I hear people talking about living things, such as birds, with the same level of empathy they might establish with a newly acquired postage stamp. Let me tell you why *I* make bird lists.

At the root of my list-making impulse lies my familiarity with the birds of my own home area — the state of Kentucky. At first, my list contained only Kentucky birds. However, when I began traveling, I found immense pleasure comparing what I found with the birds back home. Here's an example of how this works:

In Kentucky we have a single jay-bird, the blue jay, *Cyanocitta cristata*, related to Europe's Eurasian jay. It's a fairly large, flashy, blue-and-white bird famous for being both noisy and nosey; it's "nature's alarm system," for when an intruder enters its domain it screams and complains awfully. Back in Kentucky, my high-school's basketball team was known as "The Bluejays" and sometimes my fellow Kentuckians say, "Why, he was naked as a jay-bird!" referring to featherless newborn blue jays. Blue jays are at my roots.

So, imagine my pleasure when on my first trip to Mexico one day in an orchard in Tamaulipas I discovered a noisy, nosey, largish, "alarm-system" bird that was just like my blue jay, except that it was brown. It was the brown jay, *Psilorhinus morio*. The next day, on a humid slope farther south, I was even more astonished when before my eyes flitted an obvious cousin, the green jay, *Cyanocorax yncas*.

Variations on a theme! There's simply something inside most people that takes great pleasure in experiencing a theme firmly rooted in the soul, artfully and lovingly expressed in novel ways — whether it's Beethoven fiddling with variations on a theme in his Kreutzer Sonata, or the God-Force evolving variations on the jay-bird theme.

Nowadays I've positively identified scrub jays, gray-breasted jays, unicolored jays, magpie-jays, bushy-crested jays, black-and-blue jays, Steller's jays, azure-hooded jays, green jays, Eurasian jays, piñon jays, gray jays, brown jays, and my good old blue jay. And I still have plenty of jays to go. And jay-birds constitute just one type of bird out of hundreds!

Yes, lists in themselves are nothing. But they can be frameworks on which we build complex, soul-stretching insights.

Improve Your Spanish

This goal is equal to "The Goal of Penetrating the Spanish-Speaking Culture" for, once you have a language, you've gained a window opening into a culture's heart.

Being fluent in Spanish, able to get along in German and to read Portuguese and easy Chinese (and I've dabbled in several other languages like Náhuatl and Guaraní) I can say that Spanish is a relatively easy language. Unlike English, if you see a Spanish word, you can pronounce it. Verb conjugation is much more regular in Spanish than in any language I know about.

Teaching yourself Spanish as you travel the Ruta Maya is as easy as carrying a Spanish/English dictionary and a small grammar book, listening to what people say, and *making an effort to talk*.

Go ahead and make mistakes. Latin America is a wonderful place for learning a second language because the people are uncommonly helpful, understanding, good-natured and appreciative when you try to speak. Memorize the verb conjugation chart, keep in mind the simple rules of pronunciation, and then go forth with a dictionary. Listen to what people say and mimic them.

One thing about pronunciation needs special mention. To utter Spanish sounds properly you must learn to use your tongue, teeth and the rest of your oral cavity in a different manner from how your mother taught you. If right now you pronounce the Spanish verb *tener* (to have) while holding your palm in front of your mouth, you'll feel a sharp explosion of air puffing from between your lips when you pronounce the "t" part; when a Spanish speaker says *tener*, there's no explosion. To make the "t," they place the tip of their tongue on the back side of their upper, front teeth, not at the mouth's roof, like English speakers. If you have good books, they'll show you exactly where to place your tongue, with diagrams. Study the "Spanish Pronunciation" guide in the front of your Spanish/English Dictionary. It says that the Spanish "i" is like the "i" in machine. Close enough. Language tapes are great.

During my most recent trip the hardest laughter I heard was among the passengers in a bus in Guatemala when paper-checking soldiers entered and a nervous Swede said to them "*Ella tiene mis papelos.*" For over two hours people took turns making one another guffaw by repeating the nonexistent word "*papelos*," and the poor Swede became known as "*Señor Papelos.*" He'd been having problems with the fact that Spanish nouns have gender, but his mistake, instead of constituting a *faux pas*, had been something to delight a whole bus of people.

One final thing: Many of the average folk met along the Ruta Maya have not had much formal education so sometimes the Spanish you hear will not coincide with what you're learning in your books. Many

Indians speak Spanish only as a second language. If you hear someone say, "*Yo tener dinero,*" which I have heard, don't throw away your conjugation chart. Just keep up your sense of humor, keep blabbing away, making as few mistakes as possible, and before long you'll have it.

Miscellaneous Useful Spanish Sentences

Queremos darle una gratificación de ___ pesos/quetzales.
   We want to offer you a tip of ___.
¿Es posible acampar aquí durante la noche?
   Is it possible to camp here during the night?
Que le vaya bien.
   Good-bye. (More or less, "May you go with my best wishes")
Mañana, ¿a qué hora sale el autobús para ___?
   Tomorrow, when does the bus for ___ leave?
¿A qué hora llega el autobús en ___?
   At what time does the bus arrive in ___?
¿Hay otros autobuses que salen el mismo día?
   Are there other buses leaving on the same day?
¿A qué hora salen ellos?
   When do they leave?
Discúlpeme, pero, ¿es posible que aquí hay una señora que puede venderme una comida de frijoles, tortillas y talvez huevos?"
   "Excuse me, but, is it possible that here there might be a lady who would sell me a meal of beans, tortillas and, maybe, eggs?"
¿Cuanto quiere Usted para un plato de frijoles, arroz y huevos?
   How much does a dish of beans, rice and eggs cost?

Get a Handle on Tropical Ecology

The main barrier to gaining a more than superficial appreciation for tropical ecology and agricultural systems is not being able to identify the plants and animals that comprise these systems. Once you have a name, you can look into reference books and see what the significance of that organism is and learn how it interacts with the rest of the ecosystem.

   For instance, a conspicuous feature of the tropical beach ecosystem is the coconut palm; go inland a bit and you don't see them unless they're planted. By looking up in the right books *Cocos nucifera*, the coconut palm's Latin name, you can discover that not only are this tree's nuts edible but also the nut shells are sometimes

used as cups, the palm's fronds are used for roofing, and its sap has
been used as a medicine and fermented into an intoxicating drink.
Add to this the insight that the palm's classic lean over the sea
actually is part of its strategy for disseminating its fruits by water, and
you have quite an interesting picture. Knowing these things, the
coconut palm takes on a real personality. Finding your beach
inhabited by such worthy species makes the beach more interesting,
and we gain a more profound insight into nature's general diversity
and complexity.

In lieu of having good field guides, except for birds, we can put
together reference libraries that at least serve part of our needs.

How Plants Succeed in the Humid Forest and Rain Forest Areas

One of the most fascinating processes in ecology is referred to as
"succession." This is the mechanism by which different species of plants
and animals succeed one another as a biological community changes,
for example, from an abandoned agricultural field to a forest. Traveling
the more humid, lowland zones of the Ruta Maya — the southern
Yucatán Peninsula, northern Chiapas, Belize and the Petén of northern
Guatemala — it's interesting to notice which plants succeed one another
when a forest is destroyed through slash-and-burn, and then left to
regenerate. Here's a general outline:

STAGE I: Upon abandonment, a cornfield quickly is invaded by such
species as the wild plantain (*Heliconia* sp.), bamboo, an acacia-like
bush called *Mimosa pigra*, and *Cecropia*. These dominate the field for
one or two years.

STAGE II: Secondary shrubs, which dominate the area three to five
years after disruption, include various species of *Piper* (the genus from
which black pepper comes), as well as *Trema micrantha*, *Heliocarpus
donell-smithii* and *Miconia*.

STAGE III: Trees dominating six to ten years after abandonment
include *Cassia grandis*, guanacaste (*Enterlobium cyclocarpum*), cohune
palm (*Orbignya cohune*), *Inga edulis*, pricklenut (*Guazuma ulmifolia*),
Spondias mombin, and various species of fig (*Ficus* sp.).

To the novice ecologist, Stage III forests look like "virgin forests,"
because they are tall and deeply shaded. However, mature forests have
completely different species. In general, species in a mature forest
require higher humidity and a much more stable environment than
species able to survive in a forest only 30 to 50 years old. Birds and
other animals inhabiting mature forests are generally adapted for
exploiting the forest's more stable, more diverse, narrow ecological
niches — and thus are rarer and more interesting — than those able to
survive in disturbed areas or regenerating forests.

Unfortunately, I can't provide specific titles to look for; the literature is too dispersed and hard to come by; you simply must search in reasonable places, and depend on lucky finds. Here's how I put together my own reference library dealing with Ruta Maya organisms:

First of all, most of the literature available is rather technical in nature. Whenever I'm near a major university library and am allowed to enter with the students, I haunt the stacks and periodical sections, prodigiously using the photocopy machine. Journals in which plants of the Ruta Maya area are treated include the *Annals of the Missouri Botanical Garden*, *Fieldiana Botany* and *Rhodora*. For example, in *Rhodora* 77:105-140, in 1975, Spellman *et al* produced a checklist of the Monocotyledoneae (grasses and such) of Belize. Of course, after you locate any such publication you should look in the publication's bibliography for mention of previous literature on this or allied topics.

One of the best journals for Central American animals is *Copeia*. For example, *Copeia* 1966(4):719-766 has a piece entitled "The origins and history of the Central American herpetofauna" ("herpetofauna" refers to reptiles and amphibians). Government publications often have surprising offerings. In 1950 the US Dept of the Interior published *Special Science Report #5*, entitled "A Fish and Wildlife survey of Guatemala." If you can just get your foot into the door of a good university's science library, you can find wondrous stuff!

Even moderately nice public libraries usually have general-information publications from which specialized information can be gleaned. For example, take a look into *Grzimek's Animal Life Encyclopedia*.

Beyond haunting libraries, your success in amassing a good tropical-ecology reference library depends more on luck than anything. Average bookstores seldom have much beside glossy, full-color coffee-table books that look good, cost a lot, but don't offer much hard-core information. Used-books stores usually produce better finds than new-books stores. The other day I bought an out-of-print book (price $2.00) by zoologist Ivan Sanderson. It details his experiences in Belize and the Yucatán, and it's just full of miscellaneous information that, once it's organized, will be very valuable to me!

Of course, if you can take a university class, or go on a packaged tour focusing on eco-tourism, you'll find that others will have done much of your reference-material organizing for you. Take what you can, where you can, and build on it.

Help Us Keep this Book Updated

We plan to update this book periodically; that's because along the Ruta Maya things are changing fast. In areas where now there is only mud and smoldering vegetation, some visionaries are talking about cableways or monorails carrying visitors over environmentally sensitive areas; at borders where travelers must now deal with a confusing miscellany of document requirements and entrance and exit taxes, there's talk of a Eurail-type pass. During upcoming years new services will appear, old ones will disappear, roads will be paved, new ruins will be discovered... Also, I've probably left out destinations that most readers think should be included.

Let us hear about these things. You'll help not only us, but also the entire eco-tourism concept. The world still is in the pioneer stage of exploring what "eco-tourism" means in the context of the Ruta Maya. By writing to Bradt Publications with your suggestions and criticisms, and sharing with us your interesting experiences, you can be a part of the process of crystallizing the eco-tourism concept. If you figure out a better way than I have to get to Loltún Cave without a car, let me know.

Leaf-Cutter Ants

All along the Ruta Maya it's hard to miss lines of leaf-cutter ants, of which there are many species; mostly you'll see them marching across woodland trails and roads. The fact that leaf cutters carry about pieces of leaves isn't nearly as interesting as what they do with their green parasols.

Leaf cutter lines usually can be tracked into a tree or bush. Some leaf-cutter species merely snip pieces of leaves from the plants but others shear off entire blades. Once a leaf-cutter ant possesses a manageable piece of leaf, it follows its long file of sisters back to its subterranean nest. Deep inside the nest the leaf tatters are chewed upon, but not swallowed; they're munched until they form a spongy mass which, when added to millions of other tiny ant-munched spongy masses, constitutes nothing less than an exquisitely managed subterranean compost heap.

This compost heap is inoculated with a special kind of fungus. It's not just any fungus; apparently it's co-evolved with the ants for, while

it can be grown in the laboratory, in the lab it does not behave in the special way it does inside leaf-cutter nests. That special behavior is this: When leaf cutters bite off ends of the fungus's migrating strands, little heads form on the strands, looking like miniature cauliflowers. And these little fungus-cauliflowers are what the leaf cutters like to eat. Somehow I'm glad that scientists can't prompt the leaf-cutters' fungus to make cauliflowers in the laboratory.

Chapter 7

The Maya Landscape

CONTINENTAL DRIFT SETS THE STAGE

Two hundred million years ago, during the Triassic Period, the earth's waters were populated by algae, sponges, coral, bony fishes and sharks; on land early dinosaurs roamed through forests of coniferous trees and ferns, but flowering plants and birds hadn't evolved yet. Only one supercontinent existed, an immense landmass now referred to as Pangaea; the vast ocean called Panthalassa surrounded it. On the Pangaea supercontinent present-day North America's Appalachian Mountains were already old, and beginning to erode.

By 135,000,000 years ago, between the Jurassic Period and the Cretaceous, the first birds had appeared and now certain plants for the first time were bearing flowers. Deep within Earth, gigantic convection currents of magma created forces that on the earth's crust caused the single landmass of Pangaea to fracture and split into a northern landmass called Laurasia and a southern landmass named Gondwanaland. Gondwanaland itself was breaking up, with India drifting north toward Laurasia, and the Africa/South America region separating from the Antarctica/Australia part.

By the 65,000,000-year-ago mark, between the Cretaceous Period and the Tertiary, modern mammals had appeared, including the first primates; dinosaurs were becoming extinct (possibly because of a global eco-catastrophe) and while the Appalachians continued to erode, the Rocky Mountains, stretching from Alaska to Central America, had been thrust up. Now the earth's landmasses were taking on shapes familiar to us, except that North America and Eurasia were still connected, as were Antarctica and Australia; but now South America and Africa formed independent continents.

Today, Australia continues plowing northward toward eastern China and Japan, and Africa is driving north toward Europe, gradually diminishing the Mediterranean. The Atlantic and Indian Oceans widen as the Pacific is encroached upon from all sides; California west of the San Andreas Fault is ripping away from the North American mainland.

Most of the Ruta Maya region rides sedately atop the giant tectonic plate known as the American Plate. In the Ruta Maya area, only southern Guatemala and Copán lie on the much smaller Caribbean Plate. These two plates grind together in the vicinity of and along a line running parallel to the Motagua Valley and the Sierra de las Minas, past Guatemala City and into extreme southern Chiapas. Friction occurring as the plates make contact generates tremendous heat and instability, and this translates into earthquakes, upliftings and occasionally erupting volcanoes.

How the weather may have affected Maya history

People studying ancient climates (paleoclimatologists) point out that in ancient times great events in human society frequently coincided with shifts in weather patterns. It's been shown that lowland cultures in southern Mesoamerica have generally flowered during periods that were relatively cool and wet.

For example, southeast Mexico's Olmec civilization collapsed around 400 BC, a date corresponding with the end of a major cool, wet period. Similarly, the 600 AD transition between the Maya's Early and Late Classic period — the Late Classic being the time of greatest energy — coincides with a change from hot, dry weather to cool, rainy times; the Classic ends when suddenly dry weather returns. Of course, when rains come regularly, both crops and cultures prosper.

Chichén Itzá's history runs counter to this trend; its energetic Postclassic period was established during a hot, dry period. However, some suggest that even this had much to do with weather. It's been shown convincingly that much of Chichén Itzá's influence resulted from its domination of the salt trade; miners collected salt in the area of Río Lagartos, using methods similar to those described in this book in the Río Lagartos section. During hot, dry periods in the Maya area, which coincided with global periods of hotter, drier weather, sea level dropped, sea water became more saline, and along the coast salt beds formed in shallow lagoons. Chichén Itzá's demise around 1250 AD coincides with a period of sudden cooling and increased rain, which would have diluted sea water; higher sea levels would have flooded salt beds.

For a more detailed look at this field, see "Paleoclimatological Patterning in Southern Mesoamerica" by W.J. Folan *et al* in the *Journal of Field Archaeology*, Vol. 10, 1983, pp. 453 to 468.

ANCIENT CLIMATES

During the eons, earth's climate has been as unsteady as its crust. In the Carboniferous Period 300,000,000 years ago, plant material growing in hot, wet swamps formed thick, peat-like deposits that were later compressed by sedimentation dumped atop them, and converted to most of today's coal resources. Just 50,000,000 years later, during the Permian Period, Pangaea's swamps had largely become wind-blown deserts.

More recently the earth has endured ice ages during which the sea level rose and fell, depending on how much of the earth's water was invested in ice. We may still be in the Ice Age — just "between glaciers." During the relatively brief time embraced by the rise and fall of the ancient Maya — a period of some 3000 years — significant climatological fluctuations have occurred in the Maya region. About 7,000 years ago the earth's climate averaged 2° C (3.6° F) warmer than today. In Europe this provided balmy conditions that must have been very pleasant; in contrast, in North America this time was uncomfortably dry. Oak forests survived in humid Europe, but vast areas of North and Central America became desert. In the Americas, species such as the mastodon, mammoth, camel, horse, giant bison and ground sloth became extinct.

However, the first native Americans survived. In the Yucatán, weather during the Maya Early Preclassic was relatively warm and dry; then until the Late Preclassic it was relatively cool and wet; then until the Early Classic it was warm and dry again. Just between the Classic and the Conquest, at least three other major weather patterns were experienced.

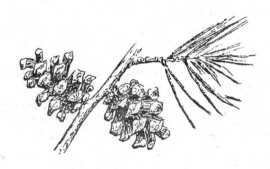

Mexican pinyon pine
Pinus cembroides

THE GENERAL SETTING

Taking the broadest view, the Ruta Maya consists of two main regions:
The cool uplands and the hot lowlands. In general, the uplands are in
the south; the lowlands are in the north (see map).

The Southern Uplands

The uplands are dissected by valleys, most notable of which are
Guatemala's Motagua Valley and the Central Depression between the
Sierra Madre chain and the Central Plateau in Chiapas. Near the
Mexico/Guatemala border, about 50km (30 miles) WNW of
Quezaltenango, stands Guatemala's Tajumulco Volcano, which at
4,220 meters (13,845 feet), is the region's highest peak; the more
famous Volcán de Fuego rises only 3,835 meters high, and Volcán de
Agua is even lower. For the sake of comparison, these peaks are
lower than Mexico's Orizaba (far from the Maya region), which rises to
5,700 meters (18,700 feet); however, Tajumulco is higher than
Europe's 4,807-meter (15,771-foot) Mt Blanc; Alaska's Mt. McKinley is
6,194 meters (20,320 feet) high, and Asia's Mt. Everest peaks at 8,848
meters (29,028 feet).

Highland vegetation zones are very dependent on local
topography. Frequently one slope of a mountain receives the
prevailing winds' moisture load being carried off the Gulf, while the
opposite slope, lying in the mountain's "rain shadow," remains in
perpetual drought. Some high ridges in Guatemala and Chiapas are
mantled with lush cloud-forest. Below cloud-forest vegetation, oak-
pine forests generally predominate. Lower still, oak-pine breaks into
a variety of tropical forest types. In deep rain shadows of peaks and
ridges, as in the Motagua area, arid savanna and cactus-rich scrub
develop.

The Northern Lowlands

Vegetational zones in the Ruta Maya's lowlands profoundly reflect
variations in geology and climate that are much more subtle than in
the south. The major feature of the Yucatán Peninsula's climate is that
rainfall diminishes toward the peninsula's northwestern corner; thus
the forest around Tikal is tall, lush and diverse in species composition,
while the forest around Uxmal about 400km (250 miles) to the north
looks stunted, scrubby and is home to a much less diverse population
of organisms. At some places in the southern lowlands average
annual rainfall is as high as 400cm (157 inches) while in northwestern
Yucatán it's as little as 50cm (20 inches).

Because the Yucatán's lowlands lie atop a great slab of porous
limestone, the little rain that does fall on the peninsula quickly drains

below ground where it's carried away in underground rivers — not pooled in accessible lakes or surface rivers. In coastal areas where the land lies close to sea level lush marshes and mangrove swamps appear, each habitat harboring its own unique assemblage of organisms.

Tropical Ecology: Miscellaneous Considerations

Deciduous vs Persistent Leaves   Despite the Ruta Maya area not having a real winter, many woody plants do drop their leaves during part of the year. Most species do this during the dry season when precious moisture can be lost through leaves. However, even in rain forests with plenty of rain year-round, as well as along rivers and lake shores, sometimes woody plants continue dropping their leaves. One purpose this serves is for a tree to rid itself of leaf-eating insect populations that, if they weren't shed occasionally, might build up year after year.

Instead of creating a new crop of leaves each year — something of a waste — many woody plants produce leaves that last for several years. Generally these are rich in chemical compounds that poison or taste bad to animals that might eat them.

Vine Growing-Strategies   Rain-forest vines have the problem that if their seeds germinate on the dark forest floor the seedling will at first receive so little sunlight that it can't grow fast, and thus must spend too much time gradually twining toward sunlight higher in the forest. Vines have two strategies for getting around this problem.

One approach is to spend the first months or years as a bush, with many branches converting sunlight-energy into carbohydrate, which is stored in underground tubers; when finally enough energy is stored in the tubers, the vine can "bolt," or grow very fast, until it reaches high into the canopy's well lighted zone.

The second strategy is to produce a big seed, with lots of energy stored in the seed's oily endosperm. When the seed germinates, a leafless or semi-leafless vine bolts from it, drawing most of its energy from the seed. Leaves are developed only after the stem has climbed high into adequate sunlight.

Epiphytes (plants living aerially, on tree branches)   The orchids, bromeliads and peperomias we see living on tree branches high off the ground have solved the problem of receiving enough light. However, these plants must be content with what water and nutrients they can find there, which is never very much; thus most epiphytes are rather small. Certainly an epiphyte is in no position to regularly drop its nutrient-rich leaves. Thus epiphyte leaves are almost always evergreen and rich in chemicals that somehow protect them against foraging animals.

Pollination Biology   In the rain-forest's understorey, not only is sunlight scarce, but also wind. Thus a greater percentage of understorey plants are pollinated by animals than are plants of savannahs, grasslands, marshes, etc.

Flowers pollinated by hummingbirds frequently are tubular and red to orange; bat-pollinated blossoms open at night, have lots of nectar, and are greenish white or purple.

Some flowering plants are pollinated by miscellaneous "dumb pollinators" like flies and beetles. In order to grab these pollinators' attention, the plants generally flower in spectacular, synchronous flushes and, because of low pollination success, produce many more flowers than fruits. Other plants depend on "smart pollinators" such as birds and bats. These plants rely on their pollinators to remember where they are, and thus usually blossom rather inconspicuously over a long period of time; enjoying a high level of pollination success, they produce about as many flowers as fruits.

In the stable environment of mature tropical rain-forests many relationships between plant species and specific animal species have evolved. For example, a particular fig tree may depend solely on one species of wasp to pollinate it.

Fruit Biology When a fruit is young and its seeds aren't ready to be dispersed, the fruit must be hard and bitter so that animals won't eat it. However, when the seeds are mature enough to be dispersed then the fruit must become sweet and soft, so that animals will find pleasure in eating it, and ultimately assist the plant in disseminating its seeds elsewhere — after passing through the animal's digestive tract. The chemistry involved in converting a hard, bitter fruit into a soft, pleasant-tasting one is exceedingly complex.

Many flowering species avoid these chemistry problems by having their fruits dispersed by the wind. Wind-dispersed fruits are generally only about a third of the size of animal-dispersed ones, aren't bright or otherwise conspicuous, don't taste good, and frequently possess wind-catching "wings" or "parachutes."

Liverwort

Chapter 8

People of the Ruta Maya

THE MAYA AND EUROPEAN SETTLERS

The Maya are not Extinct

Christopher Columbus, born in Genoa, Italy with the name Cristoforo Colombo and later known by his Spanish name of Cristóbal Colón, was the first European, along with his crew, to meet the Maya. On his fourth voyage, in 1502, he and his men went ashore at Guanaja Island, off the coast of Honduras, where they encountered a seagoing canoe being drawn along shore by naked and yoked slaves. The slaves' master arrogantly suggested to the Europeans that they should get out of his way, and he threatened them when they refused. The canoe was "long as a galley" and eight feet wide, made of a hollowed-out tree. In its center stood an awning of palm leaves, under which children, women, furniture and merchandise took shade. Unfortunately for Columbus's ambitions to discover a great empire, from Guanaja Island he chose to head east toward Panamá, not west toward the Yucatán Peninsula and Maya civilization.

Shipwrecked Spanish sailors who washed up on the Yucatán coast in 1511 were the first Europeans to behold Maya civilization. However, historians credit the official discovery of the Yucatán and the Maya to Captain Francisco Hernández de Córdoba and his crew who in 1517 sailed there from Cuba, hunting for slaves. In a battle with the Maya, chronicled by Bernal Díaz del Castillo in Chapter 4 of his *True History of the Conquest of New Spain,* the Captain received wounds from which he died a year later. This bloody first encounter of avaricious Europeans with the Maya portended the confrontations to come.

You could say that the Maya described by eyewitness Bernal Díaz were "Late Postclassic," though usually that term is reserved for the archeological context, not applied to living people enmeshed in an evolving culture. But defining Bernal Díaz's Indians in such a way makes an important point. That is, Maya civilization never ended, nor have the Mayans disappeared.

It's true that during the Late Classic (600-900 AD), 12,000,000 to 16,000,000 Maya may have lived in the Ruta Maya area, and that today "only" approximately 2,000,000 Maya survive there (constituting the largest single block of indigenous American people north of Perú.) Also it's true that when the Spanish came to America vast areas of the lowland Maya realm that once had been very highly populated with Maya cities now were uninhabited.

However, Columbus's traders and the warriors with whom Bernal Díaz and his crew-mates in 1517 fought a battle at Champotón certainly would not have considered themselves irrelevant vestiges of a once-great culture; clearly at least part of Maya civilization in the 16th century was still organized enough to put up a stiff fight. On a later voyage to Cozumel Island, in 1519, Bernal Díaz saw altars at which sacrifices were still being made and he witnessed rituals over which Maya priests presided, so even then certain of the more spectacular Maya traditions were being practised.

Moreover, now we know that in some of the Ruta Maya's more isolated areas, small Maya communities were keeping alive the old ways long after the Conquest was accomplished. The Itzá Maya at Tayasal, on an island in Guatemala's Lago Petén Itzá, didn't surrender to the Spanish until 1697. Chiapas's Lacandón Maya never formally surrendered. When recently I sat beside a Tzotzil speaker in upland Chiapas listening to how his parents had prayed to the moon and sun for good crops, and how even today some of his neighbors claim that God the Father is the sun-god, and that the moon is the Virgin Mary... I felt the current of a *living* "Late Postclassic" Maya culture surviving around me.

Why did Classic Maya Society Collapse?

Even today, Guatemala's Petén region and the southern Yucatán Peninsula has a relatively low population density. In places, seen from an airplane, the forest stretches from horizon to horizon, broken only by an occasional river. Nonetheless, Dr. B. L. Turner of the University of Oklahoma, after studying Maya agricultural systems, has said that if we could have flown over the Petén at the height of the Classic Period, we would have seen something akin to central Ohio today. Thus this question: What happened to all those Maya?

The corn-blight theory: By around 900 AD Maya farmers were recognizing that certain varieties of corn (maize) produced more grain than others. Eventually these varieties may have been planted almost to the exclusion of others, causing the genetic diversity of the Maya's corn crop to be drastically diminished. If at this time a disease attacked the crop, it could have destroyed nearly all of Mayadom's corn crop. The result could have been even more devastating than Ireland's potato famine of 1845, which was started with a fungus accidentally introduced from Mexico; nearly a million people died then.

Attacks by "barbarians from the north": Effects of the various invasions into Maya lands may have been more subtle and profound than mere defeat and domination. The northerners brought with them a sun god that needed human flesh to be sacrificed; the need for human flesh fostered a culture in which war and conquest were prime goals. History shows that such militaristic cultures are doomed to devour themselves as their constituent groups spend energy and resources not on creative growth, but on mutual annihilation.

Rebellion by Maya commoners against their disengaged, self indulgent hierarchy: The Maya's accomplishment in developing an amazingly accurate calendar indicates that their hierarchy was obsessed with abstract notions. It is human nature for those fixated on abstractions to disregard practical matters. Thus we can visualize the ancient common citizens of Mayadom, seeing nothing useful coming from their higher ranks and feeling tyrannized from having to contribute labor to the rulers' various projects, rebelling. As Arnold Toynbee has demonstrated, again and again in history cultures evolve through the same stages: Warfare > The Universal State > Tyranny > Fission.

Soil Depletion through Slash-and-Burn Agriculture: This theory comes to mind to anyone who in the Petén sees considerable tracts of savannah in places where it seems that the climate would support dense, humid forests; surely these savannahs result from the ancient Maya having ruined the soil. This theory is attacked from two directions. First, students of paleoclimatology say that 4,000 years ago the Petén was much drier than now. Thus the Petén's dense forests are invading former natural savannahs, not the other way around. Second, it's pointed out that one of the first lowland Maya centers to be abandoned was Quiriguá, though its soils are perpetually enriched by flooding of the Río Motagua.

On the other hand, evidence at Copán may support the soil-depletion theory. Copán is located in a mountain valley that during the Late Classic Period was probably overpopulated. Though the last monument there was dedicated in 822 AD, dates from obsidian blades found in the valley suggest that the population itself did not disappear until 1200. This points to a gradual decline resulting, perhaps, from exhausted forests and farmland. Pollen analysis shows that at Copán in 1200 AD the forest began returning.

Hurricane: Along the Yucatán's eastern shore you'll be astonished at the damage caused by Hurricane *Gilbert* in 1988. However, hurricanes lose much of their force when they move inland. It's hard to visualize a hurricane destroying an entire civilization, especially when its major centers lie so far inland. In Chapter 10 of *Relación de las Cosas de Yucatán*, Landa describes a hurricane that one evening at 6pm knocked down all the trees in a region and killed wildlife. However, Landa points out that despite this vast destruction the Maya rebuilt and for some years afterwards prospered.

Epidemic: In the same chapter mentioned above, Landa reports that after the hurricane the Maya enjoyed 16 years of good weather and health, the last year being the best of all. But then came a pestilence that lasted 24 hours, killing so many people that "a lot of fruits went unpicked." Of course, this occurred long after the Maya civilization already had collapsed, and the Maya's disease is presumed to have been introduced by the Spanish. However, any high-density population is particularly vulnerable to epidemics.

Earthquake: When we speak of the fall of Maya civilization we're referring to the end of the Classic period in the lowlands. Lowland bedrock in the Ruta Maya area is stable limestone; the Maya lowlands simply would not have been shaken so severely that their civilization would have been destroyed.

Climatological Change: Paleoclimatologists point out that Maya culture blossomed during a climatological period that was relatively cool and moist. However, during the 9th century (Late Classic) the weather became so dry that in the lowlands the intensive cultivation practised by the Maya probably became impossible. Recent studies show that at Río Azul, Calakmul and Copán during the Late Classic Period many Maya were showing signs of malnutrition. This suggests a long-term problem such as an extended drought. If the civilization was already suffering from one or more disasters, a long drought could have triggered the final collapse.

		MAYA WORLD HAPPENINGS	REST OF WORLD HAPPENINGS
PRECLASSIC — EARLY	2000 BC	• Maya ancestors migrated from Pacific coast of southern Mexico to upland Guatemala	• Phoenicians develop an alphabet • Olmecs settle on Mexico's Gulf Coast
PRECLASSIC — MIDDLE		• First villages in Maya lowlands	
PRECLASSIC — MIDDLE	1000 BC		•Carthage established
PRECLASSIC — MIDDLE			• Greece's Golden Age
PRECLASSIC — LATE	500 BC		• Plato & Socrates alive
PRECLASSIC — LATE	300 BC		• Conquests of Alexander the Great
PRECLASSIC — LATE	BC / AD	• A recognizably Maya civilization emerges	• Rise of Roman Empire
CLASSIC — EARLY	300 AD	• Teotihuacan influence at Kaminaljuú	• Huns invade Europe • Fall of Roman Empire
CLASSIC — LATE	600 AD	• 12 to 16 million Maya alive	• Chinese poet Li Po born • Charlemagne rules
CLASSIC — LATE	900 AD	• Major building ends; monument carving ends; dramatic population decline	• Vikings visit Vinland
POSTCLASSIC — EARLY	1200 AD	• Chichén Itzá collapses; Mayapán established	• Magna Carta issued • Marco Polo's journeys
POSTCLASSIC — LATE	1500 AD	• Mayapán abandoned 1697: Maya at Tayasal surrender to Spanish • Today about 2 million Maya survive	1475: Michelangelo born 1502: Columbus meets Maya 1521: Cortés defeats Aztecs

A GENERAL OUTLINE OF POSTCONQUEST HISTORY

History like a Spicy Soup

The Ruta Maya's postconquest history is extraordinary and hard to get a handle on. Though Europeans who recall the shifting alliances, mindless violence and general anarchy of such Old World happenings as the Thirty Years War may feel at home dealing with Latin history, North Americans can have trouble. We habitually conceive of history as a kind of linear evolution, with each year neatly designated as belonging to this or that period, which came about because of this or that battle, presidential election or natural disaster...

Latin history is by no means "linear." We do indeed find great events in it, such as Cortés's conquest of the Aztecs; but usually explaining such happenings requires so many footnotes — and the impact speaks so powerfully to the emotions and is so closed to statistical analysis and neat evaluation — that eventually we're left with a feeling more like heartburn than enlightenment.

In the case of Cortés's adventures, for example, we're simply stunned by the Spaniards' unbridled rapacity and readiness to shed blood. Also, what are we to make of the fact that the Aztec Empire was already on the verge of collapse when Cortés arrived, that Montezuma couldn't make up his mind whether Cortés was a god or not, and the incredibly complex political intrigues between Cortés, Cuba's Governor Velázquez and King Charles V? And what about Cortés's shady liaison with his female slave Malinche, whose interpretive abilities were absolutely essential to the Spanish conquest? And finally Cortés dying a frustrated, unappreciated, powerless man?

Of course, being confused by facts is wonderful. What's the use of looking at history if it's not to nudge ourselves into new perspectives and understandings?

Dividing Up the Indians

After Mexico and Central America were conquered, under the *encomienda* system developed by the Spanish in the West Indies, large parcels of land and their Indian inhabitants were allotted to Spanish conquistadors and political bigwigs; in order to stay on the land, Indians had to pay tribute, and often perform personal services. Theoretically, the Spanish were taking responsibility for saving the souls of the pagan Indians by converting them to Christianity; the *encomienda* system facilitated this, while rewarding the Spanish overlords for their trouble.

Functionally, the *encomienda* system was slavery; huge numbers of Indians died during its implementation. When Spanish royalty and the Dominicans began feeling guilty and tried to suppress it, the system proved to be too profitable to stamp out easily. However, it eventually developed such a bad name that in 1542 the New Laws of Las Casas were promulgated, defining Indians as free subjects of the King; forced Indian-labor was prohibited. Black slave labor and wage labor by the Indians were substituted. However, wages paid the Indians were so inconsequential that essentially not much changed for them.

The *encomienda* system evolved into the *repartimiento* system, which gave government the right to force its citizens to perform work necessary for the state. This meant that now the Indians only had to spend about a quarter of their year working "for the state," but abuses were so frequent and widespread that for many it was no better than the *encomienda* system.

Two centuries after the conquest, in 1821, the entire region gained independence from Spain. For the Maya, things now got worse. Under the earlier *encomienda* and *repartimiento* systems there had been no huge plantations growing such crops as sugar cane, cacao, coffee, indigo, tobacco, and henequen. By the time Independence came, such plantations did exist and landowners, mostly of Spanish origin, entrapped unsophisticated Indian laborers by offering advances on their wages, then at high prices selling them necessities at company-owned stores; soon the Maya found themselves inescapably but legally in debt, and thus vulnerable to punishment if caught trying to escape.

Thus the *repartimiento* system was replaced by *peonage*, a system in which Indians, Blacks and even some whites sunk into serfdom. In Mexico in 1915 a decree against peonage was issued, but in practice it continued. Today, as you travel the Ruta Maya, you will see for yourself what has evolved from peonage.

MAN AND NATURE ALONG THE RUTA MAYA

A similar story of exploitation can be told with regard to nature, though in that account we find much less mention of efforts to contain the greed forming the main impulse behind it. To gain a graphic understanding of how this history of exploitation has affected the Ruta Maya landscape, go to page 474 of the October, 1989 issue of *National Geographic* magazine and study the satellite photo of the Ruta Maya heartland — the western Petén and eastern Chiapas. Before I saw that image I had thought that much of the Lacandón jungle was still fairly intact. But, in this picture, anyone can *see* what's left. That picture supports a recent Voice of America statement on my shortwave radio that more than half of the Lacandón Jungle has already been destroyed, largely through illegal timber cutting and oil exploration.

Books Written by the Maya

Before the conquest, the Maya wrote books. Of the thousands that must have existed, only three or four survive; mostly they were destroyed by the Spanish, who considered them to be filled with abominations.

The surviving books are written on long strips of paper made from the pounded inner bark of the fig-tree, glazed with a thin layer of white plaster, and folded like screens. Though early sources report that the Maya wrote on the topics of "science," history and prophecy, and that they set down songs and genealogies, the ones we have today deal only with ritual; they were compiled during the Postclassic.

The three books extant today are referred to as codices. A codex is simply a manuscript of a major work such as the Scriptures or the classics. The finest of the three Maya codices is the 78-page, 20-cm high (eight-inch) and 3.6-meter-long (11¾-feet) Dresden Codex, which in the late 1800's the German Ernst Förstemann used to determine how the Maya calendar works. Plate 83 in Coe's *The Maya* shows a page of this codex. Page 780 of the December, 1975 issue of *National Geographic* magazine shows in color a section of the 6.7-meter (22-foot) Madrid Codex, which once guided Maya priests during divination rituals relating to hunting, weaving, planting, bee-keeping and rain-making.

Twice during the colonial period certain Maya writers saw that their ancient ways were being displaced by lifestyles forced upon them by the Spanish, and wrote books dealing with the old ways. In the highlands of Guatemala the myths and history of the Quiché Maya were set down in a book written in Quiché, but using European script. Today this work is referred to as the **Popol Vuh**.

In Yucatán a very similar thing happened, but this time the subject matter was a blend of medical recipes, notes on astronomy and astrology, and material on both the Spanish and Maya calendars. This compilation is referred to as the **Books of Chilam Balam**.

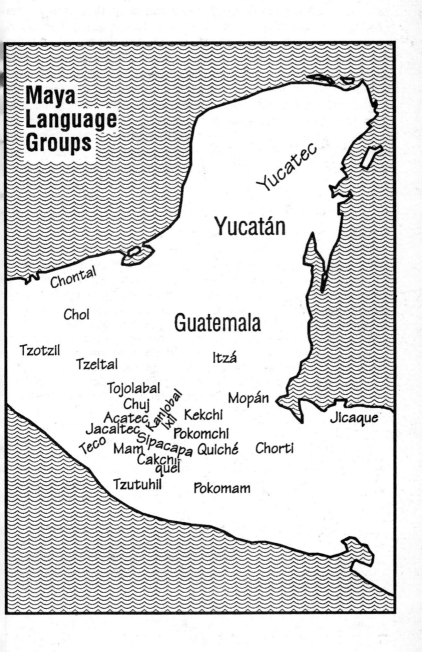

Maya
Language
Groups

Yucatec

Yucatán

Chontal

Chol   Guatemala

Tzotzil   Itzá
        Tzeltal

            Tojolabal
              Chuj   Mopán
          Acatec Kanjobal
      Jacaltec   Ixil   Kekchi   Jicaque
    Teco   Sipacapa Pokomchi
        Mam   Quiché   Chorti
          Cakchi-
            quel
        Tzutuhil   Pokomam

LANGUAGES OF THE RUTA MAYA

Today a traveler along the Ruta Maya hears two dozen distinct Maya-family languages. If at dusk you saunter through the village across the lake from the entrance to Quintana Roo's Cobá, you'll hear Yucatec; if you hike the trail behind the ruins of Palenque, to the village of Naranjo, you'll hear people on the trail as they pass speaking Chol and Tzeltal; if you wander through the *mercado* in Poptún, Petén, and hear an Indian language, it'll probably be Mopán.

And these *are* languages, not just dialects. Yucatec is as different from Tzeltal as English is from Dutch. Of course, some of the languages are more closely related to one another than others; thus Kekchi, Quiché and Cakchiquel are considered to belong to the Quichoid group of languages, while Tzeltal, Tzotzil and Chol belong to the Chiapan group. In general, Yucatec is the language spoken through the entire northern Yucatán Peninsula, but farther south the more mountainous the terrain becomes the greater is the diversity of languages.

In the streets of Yucatán cities such as Mérida, Cancún and Campeche, little or no Maya is heard — just Spanish. In the Yucatán Peninsula, Maya is mostly restricted to small, isolated towns and villages, and even if a town is small and isolated there's no guarantee that a single word of Maya will be spoken.

On the other hand, if you explore the highland communities around San Cristóbal de las Casas or if your bus stops at a village in the Guatemalan highlands, you may hear *only* Maya languages. Incidentally, men in these villages usually speak Spanish much better than the women, though women nearly always know enough Spanish numbers and business words to conduct *mercado* transactions. Because many Indians consider their neighbors who speak only the local Maya language to be unsophisticated, it's best when you address an Indian in Spanish not to first ask if the individual speaks Spanish. To do so, at least in the Indian's mind, may be to suggest that he or she is socially backward.

In Mexico many isolated villages are *ejidos* — commune-like entities established by the government. Frequently entire *ejido* populations have been transported from distant overpopulated highland districts of Mexico where only Spanish or Native American languages unrelated to the Maya family of languages are spoken. In Chiapas, especially near Guatemala, many communities are composed of Guatemalan refugees, which may speak Spanish, or Maya languages not previously found in Chiapas. In parts of English-speaking Belize you find communities of Spanish-speaking immigrants from Honduras, as well as native Spanish-, Yucatec- and Mopán-Maya speakers.

Famous Names

Aguilar, Gerónimo de   Along with Gonzalo Guerrero, Aguilar was a shipwrecked Spaniard enslaved by the Yucatec Maya in 1511. These two men thus became the first Europeans to live in the Maya area. Aguilar joined Cortés's expedition when it landed on Cozumel Island in 1519. His ability to speak Maya immensely helped Cortés during the ensuing conquest of the Aztec.

Alvarado, Pedro de   The chief lieutenant of Hernán Cortés during Mexico's conquest. See page 71.

Catherwood, Frederick   English artist whose drawings in John Stephen's book *Incidents of Travel in Central America, Chiapas, and Yucatán* (published in 1841) introduced the world to Maya archeology.

Coe, Michael D.   Author of one of the most accessible and widely read Maya-oriented books for the layman, *The Maya* (see Bibliography). He also published *Mexico*, dealing with Mexico's ancient non-Maya peoples, particularly the Olmec, Teotihuacan and Aztec civilizations.

Cortés, Hernán   Spanish conquistador and conqueror of Mexico. In 1521 he defeated the Aztec empire of central Mexico. The Aztec's king was Montezuma and their capital was Tenochtitlán, on the present-day site of Mexico City. Cortés began his expedition by stopping at Cozumel Island. The entire expedition was chronicled by one of Cortés's soldiers, Bernal Díaz del Castillo.

Díaz del Castillo, Bernal   Conquistador and chronicler who accompanied the first three Spanish expeditions to Mexico. Though his *Historia Verdadera de la Conquista de La Nueva España* mostly deals with Hernán Cortés's conquest of the Aztec nation, it also contains some of the first eyewitness accounts of Maya society.

Grijalva, Juan de   Spanish explorer who in 1518 commanded the third Spanish expedition to Mexico. He voyaged from south of Cozumel Island on Yucatán's east coast, all along the peninsula's northern and western coasts, and up Mexico's Gulf Coast as far as Veracruz. He was the first Spaniard to hear of the Aztec empire.

Guerrero, Gonzalo   Along with Gerónimo de Aguilar, he was a shipwrecked Spaniard enslaved by the Yucatec Maya in 1511. Unlike Aguilar, Guerrero refused to join the Cortés expedition when it landed on Cozumel Island in 1519. He tattooed his hands, pierced his nostrils, lips and ears, married a Maya woman and fathered the New World's first *mestizo* children, thus becoming the first European to "go native" in America. Later he led Maya war parties against the Spanish invaders and is believed to have died fighting the Spanish.

Hernández de Córdoba, Francisco Spanish explorer; in 1517, sailing from Cuba on a slave hunt, he discovered the Yucatán Peninsula, and thus also the American mainland. In a fight with the Maya at Champotón he suffered wounds from which he died upon his return to Cuba.

Landa, Fray Diego de The fanatical bishop of Yucatán who burned all known Maya books, or codices, because he considered them blasphemous. Headquartered in the town of Izamal about 60km (37 miles) east of Mérida, in the name of converting the Indians to Christianity he committed such barbarities that eventually he was recalled to Spain. Despite his behavior, Mayanists are indebted to him, for while in Spain during his recall he wrote *Relación de las Cosas de Yucatán* (On the Things of Yucatán), which today serves as the main account of Maya life as it was during the Conquest.

Maudslay, Alfred Having explored the Maya region in the late 1800's and published his findings with magnificent photographs and maps, this Englishman qualifies as the first serious Maya archaeologist.

Stephens, John L. American explorer who in the mid 1800s visited over forty Maya sites and wrote about his discoveries, as well as many incredible adventures in the politically and socially unstable region, in his book *Incidents of Travel in Central America, Chiapas, and Yucatán* (published in 1841). Accompanying him was the English artist Frederick Catherwood, who contributed magnificent drawings of ruins.

Thompson, J. Eric S. (Sir Eric) English author of the classic *The Rise and Fall of Maya Civilization*. Often he's referred to by such sobriquets as "The dean of modern Maya archeology."

Chapter 9

Fundamentals of Maya Archeology

THE PREHISTORIC DEVELOPMENT OF MAYA CIVILIZATION

Ice-Age Precursors

It's believed that modern man, *Homo sapiens*, arose in Africa about 100,000 years ago. In China, at Liujiang, remains of modern man have been found dating from about 67,000 years ago. Modern humans reached Siberia 30,000 years ago.

At that time a massive glacier — the most recent of a series of several — covered much of northern North America. In North America this moment in geologic history is referred to as the Wisconsin glacial stage. When the Wisconsin stage's glacier stood at its most advanced position, so much of the earth's water was invested in its ice that worldwide sea level stood 60 meters (200 feet) lower than it does today. Many parts of the earth that previously had been submerged beneath the oceans now lay high and dry. Significantly for mankind migrating across Siberia 30,000 years ago, one of those formerly submerged but now dry parts of the earth was the area between present-day Siberia and Alaska; in short, now humans could walk across a land bridge connecting Eurasia and North America.

Today no one knows for sure whether 30,000 years ago people really did migrate from Siberia into North America. At Pikimachay in Perú, remains *suggest* a date of 22,000 years ago; at Boqueirão da Pedra Furada in Brazil, a site *hints* at being visited 32,000 years ago, and at Monte Verde in Chile findings *intimate* habitation 33,000 years ago... ! Despite these unsubstantiated dates, it's possible that when humans crossed the land bridge into Alaska they could proceed no farther because their passage was blocked by ice.

By 12,000 years ago probably enough of the Wisconsin glacier had melted for an ice-free corridor to have formed in western Canada, and this would have enabled humans to migrate southward. The earliest undisputed traces of inhabitants on the American continent are dated from about 11,000 years ago.

Today we refer to these earliest native Americans as the Clovis people. They were late Pleistocene (Ice-Age) hunters of mammoth, bison and other animals, and their spears were equipped with stone (usually chert) points. Clovis spearheads were characterized by the presence of chipped-away depressions, or flutes, in the point's base, where the spear's shaft fitted. In the Americas, finding a "fluted Clovis point" *in situ* is a dream of every archeologist and amateur excavator. In the Ruta Maya area, in San Rafael in the pine-mantled hills just west of Guatemala City, some years ago a picnicking schoolboy stumbled across a fluted Clovis point; certainly the Clovis people roamed at least part of the Ruta Maya area millennia before Maya civilization began.

Fluted Clovis point (about 13cm — 5 in) long

"Archaic" Cultures between ± 7000 BC and ± 2000 BC

Coe refers to the time after the mastodon-hunting, cold-weather Clovis people, but before Maya civilization first appeared, as the Archaic Period. North America at this time was much hotter and dryer than it is today. The big game the Clovis people had hunted died out; people of the "Desert Culture," which extended from southern Oregon all the way into southeastern Mexico developed lifestyles based on the collection of seeds and roots of wild plants, and upon the killing of small animals.

Between 3,000 and 2,500 years ago a network of chiefdoms stretched from central Mexico to the Pacific coast of Guatemala and El Salvador; you could say that among these chiefdoms a certain *Mesoamerican culture* existed. Even at this early time before any way of living had coalesced into something that could be called the beginnings of Maya civilization a vigorous exchange of goods and ideas was taking place among the chiefdoms. Such commodities as jade, obsidian, sea shells, magnetite and pottery were exchanged. One idea that seems to have traveled rapidly was the concept of pottery vessels bearing stylized designs such as the lightning motif.

Maya Agricultural Systems

Around 900 BC, early Preclassic Maya in the Yucatán Peninsula's lowlands began practising slash-and-burn agriculture. In slash-and-burn, after a plot of cleared forest land produces a few crops — usually after three or four years — weeds begin choking out the planted crops, plant-eating insect populations build up, nutrients leach from the soil, and the fragile soils themselves erode and compact. Eventually the farmer moves to a new part of the forest, fells some trees, burns them, and starts the cycle over again, while the old plot lies fallow, reverting back to forest. (See box on plant succession.)

Formerly it was believed that the slash-and-burn practices we see today were carried over from ancient Maya times. However, it has now been calculated that land cultivated with the slash-and-burn system, with corn being the staple crop, has a carrying capacity of 150 to 250 people per square mile. In the Maya lowlands this population density was reached by the Late Preclassic period, around 300 AD. By the end of the Late Classic (900 AD), population densities had risen as high as 2,600 people per square mile in urban areas and between 500 to 1,300 inhabitants in more rural areas. Clearly, the ancient Maya developed agricultural systems more sophisticated than slash-and-burn.

Probably the first "innovation" (one that was detrimental to soils and the local ecosystem) was simply to shorten the fallow period so that available land was cropped before fully reverting to forest. By 300 AD (Early Classic) continuous cropping became possible on terraced fields. Terracing slowed downhill erosion, built up thicker soils, and retained moisture during dry spells. Even steep slopes were terraced and drainage channels were dug through swamps, using excavated dirt to elevate other planting surfaces. To date there's little evidence of large-scale irrigation. In Belize, studies of ancient raised fields have suggested that the ancient Maya not only terraced their fields, but also used green manure and mulch. Night soil (feces) was used as fertilizer.

Ancient Maya agriculture was hardly limited to corn, beans and squash. Plant remains recovered from ancient fields and buildings show that the Maya diet included sweet potato, cassava, guava, chili, avocado, *chicozapote* fruit and breadnut, amaranth and anona. Fiber, resin and bark was taken from other plants. This mix of species was cultivated or maintained in fields, kitchen gardens and orchards, and simply collected from the forest. It was a labor-intensive system far removed from today's simple slash-and-burn.

The Preclassic Period between ± 2000 BC and ± 250 AD

Though new findings might soon cause a radical rethinking of the story of how Maya society began, today a prevalent interpretation is that around 2000 BC the Maya's ancestors migrated from the Pacific coast of southern Mexico (the region of the Isthmus of Tehuantepec) into highland Guatemala. From there, they expanded northward along river valleys into the Yucatán Peninsula's lowlands; probably the first lowland Maya villages were occupied around 1200 BC.

By 400 BC the Maya lowlands were thickly populated by farming communities consisting of several hundred people. Slash-and-burn agriculture produced the main crops of corn, beans and squash, as in much of the Ruta Maya area today. This is not to say that slash-and-burn has been practised continuously since the Maya's arrival. It's estimated that the carrying capacity of land being farmed under the slash-and-burn system is between 150 to 250 people per square mile. By 300 AD, at the beginning of the Classic period, Maya population density surpassed this figure.

What caused the Archaic bands of root-diggers and rabbit-clubbers to settle down in the Ruta Maya area and initiate the Maya Preclassic? Possibly the climatical shift from hot and dry to relatively cool and rainy weather was the main triggering mechanism. Maybe advancements in agriculture caused or facilitated the change. It's even possible that the Maya Preclassic blossomed because of a single event: An increase in the productivity of ancient corn (maize) about 2,000 years ago.

Corn was originally domesticated in the highlands of central Mexico about 7,000 years ago. An increase in productivity 2,000 years ago could have resulted from a chance genetic event in a corn population such as a mutation or an accidental back-crossing of the primitive corn plant with its offspring, *teosinte*. The progeny of such genetic intermixing, if they survive to maturity at all, are commonly sterile or in some other way inferior to their parents, but very rarely the new genetic combination results in a being that in one or more respects is superior. Nowadays evidence is growing that all mankind can be traced back to a single African woman; maybe such a chance genetic event in man is responsible for our explosive success as a species.

At any rate, if such a thing did occur in a corn population 2,000 years ago, a resulting drastic increase in productivity could have revolutionized human agricultural potential. Moreover, properly cultivating the new corn plant would have required the establishment of permanent or semipermanent villages. In such villages social life would have begun evolving at a rate surpassing anything possible for people roving about in small, dispersed bands grubbing roots and clubbing rabbits.

At this point something must be said about the Olmec civilization, which during the Maya Middle Preclassic Period flourished along Mexico's Gulf Slope in the vicinity of Veracruz. The main Olmec site of La Venta was occupied between 800 and 400 BC. The La Venta site (now largely demolished by oil operations) is 2½km long (1½ miles) and its main structure is a 33.5-meter-high (110-foot) clay pyramid. La Venta shows that the Olmecs already had developed a sophisticated culture at a time when Maya civilization was still in its embryonic stage.

For years it was assumed that Maya society more or less derived from Olmec society. Michael Coe, in his popular 1962 book *Mexico* says that, "There is now not the slightest doubt that all later civilizations in Mesoamerica, whether Mexican or Maya, ultimately rest on an Olmec base." Today's archeologists believe the Olmec civilization had considerably less impact on Maya development than previously thought. Olmec society seems to have experienced its rise and fall too early to have much benefitted the Maya.

El Mirador, located in the extreme northern Petén region (see "Exploring a Vast Maya City, El Mirador," *National Geographic* magazine, September 1987) may be the Maya's greatest Preclassic site; it flourished between 150 BC and 150 AD. Its Tigre pyramid, rising 18 storeys, possibly is the largest structure ever built by the Maya. Nonetheless, Preclassic El Mirador lacks the accomplishments associated with Classic Maya civilization: There are no carved stone stelae bearing hieroglyphic writing, no hint of advanced calendrics or mathematics, no sumptuous palaces, and no corbelled vaulting.

Nonetheless, by the end of the Preclassic, a vigorous Maya Civilization certainly was already well established. Besides El Mirador, many preclassic sites throughout the Ruta Maya region were built with the typically Maya features of temples being arranged around plazas, pyramids with stairways climbing up their fronts, tombs holding lavish burials, and frescoes portraying naturalistic subjects.

The Classic Period between ± 250 AD and ± 900 AD

Traditionally archeologists have technically defined the Maya Classic Period as that span of time during which the lowland Maya used the Long Count Calendar on their monuments. Classic Tikal's Stela 29 bears the very early Long-Count date of 8.12.14.8.15, which calculates to 292 AD.

One of the most dramatic events of early Classic Maya history was the fact that many cities in the Maya area fell under the influence of Teotihuacan, about 965km (600 miles) to the northwest. It is not known whether "fell under the influence" means "militarily subjugated," or "entered into close commercial relationship with." What is known is that by 300 AD Teotihuacan's empire was perhaps even grander and more powerful than that of the Aztec civilization, which would reach its acme in the same Mexico-City location some 1,100 years later. Goods from Teotihuacan show up at Guatemala's Kaminaljuyú a little after 400 AD. Nor was Teotihuacan's influence restricted to the Maya highlands. At Río Azul, in the Petén lowlands where the boundaries of Guatemala, Mexico and Belize meet, abundant Teotihuacan-style vessels have been found. (See "Río Azul, Lost City of the Maya" in the April, 1986 issue of *National Geographic* magazine.)

Despite the highlands constituting a very sizable portion of the Ruta

Rethinking the Maya

The most popular and accessible books on Maya archeology, such as Coe's *The Maya* and Thompson's *The Rise and Fall of Maya Civilization*, project an image of ancient Maya society that is out of date today.

For instance, traditional literature emphasizes that because Maya hieroglyphics include so many calendrical notations, the Maya must have been obsessed with calendrics — they "worshipped time." However, now it is understood that often the Maya named their children after the day on which they were born. Therefore, a person's name appearing in text, the context of which is not understood, would look like a calendrical notation. And Maya texts very frequently relate the exploits of people. Though today we still believe that calendrics were important to the Maya, now we see them less obsessed with time than earlier. A revolution in thought also is taking place with regard to the Maya Preclassic period. Though the Maya's greatest intellectual and artistic achievements still are considered Classic accomplishments, now it's apparent that Preclassic cities, such as El Mirador, managed to support very high population densities; huge temples were built, intensive agriculture was practised, and the people recognized sophisticated religious symbolism.

Similarly it's becoming apparent that the Maya Postclassic was not necessarily a time of abject lethargy and degeneration. In fact, today the boundaries between Preclassic, Classic and Postclassic are becoming less clearly defined.

Nowadays new field methods and analytic techniques, as well as a growing interest in man's historical interactions with his natural environment, are redirecting studies *away* from such topics as the genealogies of the Maya upper class, *toward* questions such as those dealing with community and economic organization, ancient agricultural systems, and other man/ nature interactions.

In short, the more we know, the more we see that we need to know more.

Maya area, all the great *Classic* Maya sites — Chichén Itzá, Uxmal, Tikal, Palenque, Uaxactún, Copán, Caracol — lie outside the highland region. During the Classic Period Maya culture in the highlands seems to have lost its vitality. In the lowlands, however, Maya building, monument-erecting and science continued to evolve vigorously. During the Late Classic the Río Bec, Chenes and Puuc styles crystallized, each with its own characteristics.

Nonetheless, *something* happened that caused Classic Maya Civilization to end. The Classic Period ended when at center after center the tradition of erecting commemorative stone stelae was abandoned; the last Long Count date to be recorded was 10.4.0.0.0 at the end of the 9th century. Except for Puuc sites in the north, which were occupied until around 1000 AD, the great centers were abandoned. The questions of why these sites were abandoned, and what happened to the millions of people who once lived there, are two of the most fascinating questions facing archeology today.

By the way, some archeologists would bring the end of the Classic period closer to our own time because of the survival of the Puuc cities of Uxmal, Sayil, Kabáh, Labná and Oxkintok until around 1000 AD. Some might even say that the Classic period survived until Chichén Itzá's downfall in 1200.

The Postclassic Period between ± 900 AD and the Spanish Conquest in 1521

The history of the Yucatán-Maya's Postclassic period is dominated by the Toltec. The Toltec were a non-Maya people who spoke a language related to Aztec. Like the people of Teotihuacan who preceded them, and the Aztec who came after them, the Toltec's home was central Mexico; shortly after 900 AD they were settled at Tula, just north of Mexico City's present location. *Legend* has it that the Toltec king's name was Topíltzin, also known as "Feathered Serpent" and Quetzalcóatl. In the late 10th century a power struggle developed between Quetzalcóatl and some of his militant followers; Quetzalcóatl lost, escaped to the Gulf Coast, and set sail, it's said, on a raft of serpents, someday to return to save his people.

Whatever happened to King Topíltzin/"Feathered Serpent"/Quet-zalcóatl, Maya *legend* has it that in the late 900s (at the dawn of the Maya Postclassic) a man calling himself Kukulcan (translating to "Feathered Serpent") arrived from the west, wrested Yucatán from its Maya lords, and established his capital at Chichén Itzá. Murals in the Temple of the Warriors at Chichén Itzá, and some scenes on golden disks fished from the nearby Sacred Cenote, show Toltec forces arriving by sea, reconnoitring a coastal Maya town. A fresco in the Temple of the Tigers commemorates the Toltec beating the Maya in a battle. But one wonders if these scenes portray real historical facts, or whether they're just propaganda associated with "historical revisionism." Maya legend and Maya documentation are notoriously hard to separate.

Following the Toltec "invasion," (whatever it was) Uxmal and most other important Maya sites apparently were abandoned; Chichén Itzá was "done over" à la Toltec Tula. A hybrid architecture evolved, half Maya and half Toltec, as well as a hybrid religion and a hybrid society. One needs only to see Chichén Itzá's mingling of Toltec feathered-serpent motifs with Maya masks of the long-nosed sky-serpent to believe this. In the northern Maya lowlands, Toltec influence, at least for a while, seems to have translated into some kind of "hybrid vigor" that produced new buildings and advancements in art. Nonetheless, inexplicably, in the 1200s the ruin that today we call Chichén Itzá was abandoned, and henceforward we hear nothing more of the Toltec.

The Postclassic Maya story is not yet over, for around 1200 AD a group of people called the Itzá entered the picture. They first settled in a place called Chakanputun, which was possibly coastal Champotón along the Campeche coast; they may have been Mexicanized, trade-oriented Maya, or maybe they were something else. Anyway, in about 1200 AD, for reasons not perfectly clear, the Itzá left their home and wandered into the interior.

First they went to Lago Petén Itzá where Flores now stands, and then they wandered up the eastern coastline of Belize. Finally they turned inland, found the ruin now called Chichén Itzá, and occupied that splendid but neglected old ruin. In the late 1200s the Itzá founded Mayapán; Maya hands built according to Itzá plans. Eventually Mayapán became the last great Maya capital of the northern lowlands, holding perhaps 12,000 inhabitants. Significantly, workmanship at Mayapán is shoddy and uninspired, and the city seems to have been arranged in a completely haphazard manner. The Itzá definitely were not the Toltec.

The Itzá maintained their control over the Maya for only a couple of centuries. In the mid 1400s revolt brought down Mayapán and the city was destroyed and abandoned; over in Chichén Itzá the by-now-Mayanized Itzá once again were forced back onto the road. Now they made their way back to Lago Petén Itzá, which their ancestors had seen 250 years earlier. On the splendidly isolated island where Flores stands today they established the city of Tayasal which eventually would assume an honored place in Maya chronology when, in 1697, it became the last Maya stronghold to fall to the Spaniards.

Just think: In 1682 when Philadelphia was founded by William Penn, just 3,000km (1,800 miles) away in Tayasal, Maya priests were busy chanting ancient rituals set down in books in hieroglyphics!

MAYA ARCHITECTURE

A typical Classic Maya site consists of several platforms or mounds with steps leading up their fronts, topped by various kinds of buildings. Around these structures lie broad plazas or courtyards. The most prominent building in a cluster is usually the temple-pyramid, which towers above all other buildings. The pyramid is composed of a rubble core covered with a veneer of limestone blocks. The temple atop the pyramid contains one or more rooms, the walls of which are generally plastered with stucco and inclined toward one another so that "corbelled vaults" are formed. Frequently the Maya built their pyramids over one another, so that today when they're excavated layer after layer can be removed, onion-like.

The corbelled vault is sometimes mentioned as the most characteristic single element of classic Maya architecture, so it is a concept to be understood. "Vault" is simply an architectural term referring to a room in which the ceiling or roof is arched or arch-like. The Maya never mastered the graceful curved arch; their vaulted arch rather is composed of two inclining (corbelled) walls meeting at the summit where they are capped with flat stones.

Corbelled vaults don't strike us as being particularly elegant, and arches of various kinds were used in other cultures, such as the ancient Chinese, Egyptian, Babylonian and Etruscan, long before the Maya came up with it. However, in the context of the New World, it can be pointed out that the other great American civilizations, the Aztecs and the Incas, never discovered arches and vaulting.

A second architectural characteristic of many Maya temples is the roof comb — usually a highly ornamented "crest" built lengthwise atop the temple, apparently for no other reason than the aesthetic one of lending height, dignity and lightness to a structure that otherwise might look rather squat and heavy.

A third feature of Maya architecture is that temple façades are frequently highly embellished with painted or otherwise ornamented stucco. The term façade refers to a building's main exterior face or faces; stucco is a kind of cement or plaster similar to concrete and composed partially of lime. When visiting Maya ruins it's important to keep the ornamented-stucco feature in mind, for most ruins we see today have lost their stucco. We see bare, rough, unpainted stone, which conveys a rather somber effect, where the ancient Maya beheld shockingly red-stuccoed temples perhaps further ornamented with bizarre stucco god-masks. The original effect of Maya architecture must have been anything but somber. Sometimes, as at Quintana Roo's Kohunlich, the stucco masks still are intact, and some of the red coloring material still is visible.

Ball courts are present at many Maya sites. Though the ball game is not found in native American cultures north of Mexico, or south of the Maya area, in Mexico it's a feature of numerous non-Maya sites. El Tajín of the so-called "Classic Veracruz Civilization," about eight kilometers (five miles) west of Papantla in northern Veracruz, is home to no less than seven ball courts. When the king of Texcoco predicted that Montezuma II's Aztec kingdom would fall, a ball game was played, the outcome of which was supposed to determine if the prediction was true; Montezuma II's team lost, the ball game's results indicated that the prediction was true, and history has proved both the king of Texcoco and the ball game's augury to have been correct.

Within the Maya region, ball courts, and presumably the ball games themselves, are very different from one another. The court at Chichén Itzá, built during Toltec times, is the largest and finest in all of Mesoamerica. Its two parallel walls are 87 meters long, eight meters high and 61 meters apart (272 feet long, 27 feet high and 199 feet apart) and each wall is equipped with a stone ring or hoop through which the ball passes. Inside Chichén Itzá's ball court you could place several courts of the kind found at Kohunlich, which not only are much smaller, but also with low walls, the bottom portions of which drastically jut inward, and no stone rings are apparent.

Larger Maya sites with ruins spread over a large area also are equipped with causeways. In its general sense the term causeway can be applied to any highway or paved way, but in the context of Maya archeology it usually refers to a rather broad, straight, stone-paved way that may be raised somewhat above surrounding ground. Sometimes the Maya seem to have been carried away with their causeways, sending them shooting across the landscape for who-knows-what reason. Usually these extra-long causeways are referred to by their Maya name, *sacbe*, which means "white road." At Quintana Roo's Cobá, *Sacbe* No 1 travels no less than 100km (62 miles) toward the west, to the minor ruin of Yaxuná, about 19km (12 miles) southwest of Chichén Itzá. Sometimes impressive Maya *sacbes* end at tiny temples that seem to have been of slight importance. Many archeologists believe that these highways' function must have been less for commerce than for ceremony.

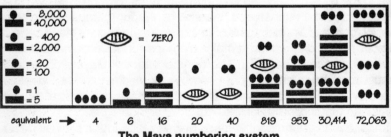

The Maya numbering system

Chapter 10

Maya Art

Probably the most exciting Maya paintings are those portraying important events in Maya history or mythology. The wall painting in Chichén Itzá's Temple of the Warriors showing canoe-borne Toltec warriors reconnoitring the Maya coast is a wonderful example. At first this painting looks like the rather unsophisticated drawing of a child, for it shows no sense of perspective; seen from the ocean the nearby Toltec in their canoes are the same size as the Maya on land in the background, attending their every-day business. The water around the Toltecs' canoe is populated with so many kinds of marine life that it seems a childish fascination with novelty put them there.

However, after becoming more familiar with Maya art the lack of perspective in the Temple of the Warriors mural takes on new meaning. One begins to feel that the artist simply had been less concerned with aesthetic niceties than with dramatically portraying the Maya on land not expecting at all the pending, very momentous Toltec invasion. Also, by showing the sea so populated with marine life the artist seems to be expressing his satisfaction that after the Toltecs' long journey they'd discovered a bountiful place that was nothing less than a land of milk and honey!

Wandering around Chichén Itzá it's interesting to try to identify from their dress the nationalities of the various warriors appearing in murals and carvings. One warrior will have a bird effigy on his headdress, a back shield and an eagle-emblem breast ornament, so he will be equipped exactly the way Toltec warriors are portrayed at Tula north of Mexico City. Another warrior will be armed with a round shield, a spear-thrower and darts; these are Itzá warriors whose shields were more protective than the Maya's flexible, elongated things, and whose spear-throwers and darts were superior to the Maya's simple spears.

Maya art is full of symbols and symbolic situations that to the ancient Maya conveyed considerable information. For example, in a mural at Bonampak we see a head chief wearing a jaguar tunic, taking a man by the hair; grasping by the hair symbolizes capture. Two sculptures at Palenque show a chief on a throne being offered a fine headdress surmounted by quetzal feathers; this symbolizes submission of power on the part of the giver. On an incised bone found at Tikal, instead of drawing water beneath a canoe, shells were drawn symbolizing water.

Not all symbols are so easy to interpret. For example, consider the tulip-shaped flower symbol often referred to as the water-lily motif, and frequently seen as a figure in headdresses. Apparently the Maya considered the netherworld as existing below the surface of water, as at Chichén Itzá's Sacred Cenote. Of course the water lily is rooted in this submerged world, so we can speculate that when we see an individual sitting cross-legged and staring into space, with a water lily growing from his head, the water lily indicates that this is a seer in communication with the netherworld. The water lily of the Ruta Maya, *Nymphaea ampla*, has a cousin in Africa, *Nymphaea caerula*, which is used as a narcotic among certain groups. If the Maya water lily proves to be hallucinogenic, this will be even stronger evidence to support the water lily's netherworld interpretation.

Other symbols are even more obscure, and may never be interpreted because we have lost the train of Maya thought. For

Carved figure at the entrance to Copan's staircase

example, the Maya considered the number nine as symbolizing purity and freshness. Sir Eric Thompson leads us through the Maya thought-process accounting for this association. The god of the number nine, he says, is the Chicchan snake god, who is represented by the *yax* sign. It so happens that *yax* also signifies green, with the added connotation of purity and freshness. Thus the number nine equals purity and freshness. A parallel in US culture, Thompson suggests, would be if someone were to sketch a military figure standing in a boat instead of writing the word Delaware... Most US schoolchildren would identify the military figure in the boat as Washington crossing the Delaware River, on his way to trounce the British.

When we speak of murals, we're referring to paintings done in stucco and applied to walls. Stucco is simply plaster, based on lime, and the Maya were masters at working with it. One problem with stucco is that it dries rapidly. The Maya added a bark extract and other substances that kept the stucco malleable for a long time, enabling the artist to work in great detail. Today the Maya's stucco-working secrets are forgotten; now no one can duplicate the Mayas' works of art. Curiously, when Maya artists wanted to portray a human, first the person was drawn naked, and then clothing was added layer upon layer.

Even an amateur can develop a certain knack for recognizing the periods during which certain Maya art was produced. As you view Maya art, note that in earlier work — Preclassic and early Classic — great attention is given to detail, yet there's a certain heavy, plodding feeling about it. Later works suggest that artists became more interested in concepts than in particulars... or maybe they just changed to mass-producing their work for business reasons, and no longer felt like bothering with details.

Early work is angular, ponderous and substantial; late work is roundish, executed with a flair, but somehow superficial.

Section of mural at Bonampak

PART TWO

Ruta Maya Destinations

Yucatán Peninsula

Chapter 12

The Yucatán Peninsula

THE SETTING
Geography

The Yucatán Peninsula's landscape is one of small rolling hills, or simple flatness. Geologically it's comprised of a massive low-elevation slab of limestone. This limestone bedrock has profoundly affected both the region's biology and native cultures. At the very root of this powerful influence of bedrock over life lies a simple chemical formula:

$$CaCO_3 + H_2CO_3 \rightarrow Ca(HCO_3)_2$$

in other words:

limestone (calcium carbonate) + carbonic acid → calcium bicarbonate (in solution)

The equation's carbonic acid forms naturally when atmospheric carbon dioxide (forming about one percent of the air we breathe) spontaneously combines with water. Rainwater fresh from the sky is slightly acidic, even when uncontaminated by air pollution. Limestone is always cracked and fissured, so during the eons, as slightly acidic rainwater has percolated down through the peninsula's fractured bedrock, dilute carbonic acid has eaten away at the limestone, changing rock-hard calcium carbonate to calcium bicarbonate, which leaches away in solution. Calcium bicarbonate further disintegrates into gaseous carbon dioxide, water, and calcium ions. Thus, what once was hard limestone rock evaporates into the air or flows away in groundwater, leaving empty space. Given enough time and flowing, acidy water, a tiny fissure in limestone bedrock becomes a mighty cave.

It's interesting to look at a good map of the Yucatán. Where are the rivers? Maybe you can find one or two down in the extreme southern lowlands, or near the marshy coasts; but among the interior's low, rolling hills, a good river is impossible to find. That's because water in this region flows underground. Occasionally a stream appears such as the one running from near the ruin of La Muñeca to near Conhuas (southwest of Xpuhil). However, you'll look in vain for its outlet into the ocean or a larger river, for it ends by flowing back into the ground!

Needless to say, this paucity of surface water must have been as hard on the ancient Maya as it is today on the region's new settlers. No wonder that at Chichén Itzá the water-filled Sacred Cenote — a huge sinkhole resulting when a cave collapsed — was regarded with such reverence.

Biology

Because the entire Peninsula is low in elevation, nowhere in the Yucatán do we the find cloud forests, oak/pine forests, or cactus-populated, rain-shadow deserts such as those found in mountainous Guatemala and Chiapas. More than anything the region's biota reflects a pattern of rainfall that in the south is ample, but which toward the northwest rapidly diminishes. While Xpuhil in the south can receive 1.6 meters (over five feet) of rainfall a year, and the surrounding forest is relatively lush, averaging maybe 10 meters (30 feet) tall, Mérida in the northwest receives only about a meter of rain, and the surrounding forest is low, scrubby "thorn forest."

Marsh vegetation is well developed along the coast, and here and there in the interior, as along the Laguna de Silvituc about 25km (16 miles) east of Escárcega. Aquatic plants growing in the lake's waters include the bladderwort, *Utricularia* sp. (bearing underwater bladders that entrap small aquatic life), species of water-lily, *Nymphaea* sp. and the beautiful, free-floating, violet-blossomed water hyacinth, *Eichhornia crassipes*. Mangrove

Red mangrove
Rhizophora mangle

forests with their own unique assemblages of plants and animals are found along the Yucatán's coast in several places, as at Celestún and Río Lagartos.

A greater diversity of bird-species is found in the Yucatán's humid

Notes on Some Special Trees in the Yucatán Peninsula and the Petén

Some of the most important and interesting trees in the more humid forests of the Yucatán Peninsula and the Petén belong to the fig family. These include the chicle-producing chicozapote, *Achras sapota*, the *ramón*, or bread-nut tree, *Brosimum alicastrum*, (which produces edible chestnut-like fruits and a superior browse for animals), wild fig trees of the genus *Ficus*, and the useful gumtree, or *hule*, *Castilla elestaca*.

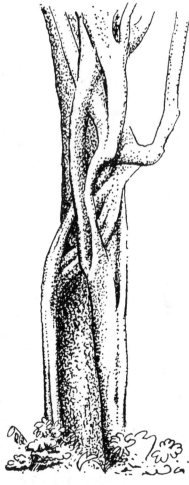

The gumtree has dark, foot-long, leathery, hairy leaves and produces a milky sap that in the past was the source of Panama rubber, used for fabricating rubber coats. The ancient Maya and Aztecs used this rubber for making the ball used in their ball games. Panama rubber shouldn't be confused with Pará rubber, from the Brazilian *Hevea brasiliensis*, which is considered to be of superior commercial quality. In the past the juice of the moonflower, an attractively flowering, twining vine of the morning-glory family, was used to cause the gumtree's milky sap to coagulate.

In the Yucatán as one travels northwest the landscape becomes more arid, members of the fig family become less common, and members of the bean family become dominant. Often these trees are acacia-like, with feathery compound leaves composed of small leaflets, and twigs armed with spines. Be careful walking along trails through the northern-Yucatán forests, for stepping on spines and grabbing spiny branches is a greater possibility than being attacked by snakes and scorpions!

Strangler fig on host tree

south and east than in the arid northwest. In humid areas, especially at dawn and dusk, large, raucous flocks of Aztec parakeets and white-fronted parrots wing overhead, and in the forest one of the most distinctive sounds is that of the keel-billed toucan, which calls like a gigantic cricket frog.

Some of northern Yucatán's birds are especially interesting because they are mainly Caribbean species — not mainland Mexican. For instance, the Caribbean dove found locally in northern Yucatán is distributed in Jamaica, Grand Cayman and St. Andrew. The Caribbean elaenia is found on the Lesser Antilles and islands off the Yucatán Peninsula. The stripe-headed tanager is distributed in the Bahamas, Greater Antilles and, in Mexico, only on Cozumel Island.

The People

In the Yucatán Peninsula, much in contrast to the Ruta Maya's southern highlands, one Maya language predominates — Yucatec. Moreover, most foreign, Cancún-type visitors to the Yucatán Peninsula probably never even hear Yucatec, for in the medium-sized and larger cities Spanish has supplanted it. Yucatec is the language of small, usually isolated villages. If at Cobá you walk to the village on the other side of the lake you'll find nearly everyone there speaking Yucatec. Unlike Guatemala and highland Chiapas, in the Yucatán you will not see many people wearing traditional dress, nor will you easily find colorful, open-stall *mercados*. Though the Yucatán has more than its share of spectacular Classic ruins, here modern society has usurped traditional Maya ways much more thoroughly than in the southern

How do You Pronounce "Xpuhil"?

Xpuhil, Xcalak, Xkukican, Xkichmook, Xtampak, Xul, Xtampak... Maps showing Yucatán place-names are thick with words beginning with *X*. The reason is that in certain Maya dialects *X* means "place" or "the place of... ".

The short answer to how these place-names are to be articulated is that *X* should be pronounced as if it were *Eesh*. Thus "Xpuhil" should exit the mouth sounding something like "eesh-puh-HEEL." Of course, there are complications.

In some parts of the Ruta Maya it's hard to hear the "ee" before the "sh"; thus Xpuhil becomes "shpuh-HEEL." None the less, the "eesh" seems to be more popular. Elsewhere the convention of using an X to designate the *eesh* sound has not been followed. Thus just west of Cobá we find the ruin of Ixil and south of Chichén Itzá there's the town of Ishmul.

highlands.

The northern part of the Yucatán Peninsula is much more densely populated than the southern part and northern Guatemala. Until recently the southern part of the Maya lowlands had remained almost unpopulated, except for near the coasts. Formerly both had many Maya cities; the question of what happened to the Maya of the southern Yucatán and northern Guatemala is *the* mystery of Maya archeology.

Nowadays, both in Guatemala's northern Petén District and the southern part of the Yucatán Peninsula, population density is increasing rapidly, not only because of high birthrates but also as a result of various government programs designed to "open up the frontier." On my most recent trip through southern Yucatán, one day I was waiting for a bus on the road between Xpuhil and Escárcega, next to the settlement of Ejido Felipe Ángel, population 25 souls. A fellow came by on a bike, paused to chat, and said, "Tomorrow the Mexican government is sending 70 people here from the highlands, near Mexico City. Those people are supposed to live here for the rest of their lives, making a living on the land the government gives them. Too many people live in the highlands, but here we don't have enough."

Society in the Southern Yucatán Peninsula has a special pioneer flavor. Hanging around Xpuhil and visiting some of the surrounding settlements, for instance, you see the rough-and-tumble, the down-and-out, the hustling-upwardly-mobile, the socially conscious, the social outcasts... all mingling vigorously.

Mexican freetail bat
Tadarida brasiliensis

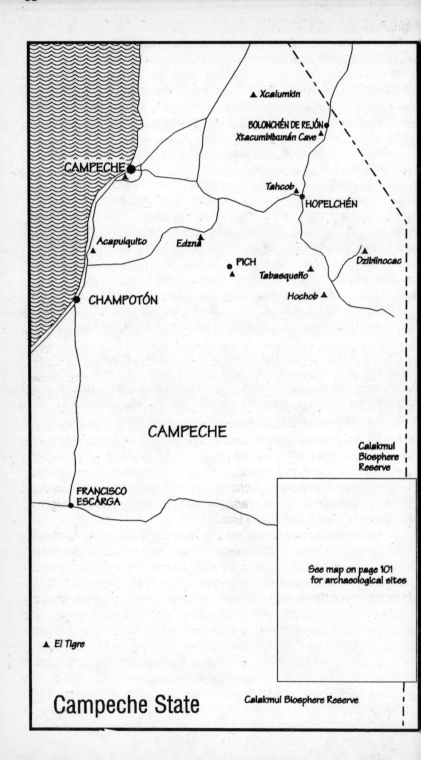

Xcalumkin

BOLONCHÉN DE REJÓN
Xtacumbibunán Cave

CAMPECHE

Tahcob

HOPELCHÉN

Acapulquito   Edzná

PICH   Dziblinocac
                   Tabasqueño
CHAMPOTÓN
                          Hochob

CAMPECHE

Calakmul
Biosphere
Reserve

FRANCISCO
ESCÁRGA

See map on page 101
for archaeological sites

El Tigre

Campeche State   Calakmul Biosphere Reserve

PLACES TO VISIT

Campeche State

Xpuhil

Archeological orientation

If you want to have "the Río Bec architectural style" firmly planted in your mind, without hiking all the way to Río Bec, Xpuhil is the place to go. Its Late Classic, steep-sided pyramids with steps too narrow to climb, leading to dummy temples with showy roof combs are exemplary of the strange Río Bec style.

Logistics

Both first-class and second-class buses stop at the town of Xpuhil, which lies about a kilometer east of the ruins. Most second-classers will be happy to carry you on to the ruins if you make clear your wish to get off at *la ruina de Xpuhil*. To reach the ruin from town, just walk westward toward Escárcega, to a little beyond the hill's crest and the big, thatch-roofed restaurant on the left; the ruin's entrance lies on the right. The ruin is so near the road and the space between the grounds and the highway is so narrow that, unlike most other Mexican ruins, the custodians prefer for you not to camp outside the entrance. However, they do offer a free alternative, in the form of a camp owned by the Instituto Nacional de Antropología, where the custodians themselves live, back in the town of Xpuhil.

Apparently at one time there were plans to develop this camp for there are several thatch-roofed bungalows. However, these have fallen into such disrepair that it's preferable to sleep in a tent or camper. To ask permission from the custodians to stay in the camp you can ask, "*¿Es posible dormir esta noche en el campamento en el pueblo? Tenemos una tienda de campaña.*" — "Is it possible to sleep tonight in the camp in town? We have a tent."

To reach the campground, return to Xpuhil's crossroad and take the road north, toward Dzibalchén. On this highway walk no more than a few seconds before exiting onto the first road on the right, which at this writing is just a muddy, one-lane path dipping into marshy ground. Walk for about three minutes until white-walled huts with collapsing thatched roofs appear on the slope to the left. No services are available. If you need to use a toilet, the proper question is, "*¿Donde puedo irme al monte?*" The word *monte* refers to the surrounding woods; you're asking which direction you should walk into the woods to find the place where people relieve themselves. Don't forget a *gratificación* for the custodian who helps you get settled here.

At the moment no hotels or formal guest rooms are available in Xpuhil, though this may soon change because new settlements are springing up everywhere in this part of the Yucatán, and Xpuhil is becoming the main city for a lot of people living in isolated communities. In fact, Xpuhil is a good place to sit someplace out of the way and savor real frontier-town bustle — a steady influx of Indians hitching into town in the backs of pickup trucks, bringing bags of corn and beans; hard-bitten backwoods folks buying machetes and hoe handles; young men celebrating their infrequent visit into town by getting monstrously drunk...

If you want to camp in town but can't cope with staying where *monte* means "toilet," or if you want some information about visiting some of the area's more isolated ruins with a guide, visit the thatch-roofed restaurant atop the hill near the ruin — the **Restaurante El Mirador Maya**. The owner of this pleasant place, Sr Moises Carreón Cabrera, and a strayed Frenchman by the name of Serge Riou, are at your service, and are very well informed and supportive of our kind of eco-tourism.

The idealistic Serge, known hereabouts by the name of Checo, speaks passable English, as well as fluent Spanish and his native French; he makes Xpuhil his home all through the year except from May to mid June, when he returns home to France. At this writing he's organizing tour itineraries and beginning to involve local people in eco-tourism. As a guide himself, Checo takes groups no larger than five. His current fee is about US$80 per day, per group. He prefers to walk to isolated ruins, even if they're served by dry roads that a 4 x 4 could manage. With Checo a walking trip to the ruins of Hormiguero and Río Bec takes four days.

Becan

Archeological orientation

Becan is famous for the moat around its main temple area. Originally the moat was two to four meters deep (seven to 13 feet) and three to about 24 meters wide (ten to 80 feet), and spanned by seven stone causeways; it's about 1.9km (1.2 miles) in circumference. In one of Becan's structures several passageways have been discovered; these were possibly used during ceremonies involving mysterious visitations by gods. Deposits of charred debris and bone material taken from the site indicate that it was attacked about 450 A.D. (Early Classic).

Logistics

Becan lies about six kilometers (3.7 miles) west of Xpuhil, clearly visible half a kilometer off the highway. In Xpuhil it's easy to find taxis eager to ferry you this distance, and to Chicaná just two kilometers (1.2 miles) farther west. The *taxista*'s standard fare for this distance of paved road is around US$3.00 — about ten times the fee for riding in

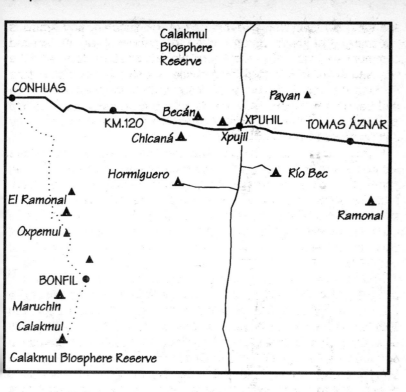

pickups the much more difficult 14km between Xpuhil and the entrance road to Hormiguero.

One way to land a less expensive ride is to wait at the crossroads in Xpuhil until you see a westward-pointing pickup truck loading passengers, and see if you can go with them. "*¿Pasan ustedes la ruina de Becan?*" you can ask the pickup-owner — "Do you pass the ruin of Becan?. "*Y, ¿cuánto cuesta el pasaje?*" — "And, how much is the fare?" Second-class buses, which stop anywhere you wish, run much less frequently between Xpuhil and Escárcega than between Xpuhil and Chetumal. The few that do generally head eastward in the morning, westward in the afternoon.

Becan ruin is accessible by a dirt road marked with a sign; the entrance is next to a small store or kiosk. Probably this road is passable even during the wet season. The dirt road ends at the custodian's office, which stands across the moat from the main ruin. After paying your entrance fee, you're allowed to camp overnight in the parking area next to the moat. Though from here you enjoy a splendid view of the main pyramid, the area is too small and exposed to make a good camping site. It's about large enough for one large camper, or two or three tents.

Chicaná

Archeological orientation

Chicaná is a modest site showing influences of both the Río Bec style and the Chenes style. A reconstructed building one story high stands on a platform with rounded corners, characteristic of the Río Bec style; a baroquely ornamented temple door representing the gaping mouth of a monster, with teeth projecting over the lintel, reflects the Chenes style.

Logistics

The ruin of Chicaná lies about one kilometer (⅗ mile) south of the highway, about two kilometers (1¼ mile) west of Becan and thus eight kilometers (five miles) west of Xpuhil. Though Chicaná is a small ruin, it's in a more pleasant, peaceful setting than its two neighbors up the road; a grassy parking lot easily accommodates three large campers. Becan's parking lot/camping area is an excellent place to sit at dusk watching Aztec parakeets cavort in the treetops across the drive, while Yucatán gray squirrels, *Sciurus yucatanensis*, leap from tree to tree in the nearby ruin area. Next to the custodian's office grows a tree with egg-shaped, apple-sized,

Anona

slightly scaly fruits. This is the famous anona, or custard apple, *Annona reticulata*, the fruits of which have sublimely sweet flesh that melts in the mouth; though planted in the tropics worldwide, it's native to tropical America.

Hormiguero

Archeological orientation

In the Río Bec style, Hormiguero's claim to fame is a well preserved pyramid on which stands a temple with a richly ornamented monster-mouth door.

Logistics

If you've been itching to hike to one of the more isolated ruins you've probably been eyeing on the map the cluster of ruins south of Xpuhil — Hormiguero, Río Bec, Tortuga, La Muñeca, El Palmar, and others. Of these, probably Hormiguero is the most accessible. However, unless you hire a guide, even Hormiguero should be visited only by hikers with a fair amount of experience in navigating, and who can with certainty find their way back if they lose their direction.

Becoming disoriented on the way to Hormiguero is easy not because the ruin lies deep in the trackless jungle, but because the area is so rapidly being opened to settlement — despite the ruin lying well within the Calakmul Biosphere Reserve. In places fresh dirt roads and trails to new cornfields can easily be confused with the main road. Only in a small area right around the ruin is the road like a tunnel through the jungle. If you don't trust your ability to navigate, but really can't afford to pay Checo to accompany you (see Xpuhil section), you might try this approach to get to Hormiguero:

No bus service is available heading south from Xpuhil, so at the town's crossroads try to spot a pickup truck loading up with passengers heading south — or walk a couple of kilometers out of town, and hitch from there to avoid local traffic. At least early and late in the day there's plenty of truck traffic on this gravel road and hitching is an honored institution, so you probably won't need to wait for long. Since most drivers on this road don't know about Hormiguero, you might need to specify that you want off about 14km (8.7 miles) south of Xpuhil, at the entrance to the village known as Ejido Castellot, which lies about 100 meters off the road, on the right. Beside the road there should be a small, rusty sign announcing "Ejido: Eugenio Echeverria Castellot N° 2." After your ride most drivers expect a small *gratificación* of about US 30¢.

As you hike the main dirt road heading west through Ejido Castellot, probably some boys or young men will run out offering you their guide service. Later when your path becomes obliterated because of a new cornfield, you'll be glad you hired one. If you want them to guide you to the ruin, then leave you so you can camp there overnight, you can say, "*Cuando llegamos a la ruina, usted puede regresar a su pueblo solo. Cuando regreso, no necesitaré a un guía*" — "When we arrive at the ruin, you can return to your village alone. When I return, I won't need a guide." If you want to try finding Hormiguero all by yourself, here's how:

Just keep walking on the dirt road heading westward through Ejido Castellot. After half an hour you come to a quadrangular, 50-meter long pond (on the left) and probably some women washing clothes. After thirty more minutes turn right on the road that at this writing is less used than the road continuing straight. The road on which you've been walking points south at 200°; the grassy road to Hormiguero heads west at 290°. Now follow this grassy road through cut-over secondary woods and cornfields. After five minutes a road leads to the left, but don't take this. Try to stay on the "main road" for about 35 more minutes. If suddenly the vegetation looks more intact, that may be the ruin coming up.

The road to the ruin is passable with a 4 x 4 during dry weather, but low-hanging tree limbs can be a problem. In at least one place it's briefly rather steep and could be very slick when wet. Even in the dry season a few muddy places can give problems, and along these quagmires there may be no trees large enough to winch from. Also, frequently portions of the road are buried beneath four-meter wide, half-meter-high anthills! Surely this remarkable kind of ant domicile is responsible for the ruin's name, for *hormiguero* in Spanish means "anthill."

I agree with Checo that the road to Hormiguero — at least the last section — should not be driven. Vehicles will only mess up the road for those of us who prefer walking, and it distracts from the sensation of eventually coming upon the main pyramid with its monster-mouth door standing majestically "in deep jungle." The moment of finally arriving in front of this pyramid, because of the difficulty in getting there, its isolation, and the dense forest around it, rates as one of the premium experiences available along the Ruta Maya.

At Hormiguero there's no office, no parking area and no cleared plaza — just rank forest and the ruins. Beneath some trees lies an excellent spot for camping, where you can visualize yourself lying in your tent at night, dreamily gazing through the tent's screened window, viewing the pyramid by moonlight. However, for the sake of security, if you decide to camp here, remember that everyone who saw you between here and Ejido Castellot has been able to figure out where you were heading, and they know that this one spot beneath the trees is perfect for camping. I chose a random spot in the forest where I couldn't see anything interesting, but where no one would ever find me, except by chance.

Río Bec

Archeological orientation

Río Bec is famous because an architectural style has been named after it (see page 109). It's a large, unrestored site spread over a wide forested area.

Logistics

Río Bec is in Quintana Roo, but it's being considered here because its access road is in Campeche. The same broad gravel road that connects Xpuhil and Ejido Castellot carries us to the entrance to the dirt road to Río Bec. Probably the driver of the truck on which you're hitching won't know the whereabouts of the entrance to Río Bec so you may need to help him by saying that it's between the small villages of Campanario and La Lucha, heading eastward (on the left, if you're heading south from Xpuhil).

The trail to Río Bec passes through forest that is much less disturbed than along the road to Hormiguero; therefore it's much more pleasant and interesting. At this writing it's impassable even for 4 x 4's because a bridge is out. Though staying on the right road is a simple matter, you'd do best to have a guide lead you to the ruins. The problem is that the ruins lie a little off the road, well hidden by the forest, and you can walk right past them. Either have Checo accompany you, or hire someone in Campanario or La Lucha as a guide. If you want to stay a while at the ruin and walk back alone, the experienced hiker should have no problems.

Calakmul

Archeological orientation

At Calakmul we find a pyramid rising 53 meters (175 feet) from a base covering two hectares (five acres). So far, 6,750 structures have been mapped here; magnificent jade masks have been found and a peak population of 60,000 has been estimated for the site. Though more stelae have been recorded at Calakmul than at any other Maya site, major excavations still haven't been conducted. Like El Mirador and Caracol, Calakmul is one of those giants of Maya archeology that someday may qualify as a destination for average tourist itineraries, but right now it's just too hard to get to for most people.

Logistics

Calakmul is accessible by a 30-km-long (18.6-mile), deeply rutted, tunnel-like road through the forest. Trekking there should be attempted only during the dry-season months of March and April; in 1981, 4.9 *meters* (16 *feet*) of rain were recorded nearby! Moreover, without proper guiding this trip can be a bit dangerous because of the area's thriving drug-running and tomb-looting industries. If you want to get to Calakmul, talk to Checo (see the Xpuhil section).

By the way, in the 723,000-ha (2,792-sq-mile) Calakmul Biosphere Reserve surrounding the ruin live five of the six species of cat native to Mexico: The jaguar, the margay, the puma, the ocelot, and the jaguarondi. Among the birds found are the ocellated turkey, great curassow and ornate eagle — all threatened species. This all sounds very good, but if you go to any of the ruins profiled above you'll see an astonishing amount of slash-and-burn destruction inside the reserve.

The only way I can see that the region's ecology might escape complete disruption is for eco-tourism to be developed. Only when everyone sees more money coming from eco-tourism than from traditional development (which includes illegal timber harvesting and tomb looting) will anything be saved. If you pay Checo and his crew of local guides to take you to Calakmul, or any of the other ruins, you'll be at the forefront of conservation efforts.

ESCÁRCEGA

At Escárcega, also known as Francisco Escárcega, the Ruta Maya's southern-Yucatán route connects with the main road between Palenque and Mérida. Escárcega is a smallish, unassuming, quintessentially Mexican town. At dusk its little plaza is positively vibrant with local folks coming out to sit in the cooling air, gossip, watch the children play and to snack. There's just something about a small-town Mexican plaza at dusk that is beautiful — somehow a coming-together of all the culture's best impulses.

Concerning the plaza's snacks, you should try an *elote* — steaming-hot sweetcorn smeared with mayonnaise and sprinkled with grated cheese and optional chili powder. Lodging in Escárcega ranges from US$2.00/night *pensiones* to upscale hotels. A clean room with its own bath, hot water and a ceiling fan, within a block of the plaza, costs about US$5.00. The second-class bus station Autobuses del Sur lies just three or four blocks from the plaza; the first-class ADO station stands about half a kilometer away, on the main highway on the northern side of town.

THE ROAD BETWEEN ESCÁRCEGA AND CAMPECHE

Between Escárcega and Champotón, for 84km (52 miles) Hwy 261 crosses low, flat land on which one sees cow pastures, every degree of weediness and hacked-on secondary forest, an occasional banana plantation and a few small villages; one is thankful for vultures flying overhead, for breaking the monotony. In coastal Champotón people fish for sawfish and small shark; the town is equipped with several hotels, including three on Calle 30. Here **Hotel Snook** earns three stars. Moreover, this quaint little seaside town has some history.

In Bernal Díaz del Castillo's *True History of the Conquest of New Spain*, in Chapters Four and Nine you can read Díaz's eyewitness accounts of fighting that in 1517 and 1518 took place in this general vicinity. Moreover, many suppose that the town of Chakanputun, from which the Itzá were driven around 1200 AD (eventually settling in Chichén Itzá and Guatemala's Tayasal) was at or near present-day Champotón. It's easy to see why Champotón enjoys such an estimable history: It lies at the mouth of the Río Champotón, the first fair-sized river to be met when coming from the arid north.

North of Champotón, Hwy 180 runs right along the coast, affording many fine views of the Gulf. For the first five or so kilometers north of town a simple wire fence stands between the highway and the beach, but then the fence peters out and plenty of possibilities arise for beachcombing and birding. After exiting a second-class bus or parking your car along the road you can walk along the beach for hours. Among the birds you might spot are brown pelicans, olivaceous cormorants, magnificent frigate-birds, laughing gulls, royal terns, white ibises and roseate spoonbills. Occasional mangrove lagoons and tidal flats are home to mangrove swallows and mangrove warblers.

However, this beach is not famous for swimming. The water looks turbid and the beach itself is more muddy than sandy. Toward the north, the muddy shore evolves into a rocky one. Campgrounds and hotels are surprisingly absent from this shore, though about five km (three miles) north of Acapulquito the four-star but somehow forlorn-looking **Siho-Playa Hotel**, with a splendid view of the brooding Gulf, tries hard to be first-class; its rooms go for as little as US$23.00.

About 30km (19 miles) south of the city of Campeche, Seyba Playa is a busy, colorful little fishing village with fishermen mending their nets in the shade of coconut palms; the whole town smells of fish, which is to be expected because people here make their livings on octopus, white sea-bass, halibut and small shark. If you're in the mood for swimming, follow signs to Payucan, where the beach is touted as being "composed of polished grains of sand, lapped by moderate waves, and giving way to a gentle slope beneath transparent water."

For our purposes, probably the most interesting place in the large, bustling, modern town of Campeche (three four-star hotels and an assortment of lesser-stars) is the bus terminal, served by several lines. Frequent first- and second-class service is available at practically all hours for points south and north. However, if you're interested in ruins to the east and northeast — the Chenes group, Uxmal and other ruins of the Puuc region — service is less bounteous.

Highway 261 between Campeche and Mérida, which the Ruta Maya follows, no longer is the main highway connecting the two cities. Now most north/south traffic follows Hwy 180, which lies far west of the main ruin zone. Traffic on Hwy 261 south of Uxmal consists mostly of tourist travel and people living in isolated settlements "going to town" in Campeche and Mérida. If you're taking the bus to any of the ruins between Campeche and Mérida, such as Uxmal, at the bus station in Campeche note current scheduling at the second-class bus-line called Camioneros de Campeche, which serves *las ruinas*. At the time of this writing, buses of this line depart in the direction of Uxmal approximately every two hours; on many of them there's standing-room only.

Edzna

Archeological orientation

Edzna's architecture manifests the Chenes architectural style (See box page 109). Its buildings, arranged around two nuclei, cover an

The Río Bec, Chenes and Puuc Architectural Styles

Among ruins manifesting the strange Río Bec style are Río Bec, Xpuhil, Hormiguero, Chicaná and Becan. Xpuhil, the most accessible example, demonstrates exactly what the style is all about. Its main temple is flanked by three high towers that *imitate* regular temple-pyramids. The steps leading up these "pyramids" are too narrow and steep to use, and the "doorway" into the temples at the summits lead to nowhere. In short, the Río Bec style is so concerned with appearances, and unconcerned about utility, that it amounts to pure fakery. As Michael Coe says, "It is as though the Río Bec architects wished to imitate the great Tikal temples without going to any trouble." Besides false towers, the Río Bec Style is characterized by lavishly ornamented façades.

Just north of the Río Bec area lies a cluster of ruins manifesting the Chenes style. Among these are Edzna, Hochob, Tabasqueño and Dzibilnocac. Buildings in the Chenes style, similar to the Río Bec fashion, are mounted with overly elaborate, lavishly ornamented façades with sky-serpent masks; there's an affinity for monster-mouth doors. The Chenes style is void of the Río Bec's steep, narrow-stepped pyramids with fake temples atop them.

To the north of both the Río Bec and Chenes area lies the Puuc Hills, and the architectural style named after them. Uxmal is the largest Puuc site. In Puuc architecture we sense artistic impulses that are relatively more settled, less fantastic, and perhaps more self-confident than in the Río Bec and Chenes styles.

Seeing the exquisitely crafted upper façades of Uxmal's temples, and their exuberant usage of stone mosaics, emphasizing sky-serpent faces with long, hook-shaped noses we discover something approaching the Maya equivalent to the European Baroque. The Puuc style continues with the Chenes's nervous energy, but that energy is more under control and somehow less neurotic...

In this context, the Río Bec style seems to be a freakish architectural expression of a culture indulging its idiosyncrasies just before an inevitable collapse; the Puuc is more mature and conservative; the Chenes is more or less an intermediate style between them.

area of 603 ha (2.33 sq miles). In Maya the word *edzná* means something like "House of the Grimaces," which probably refers to the crest of the Temple of Five Floors, decorated with not-very-amiable-looking god-masks. In the housing group called Annex of the Knives the main building covers a more ancient foundation constructed in the Petén style.

One of Edzna's most interesting features has nothing to do with architecture; it relates to the fact that the dispersed buildings stand on a plain that frequently floods. The ancient Maya developed a network of channels that drained the area by conducting rainwater into lagoons; serving as reservoirs, these lagoons held water through the dry seasons. Channels were dug to irrigate fields.

Logistics

Roads between the town of Campeche and Edzna are paved and fairly good. At this time, Monday through Friday, a Camioneros de Campeche bus leaves Campeche at 1400 for the town of Pich (in Yucatec, *pich* means "guanacaste tree"), passing right by Edzna's 500-meter entrance road. If you can't make the Pich bus (and no new service has opened up since my visit) then you can take any of the every-two-hour buses heading for Hopelchén, Uxmal and Muna, and disembark at *el entronque* at Cayal. At *el entronque* stand some wonderfully large guanacaste trees (see box), under which you can stand as you hitch to Edzna 19km to the south. Hitching down this road is a well established practice; probably some men will be waiting in the shade with you. Another alternative, probably faster but more hectic and less interesting, is to take any of the dozens of buses heading south, and just south of Acapulquito get off at *el entronque* with Hwy 188, the road to Tixmucuy. From there you can hitch (or possibly take a bus part-way) through Tixmucuy to Edzna.

From Cayal Hwy 261 shoots south, straight at the ruin, and then at the ruin curves hard to the left, heading for Pich; Hwy 188 from south of Acapulquito connects with Hwy 261 at this same curve. No matter which route you use, you need to leave the bus at this curve (you'll see the Temple of Five Floors rising above the trees 500 meters away). At the end of the ruin's 500-meter access road, besides the ruin's entrance, stands a small, rustic cafe offering basic refreshments.

Camping is allowed in a rather weedy, junky area near the cafe. For my taste, this area is too close to buildings and family life for tent-camping. About a hundred meters from the entrance, on the right as you face the ruins, there's a small trail entering a low area that during the rainy season is submerged, but in the dry season comprises a beautiful, park-like environment perfect for camping, though mosquitoes are bad. This depression must have been part of the ancient Maya's reservoir system.

The custodian says he's thinking of clearing out some of the old canals around the main buildings so that visitors can walk down them, getting a good view of the surrounding dense forest; these would provide wonderful birding trails. Usually boys and young men are available for guide service.

At this time, theoretically, the bus from Pich to Campeche passes Edzna's entrance road around 0600 — an hour that during the winter/dry season is too early for those of us who need light to break camp. If you get stranded at Edzná and must hitch, the quickest way out is to take Hwy 188 west toward Tixmucuy, which meets Hwy 180 south of Acapulquito. If you're working north toward Mérida and don't want to go through the town of Campeche, you'll probably have to wait a while. I finally escaped by walking two kilometers up the road toward Cayal, to the agricultural research station called Campo Experimental Edzna. Here I made friends with workers who let me ride with them to Cayal when they went home for lunch.

HOPELCHÉN

At Hopelchén we make a short detour off the Ruta Maya and head south to the ruins of Hochob, Dzibilnocac and Tabasqueño; past the ruins, the road south traverses the Calakmul Biosphere Reserve and reconnects with the Ruta Maya at Xpuhil. Hopelchén is home to several well stocked grocery stores and a Pemex gas station. The hotel called **Los Arcos** lies at one of the plaza's corners, sprouting several satellite dishes on its roof. It's clean and has a restaurant; a double room with private bath, hot water and a fan on the ceiling costs about US$8.25; the **Posado Escárcega** stands at Calle 25 No. 15. Two two-star hotels are located on Avenida Justo Sierra.

In Hopelchén the paved road south leaves from a corner of the plaza and is clearly marked. Buses to Dzibalchén, the town nearest the ruins, depart from in front of a store facing the plaza; above the store in big letters is written "Escalante Heredia Hnos. y Cops." The plaza itself is a shady, friendly place. At the time of writing bus schedules seem to be in a state of flux; about five a day run between Hopelchén and Dzibalchén. Probably in the future there will be more, for settlements along this road are springing up like mushrooms, which may be bad news for the Calakmul Biosphere Reserve.

A community of Mennonites lives near Hopelchén so if you hang around the plaza long enough you'll see these people getting on and off buses and hitching rides in pickup trucks. Their religion forbids them to own and operate their own horseless carriages. The men wear black coveralls and straw hats while the women attire themselves in black skirts or aprons, darkish, heavy blouses that must be very hot in this climate, and straw hats. Since originally most of their ancestors came from German-speaking parts of Europe and most Mennonites are slender Caucasians, you might be tempted to strike up a conversation with them. However, most of Hopelchén's Mennonites speak only Spanish.

DZIBALCHÉN

Dzibalchén makes a wonderfully colorful, traditional, small-town base from which you can visit Hochob, Dzibilnocac and Tabasqueño; it has a small market and some well-stocked stores.

Also, Dzibalchén is home to English-speaking José William Chám C., an Indian providing eco-friendly services — local folks call him "Don William" (pronounced "Don Wilem"). From Don William you can rent a sturdy bike capable of surviving the bumpy gravel road to Hochob; it costs about US$3.50/day; at this writing three bikes are available. Don William is eager to serve as a guide himself. He won't state a standard fee but says that for a day of guiding "Americans give me about US$17.00, Germans give me about US$10.00, and the Dutch about US$7.50... "

You don't really need Don William to help you find Hochob, but if you're interested in Tabasqueño or some other secret places he knows about, he's certainly worth his pay. Possibly the most interesting service Don William can provide concerns lodging. If you find the hotel-less Dzibalchén area as pleasant as I do you may want to stay a while. Don William knows some local families willing to accept travelers into their homes.

To find Don William stand in Dzibalchén's plaza with your back toward the Palacio Municipal. Then walk to the plaza's far left corner and continue up that street, heading away from the Palacio, for about 800 meters, until it turns hard to the left, and continue until you see a sign that says, in English, "TOURIST INFORMATION HERE." If you get lost, almost any kid in town can tell you where "Don Wilem" lives. If you'd like to set up something with him before you arrive, his address is: Sr José William Chám C., Domicilio Conocido, Barrio "El Pocito", 24920 Dzibalchén, Hopelchén, Campeche, México.

Hochob

Archeological orientation
Hochob (pronounced ho-CHOB) is a small, minor ruin with the usual Chenes-style monster-mouth temple-door entrance, located atop a tall hill overlooking the surrounding country; not much is said about it in the literature. However, because it lies so peacefully off the beaten track, and getting there involves passing through some interesting territory, Hochob might become one of your favorite destinations.

Logistics
The seldom-traveled, one-lane gravel road to Hochob departs from the paved Xpuhil/Hopelchén road on the northwestern side of Dzibalchén, just as you enter town, coming from Hopelchén. The intersection lies across from the cemetery, beside a huge guanacaste tree, not far from the little sign announcing Dzibalchén's outskirts; our road heads 210° to the southwest. Even during the wet season four-

wheel drives should be able to make it all the way to Hochob, though toward the road's end occasionally it becomes a bit steep and rocky.

Eight kilometers (five miles) straight down this road lies the small town of Chincón, which is about as sleepy-looking and muddy as can be imagined. Coming to Chincón's plaza, take a hard left, pass by the small, whitewashed church and the basketball court, leave town, and pass across a field about a kilometer wide. Beyond the field, vegetation at the time of this writing is surprisingly intact; walking the trail in early morning provides interesting birding.

Along the road between Chincón and Hochob sometimes trails depart at right angles from our road; the locals use them for collecting building poles, and to reach their beehives. Four kilometers (2½ miles) from Chincón the road forks; take the arm leading to the left and stay on it. Soon you'll glimpse Hochob rising atop a hill. The plaza inside the ruin makes a wonderful picnic spot — shady and breezy, and most inviting for a mid-day snooze. It's immensely pleasant to perch on a breezy temple-foundation and gaze over the surrounding hilly landscape. Large flocks of screeching Aztec parakeets are impressive.

Three routes are available for leaving Hochob. The easiest option is to return the way you came. A second is to have the custodian, who frequently comes to the ruins from his home in Chincón, put you on the path to the ruins of Tabasqueño. Apparently, once you arrive at Tabasqueño, you can take yet another path that meets the Hopelchén/Xpuhil road northwest of Dzibalchén. (I didn't find out about this until later; if you explore it, send me the details!)

The third route involves circling around toward the southeast and coming out at Dzibalchén. This is a fine walk (probably passable with a 4 x 4 during the dry season) passing through a variety of habitats, including some very pretty woods; a morning bird-walk should provide an impressive list. To take this route, return to the fork, turn around as if again you were coming from Chincón, and this time take the right arm instead of the left. Fifteen minutes of walking brings you to an intersection with another road, where you should take a hard left and follow the tire marks past all exits and side roads for about an hour and a half (walking). After this period of time, a large path leads off to the left, to Dzibalchén. If you feel insecure taking an unmarked trail away from the main road, then just continue following the road, which eventually curves around and enters Dzibalchén.

Dzibilnocac

This is a small ruin distinguished by its stucco masks. You can reach it by taking the 1100 am bus from Dzibalchén to Iturbide — about 18km (11 miles); the ruin lies less than a kilometer from Iturbide. Just ask anyone in town where the trail is.

Nohcacab

On the *National Geographic* map mentioned on page 12 this ruin between Hopelchén and Dzibalchén is designated a "ruin of touristic interest." However, there's little to see here besides some piles of stones.

Tabasqueño

Tabasqueño is small but similar in interest to Hochob. Already I've mentioned the path between Hochob and Tabasqueño, which Hochob's custodian can help you find. People in Dzibalchén insist that Tabasqueño is easily accessible by a trail off the Hopelchén/Xpuhil road. They say that one needs only to go to Kilometer 35, about five kilometers up the road toward Hopelchén, take a trail to the left, go through a cattle lot, across a pasture... etc. But Kilometer 35 is unmarked and it's hard to find the path going left. The cattle lot appears to be private property and maybe someone like Don William can open the gate, but a foreigner feels uneasy doing it. When a person crosses the big pasture the 40 or so playful or hungry cattle stampede up behind you and stop just an instant before plowing over you, which is disconcerting. And if you're still interested in the trail after all this, then you can try figuring out which of the several cattle paths meandering across the field leads to Tabasqueño... If you want to visit Tabasqueño, talk to Don William about it.

Tahcob

Though maps frequently show Tahcob as a "ruin of touristic interest" just west of Hopelchén, my bus driver on the road to Hopelchén, who seemed to know everything about the area, said he'd never heard of Tahcob. And it turned out that he passed within twenty meters of it every workday, and it was in plain view! Tahcob is a tiny ruin not much larger than a gringo camper, standing in the weeds about five meters off the main road, approximately two kilometers west of Hopelchén. You can see everything about it from the road.

XTACUMBILXUNAN CAVE (BOLONCHÉN CAVE)

Back on the Ruta Maya, signs just south of Bolonchén de Rejón point us to this easily accessible, tourist-oriented cave. The idea here is to descend deep into a cave and take a subterranean walk. However, during my visit the ladder was broken and the visit amounted to looking at some rocks near the cave's entrance suggestive of massive, drowsy animals. A fine place for picnicking.

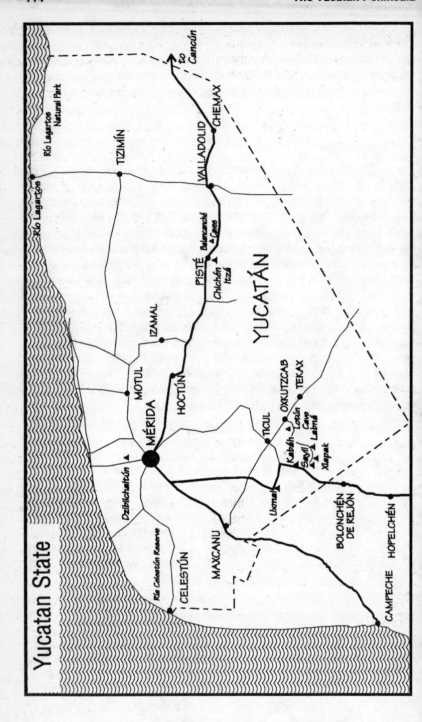

Yucatan State

Yucatán State

Sayil, Xlapak and Labná
Archeological Orientation
These three ruins, all within 10km (six miles) of one another, are fine examples of Puuc architecture, which was the dominant style in the Yucatán during the heady days of the Late Classic — it's the style seen in greatest florescence at Uxmal. Buildings of the Puuc style are characterized by "veneer masonry" — a technique by which beautifully cut stone is imbedded in concrete, rather as we might set tiles into cement. As in the Chenes style farther south, temple façades are baroquely ornamented with all kinds of weird motifs, and there's a real obsession with rain-god masks. One thing that distinguishes Sayil, Xlapak and Labná from many other ruins in the Yucatán is that here we find little or no evidence of Toltec influence on the architecture. At Labná the latest recorded date is 869 AD — the end of the Late Classic.

Sayil
At Sayil we see the magnificent Great Palace, with dozens of rooms arranged in three stories, with the upper stories set back so that the roofs of the apartment below serve the apartments above as terraces; a 64-meter long, 23-meter wide (210-foot long, 75-foot wide) stone staircase from the pyramid's base serves all three terraces. Aesthetically, such massive buildings generally have problems looking "heavy." Here the ancient Maya architects solved this difficulty by giving the second floor some very wide doorways with triple entrances formed by pairs of columns, thus breaking the monolith into lighter elements. Several other structures are worth seeing, too, including a free-standing arch that usually is considered the most impressive in the Maya world.

Xlapak
Compared with Sayil, Xlapak is extremely modest, with three fallen structures, and bits and pieces of this and that temple scattered among the weeds.

Labná
Some consider Labná's buildings to offer the finest examples of Puuc architecture. It's best known for its arch, adorned with intricately carved mosaics.

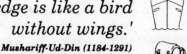

Logistics

The paved, well maintained road leading to Sayil, Labná and Xlapak leaves Hwy 261 just north of the border between the states of Campeche and Yucatán; more or less opposite the entrance lies a checkpoint for agricultural goods; at the intersection itself stands a sign reading, "Sayil 5; Xlapak 10; Labná 14." At this intersection, northbound buses pass at about 0800, 1000, 1430 and 1700; southbound buses pass around 0800, 1000, 1330 and 1630. At the time of this writing, the highway along which the ruins are clustered, and which eventually leads to Loltún Cave and the town of Oxkutzcab, is not served by regular buses. Theoretically each day one or more buses carrying tourists on packaged tours from Mérida visits each of these ruins. In Mérida, Agencia de Viajes Gonzalez, with an office in the first-class ADO bus station, can give you more information.

Supposedly, each day a bus leaves Mérida at 0800, arrives at Labná at 1000 where it spends half an hour, then for half an hour visits Xlapak, and finally at 1100 enters Sayil. On my last visit to the area my strategy was to take a regular bus to the intersection, then hike to all three ruins, enjoying a pleasant one-hour walk between each. Coming out, I'd catch the tourist bus. To my dismay, however, after camping overnight near Labná and the next morning waiting for the bus along the road, it arrived at Labná quite late after (contrary to schedule) first going to Sayil. After simply turning around at Labná instead of stopping, it zipped away, bypassing Xlapak; I was left standing beside the road, scratching my head. I ended up walking the 14km back to Hwy 261. Apparently the bus driver, instead of adhering to a fixed schedule, does whatever the passengers prefer, which frequently means "briefly visit Sayil, then make a bee-line for Kabáh and Uxmal."

Few hitchable trucks pass down the Sayil/Xlapak/Labná road and for some reason the ones that do are usually full or simply won't stop. If you do get a ride, it'll probably be in another traveler's rented car. Occasionally people in cars travel this road to Loltún Cave, which lies 19km (12 miles) east of Labná. Because of travel problems on this road, Loltún Cave is probably most accessible to the carless, independent traveler by first going up to Muna (or even to Mérida), and taking the bus down to Oxkutzcab; then hitch or walk the seven km (four miles) to the cave, which offers about 1.5km (nearly a mile) of large caverns.

Unless you have your own car or go on a packaged tour out of Mérida, the independent traveler finds visiting these ruins a bit awkward. Since Sayil is considered to be by far the most impressive ruin, one option might be simply to walk the five km (three miles) between it and Hwy 261; probably you can hike the distance faster than you can hitch. Along this five-km stretch several trails and dirt roads lead into the forest to good resting and picnicking spots. At all three ruins you can buy refreshments, books, carvings, jewellery and "Indian clothing" such as attractive *minipiles*; camping is permitted in or around each site's parking area.

Though Sayil is the most impressive of the three ruins, Labná's setting is the most natural and pleasant, and little Xlapak has the most soul. Xlapak's soul comes in the presence of Sr Isauro Tuyub May, the custodian, and his wife. As well as tourist items, sodas and crackers available at each of the three ruins, at Xlapak you can also enjoy a congenial cup of hot coffee and, if you speak Spanish, Don Isauro will tell you interesting things about the area and the ruins; be sure to ask him about the excellent wood carvings sold at each location.

Kabáh
Archeological orientation
Kabáh's buildings are Puuc in style; the main one being the Temple of Codz Poop, adorned with dozens of curl-nosed rain god masks. Two door jambs — a jamb is an upright piece forming the side of a door — bear the date 909 AD, and show figures with spear-throwers and close-fitting jackets of Toltec style. Like Uxmal and Labná, Kabáh has a fine arch; its arch marks the terminus of a causeway, or *sacbe*, linking the site with Uxmal 15km (nine miles) to the northwest.

Logistics
On Hwy 261, Kabáh lies about five km (three miles) north of the road leading to Sayil, Xlapak and Labná; the road passes right through the center of the sizable ruin complex. A large parking area with an adjoining grassy spot is available for overnight campers, but this is so close to the highway that, for security purposes, the lone camper would probably hesitate to peg a tent there. During the day the ruin is busy with tour buses mostly making one-day runs from Mérida. At this time, regular buses heading north pass through the area at about 0800, 1000, 1430 and 1700; southbound buses pass around 0800, 1000, 1330 and 1630.

Kabáh's main ruin area is cleared of trees so it is open and sunny; you can climb to a temple, perch in the shade, and with binoculars gaze into the surrounding forest at bird's-eye level. Across the highway from the main entrance the trail to the *Arco Maya* makes a good early-morning birding walk, for vegetation is kept cleared along the trail, but about twenty meters away scrubby forest rises like a wall. In such situations you can spot forest-birds that normally are too shy to get close to.

At the arch a trail worth exploring enters the forest; I was told that it goes all the way to Uxmal; if you have more time than I did, maybe you can confirm this for this book's next updating.

Uxmal

Archeological orientation

Uxmal is the largest Puuc site and one of the triumphs of Maya civilization. The Nunnery, the Governor's Palace, the Dwarf's House, the Temple of Venus, the Pigeon House, the Turtle House... These wonderful buildings qualify Uxmal as one of the "super-ruins" along the Ruta Maya, along with Chichén Itzá, Tikal and Palenque. Not only does Uxmal offer the visitor *quantity*, but also *quality*. While some ruins, such as Labná, give the feeling of having grown piecemeal, Uxmal conveys the impression of having blossomed like a flower. It's the most uniform of Maya cities, possibly the most beautiful and, to me, the city that most harmoniously and hauntingly reflects its natural environment.

Most traditional guidebooks include pages and pages of information about Uxmal and there's plenty of literature available on the grounds; I'll not repeat their information here.

Logistics

At this time, northbound buses for Mérida stop at Uxmal's entrance road at 0800, 1000, 1430 and 1700; buses for Campeche stop at 0800, 1000, 1330 and 1630. These are the same times given for their arrival at the road to Sayil/Xlapak/Labná, and at Kabáh, which sounds

---

Birds You Might See around Uxmal and Nearby Ruins

Among the bushes and in the gardens of the hotels around Uxmal, and in the cleared areas of the archaeological zone itself, here are some of the birds you might see: *common ground-dove, ruddy ground-dove, groove-billed ani, Vaux's swift, turquoise-browed motmot, tropical kingbird, kiskadee flycatcher, rough-winged swallow, Yucatan jay, tropical mockingbird, clay-colored robin, peppershrike, great-tailed grackle, melodious blackbird* and *Altamira oriole*.

Along trails or dirt roads leading into scrubby, thorny woods around Uxmal and nearby ruins, in addition to the species mentioned above you might see: *plain chachalaca, white-fronted dove, fork-tailed emerald, buff-bellied hummingbird, golden-fronted woodpecker, social flycatcher, Yucatan flycatcher, Yucatan wren, Carolina wren, spot-breasted wren, white-bellied wren, gray-throated chat, gray-crowned yellowthroat, black-headed saltator, blue bunting* and *olive sparrow*.

At night, if you hear an owl with a low, staccato whistle, probably it's the *ferruginous pygmy owl*; the low-flying *lesser nighthawk* issues a low, trilling call, and the *pauraque* calls with a hoarse *pur-we'eeeeer* whistle.

self-contradictory. However, the three stops are fairly close to one another and arrival times vary so widely that there's no point in being more precise. Moreover, you can expect schedules to change quite frequently. The main information to be derived from the above timetable is that by the time you get into the region, both from Mérida and Campeche probably there will be at least four buses a day heading for Uxmal and surrounding ruins.

Uxmal is definitely on the traditional tourist circuit. You can buy good ice cream and nearly any other touristy thing there; at dusk they put on light shows. If you've just arrived in Mexico, or have only experienced northern Yucatán, Uxmal's prices and gung-ho touristization will not strike you as particularly noteworthy. But if you've just come up from the south after being in the Xpuhil area, for instance, or even around Palenque, Uxmal's prices and attitudes will shock you.

At **Hotel Villas Arqueologicas**, as cool and pleasant as any place you could hope for and right next to Uxmal's entrance, a double room costs a little over US$50; at the **Hotel Hacienda Uxmal**, on Hwy 261 across from the entrance to the road to the ruins, with a pool and a bar, each TV-supplied room costs about US$40.

Camping is possible at Uxmal. When you enter Uxmal's office-building complex on your way to the ruins, right after passing the information booth on the left, take a left around the corner and stop at the first door, marked Oficina de la Unidad de Servicios. Ask here if you can camp in the parking area. *¿Es posible acampar en el lugar de estacionamiento?* At the time of writing camping at Uxmal costs about a dollar a night, no matter whether you're in a large RV or a little pup tent, and this must be the best bargain in town; no hookups. The parking area in which you're allowed to camp is the one to your right as you enter the complex; usually they keep it chained off. It's paved with asphalt, but enough grass is present at the edge for a tent. There are woods nearby but people use it so frequently as a toilet that camping there wouldn't be very pleasant. The main problem with this campground is the high population density. During my visit, the parking lot was tightly packed with RV's, though not a single tent was present. About four km (2½ miles) north of Uxmal the **Rancho Uxmal**, a rather small but peaceful place, offers camping for about US$2.25/night, or you can swing a hammock inside a *palapa* for about 50¢; double occupancy in some dingy room costs about US$12.00. No hookups are available unless you carry your own extension cord, and then, they say, maybe they can work something out.

MÉRIDA

If Uxmal is one of the Ruta Maya's super ruins, then Mérida is one of its super cities; abundant tourist-literature is available in the usual places.

An important Maya ruin (though not physically grandiose) lies just north of Mérida, and is a favorite destination for tourist agencies scrambling to put together day-trips. At **Dzibilchaltún** the Temple of the Seven Dolls is unique in that it features windows, a vaulted corridor and an inner chamber placed to show key solar alignments. Dzibilchaltún is further distinguished by having been continuously occupied from at least 500 BC to the Spanish conquest — a period of 2000 years.

You might also consider making a trip to the graceful and historically significant town of **Izamal**, about 60km (37 miles) east of Mérida. To Mayanists, Izamal is most famous as the headquarters of the fanatical Bishop Diego de Landa who on the one hand burned all the Maya books, or codices, he could find because he considered them to be blasphemous, but also wrote *Relación de las Cosas de Yucatán*, which is regarded as the best scholarly report existing on Maya culture as it was when the Spanish arrived. At Izamal we find a wonderful church and monastery begun in 1553 by de Landa, using stones plundered from a Maya temple. Apparently Izamal's pyramid once stood higher than its present 17 meters (56 feet), for Landa wrote that when one stood atop it, "the eye can easily reach down to the sea," which certainly is not the case today.

Since getting to some of northern Yucatán's ruins at present is impossible in regular buses, here is what a typical tour operator, Gonzalez Tours, with a branch office in the main bus station, charges for certain day-trips: A tour of the city of Mérida costs US$10.00; a minibus to Uxmal and Kabáh requires US$30.00; an afternoon trip to Uxmal, staying to see the sound and light show at night, commands US$33.00; the Sayil/Labná/Xlapak package costs US$93.00; a round-trip ticket to Chichén Itzá goes for US$30.75; and you can be carried to Chichén Itzá, see the ruins, and then later that evening be dropped in Cancún for US$40.00.

Independent travelers will be pleased with the main bus station's long list of schedules; the station stands at Calle 69 between 70 and 72. Birdwatchers, beachcombers, campers eager to overnight on isolated shores, and people with a taste for colorful destinations "at the end of the line" will find plenty to work with here.

Around Mérida you'll see plantations of a plant looking like giant *Aloe vera*. These plants are henequen, of the genus *Agave*, belonging to the agave family. (*Aloe vera*, seen frequently as a house plant and used in everything from shampoo to skin treatments, is in the lily family.) Henequen produces the strong fiber called sisal hemp, traditionally used in hammocks, bags and such. If you take a second-class bus between Mérida and Chichén Itzá, about 44km (27 miles) west of Mérida, you'll briefly leave the main road to enter the town of

Tahmek; about one kilometer west of Tahmek you'll pass a factory where henequen leaves are converted to fibers. If you're lucky you'll see stacks of henequen-plant leaves waiting to be processed, racks of drying fibers, and maybe even the big machine crushing leaves.

CELESTÚN

Significance

Celestún is a 59,130-ha (228 sq-mile) wildlife refuge west of Mérida, established around an estuary paralleling the Gulf Coast; formally it's known as the Ría Celestún Special Biosphere Reserve. Though most tourists visit Celestún "to see the pink flamingos," eco-tourists focus on other aspects of the area's incredible biodiversity.

With 230 species of bird observed there to date, of which 58% are permanent residents, the reserve is considered to be the fourth most important winter migration site in the Gulf of Mexico region. It's especially important for aquatic migratory birds such as American widgeon, blue-winged teal, northern shoveler and lesser scaup. About 30 species of migratory warblers overwinter here.

From May to September the Carey and white turtles, in danger of extinction, nest on the refuge's beaches. Boa constrictors and crocodiles can be spotted among the mangroves. Footprints of white-tailed deer and raccoons are found, as well as those of the jaguar and ocelot. Endemic orchids grow here, and at the river mouth lobsters, shrimp and many species of marine fish breed and grow.

Logistics

The refuge is accessible from the coastal fishing village of Celestún, lying 92km (57 miles) west of Mérida; Celestún stands on a kilometer-wide strip of land about 25km long (⅔-mile wide and 15 miles long), between the Río Esperanza and the Gulf of Mexico. If you're in a car when you cross the Río Esperanza into Celestún, men rush toward you calling "¿Flamencos? ¿Flamencos... ?" These are boatmen eager to carry you to isolated spots where flamingos congregate. The standard price for a flamingo trip is about US$25 per boatload; most tourists find others to go with them, to split the price.

These trips comprise a kind of acid test of whether you are a thoughtful eco-tourist, or an uninformed, insensitive snapshot-collector. For, once you've paid your money and you're out there approaching the flamingos, there's every compulsion to inch closer and closer. And all too frequently the boatmen are happy to oblige, knowing that if they do they may land better tips. Of course, the refuge's guardians work hard to educate the boatmen to stay a certain distance, so as to not frighten the flamingos and drive them away. The best thing for you to do, before any agreement is made, is to insist that the motorboat in which you travel will under no circumstance approach the flamingos any closer than the refuge's guardians permit. This will make it easier for the birds, the boatman and you. *"Ojalá que no lleguemos tan cerca a los flamencos que les molestamos..."* you can say — "I hope we don't get so close to the flamingos that we frighten them..."

Three no-star hotels in Celestún provide not-too-expensive rooms; next to the beach there's a wonderfully pleasant restaurant where you can sit in deep shadows lulled by the beach's monotonous wave-action, sipping whatever you want to sip. Usually only a handful of international travelers makes it here and things stay quiet; however, on weekends quite a few visitors from Mérida liven

American flamingo
Phoenicopterus ruber

things up. The locals say that putting a tent on the beach is OK, but you should watch out for kids who have been known to pilfer from them. Just north of town the beach becomes unpopulated and wonderfully desolate.

About four km (2½ miles) north of Celestún, on the bumpy, one-lane sand road, make a right-hand turn inland. Soon you'll come to several large, shallow ponds filled with water so salty that the salt is precipitating out. If you arrive early in the morning on a workday, you can see men collecting salt there. They wade into the ponds pulling sled-boats (usually plastic barrels cut in half lengthwise), into which they shovel wet salt from the lagoon's bottom. Then they pull the sled-boat to shore and dump the pinkish salt into piles a meter high. The salt is composed of conglomerations of salt crystals two or three centimeters (about an inch) large. When the piles drain, the salt becomes white, and then it's collected. Apparently a prime commodity of ancient Maya commerce was salt collected here and at similar northern-Yucatán sites. Today's salt-collecting methods must be very similar to the ancient Maya's.

Though one certainly wants a picture of this time-honored activity, I feel squeamish about treating the salt-collectors as a photogenic spectacle — especially because their work is hard and couldn't possibly pay much. Many men work barefoot. They told me that sharp salt crystals cut their feet and legs and the salty water burns their cuts. Some of the men seemed embarrassed to be seen doing such work. This situation is another test of the eco-tourist's sensibilities. I ended up not even taking any pictures.

Beyond the salt-collecting ponds are more ponds where in the winter large flocks of white pelicans gather at dusk. Among the year-round residents of these lagoons are the brown pelican, little blue heron, American egret, reddish egret, magnificent frigate-bird, laughing gull and royal tern. In the winter several species migrate here from the north. These include, beside the white pelican, the black-bellied plover, killdeer, spotted sandpiper, willet, sanderling, western sandpiper, and herring gull.

If at dusk you're wandering around the marshes with a pair of binoculars you may meet some folks on bicycles making sure that no one bothers the reserve's biota. Biologist Juan José Durán Najera along with Sr Matias Martín Sánchez and Sr Eliodoro Caamal Cohuo are some of the most dedicated and hard-working preservers of nature I've met; they're involved with the *Parques en Peligro* (Parks in Danger) program, supported by PRONATURA, Mexico's main environmental organization, and the *Proyecto Flamencos* (Flamingo Project), sponsored by Mexico's SEDUE and the US Dept. of Fish & Wildlife. If you see these men, share some animal crackers with them and tell them that I say hello.

RÍO LAGARTOS

Significance
Similar to Celestún, Río Lagartos is a 48,000-ha (185-sq mile) wildlife refuge known best as a place to go to see flamingos. As with Celestún, boatmen in the little fishing town of Río Lagartos are exceedingly interested in ferrying you to see the birds, and again, there's much more nature to see here than just big, pink birds. Río Lagartos is the only Mexican site included in the List of the Convention of Wetlands of International Importance.

The refuge's beaches are the most important sites for the nesting of the carey turtle and the white turtle. Along with crocodiles, white-tailed deer and various cats (including the jaguar) the refuge is home to two rare palms — the kuká, *Pseudophoenix sargentii* and the chi'it,

Gulf-Coast Turtles

Five species of marine turtle are native to the Yucatán's beaches:

Carey turtle: *Eretmochelys imbricata*
White turtle: *Chelonia mydas*
Caguama turtle: *Caretta caretta*
Parrot turtle: *Lepidochelys kempi*
Laud turtle: *Dermochelys coriacea*

Once these turtles were abundant in the region but now, due mostly to man's impact, they've largely disappeared.

Various Mexican and international organizations conduct programs to protect these animals; among these are Mexico's main environmental group, PRONATURA, the Mexican Secretariat of Urban Development and Ecology (SEDUE), and Ducks Unlimited of Mexico.

At this time eight "turtle camps" have been established along the Mexican coast. Nesting grounds are protected during the spawning period and an effort is made to protect the offspring when released. In 1989, 2,265 nests were guarded and 182,636 offspring were freed.

Nonetheless, turtle numbers continue to drop.

Trimax radiata, both in danger of extinction. Also rare species of cactus grow here. Jabiru storks and peregrine falcons are seasonal visitors; in the refuge's southern forests live ocellated turkey, *Agriocharis ocellata*, which are endemic and in danger of extinction. Mangrove swamps here are even more accessible than at Celestún.

Logistics

Go to **Valladolid**, on Hwy 180, approximately midway between Mérida and Cancún, and not too far from Chichén Itzá. Valladolid is a bustling, industrial city right in the middle of the Mérida/Chichén Itzá/Cancún tourist-pipeline so its prices are a bit higher than you'd expect, and sometimes buses are especially heavily packed; if you can take a first-class bus to Valladolid, with an assigned seat, it'll probably be worth the small extra cost.

To reach Río Lagartos from Valladolid, take an Autotransportes de Oriente bus to Tizimín, which lies midway Valladolid and Río Lagartos on the Yucatán's northern coast. In Tizimín, if the Autotransportes de Oriente bus line isn't offering convenient connections continuing on to Río Lagartos, step around the corner to the station called Union de Camioneros de Yucatán. In the latter station notice that one side of the building provides first-class service while the other side offers second-class, and that each side schedules buses at different hours; together they offer about eight trips a day. While you're in this bus station, take a look at some of the end-of-the-line destinations being serviced. San

Felipe, El Cuyo, Panabá... This looks like good exploring territory; if you find something interesting, let me know. The road to Río Lagartos is paved but a bit bumpy. An RV and a bus can pass on it if both inhale deeply.

In Río Lagartos there's a main hotel rising high above other buildings in town and with the giant word "HOTEL" written on it, costing about US$13.00 double. Several people around town offer cheaper and more colorful informal accommodation. For example, if you walk from the town's plaza to the waterfront, turn right and pass along the street right next to the water (take a camera because the fishermen's variously painted boats make wonderful shots), knock on the door of house number 188. Here Sr. Daniel Alcecer Loría will probably be tickled to show you a little building in his backyard, equipped with a couple of hammocks. Sleeping at his place costs about US$8.00.

Visiting the flamingo grounds at Río Lagartos is a little more expensive than at Celestún; the boatmen explain that here there are more submerged rocks and logs. Moreover, they speak of two different flamingo trips, one costing about US$27 per boatload and the other about US$40. On the US$27 trip you can expect to see maybe 20 to 40 flamingos; on the US$40 trip you can see hundreds. Unfortunately, at Río Lagartos such competition exists among the boatmen that several men specialize in "getting close," so, please, don't forget, *"Ojalá que no lleguemos tan cerca a los flamencos que les molestamos..."* One boatman here approached me proudly holding snapshots of a client who'd jumped from his boat and grabbed a gasping flamingo right in the middle of its slender neck!

Besides taking you to flamingo grounds, for about US$8 the boatmen will ferry you to a beach across the strait where you might be the only swimmer. And if you'd like to camp for a few days on an isolated beach where it's just you, the sunlight, the wind, the sand and the ocean, the boatmen will drop you off and on another day pick you up. If you've been for too long in the Mérida/Chichén Itzá/Cancún tourist-pipeline, two or three days of tropical-island isolation may offer the kind of calming experience you need!

Unlike Celestún, which lies on the Gulf Coast's beach facing the ocean, the town of Río Lagartos is situated on the mainland side of the inlet, so there are no open-walled seaside restaurants with deep shadows in which you can sip what you want to sip. In fact, except for its being a typically pleasant, peaceful, colorful little Mexican town with some good seafood, there's not much for a traveler to do inside the town of Río Lagartos itself.

However, there's one spot up the coast a bit that's nice for cooling the heels. Starting at the Plaza, head for the sea and turn right. Follow this bumpy sand and stone road right out of town (past the Pemex station). Soon open water will be on your left and on the right will stand an excellent mangrove swamp rich in bird-life and other mangrove biota. If the locals cease using this swamp as a garbage dump, it has the potential for being a prime attraction for those of us who enjoy observing mangrove life-forms up close.

About a kilometer beyond town you come to an open area with a thatch roof on poles (a *palapa*) about fifteen meters long and five meters wide. This stands next to "ye ol' swimming hole," a wonderful little spot with turquoise, clear water, and even some decayed steps from bygone days of glory leading into the pool. A large mangrove tree, with its maze of intertangled aerial roots, stands across the pool opposite the steps. A small wooden pier near the *palapa* juts into the inlet; a large grassy area provides a place to camp. In short, it's a marvelous place for hanging loose. Though on weekends it can be busy, during the week hardly anyone visits here except around dusk, when sometimes a car or two of local people come out just to kill time and take a dip. It's a perfect place to meet socially-minded Mexicans and to practice Spanish.

If you're a birder wanting to add the flamingo to your life list but you don't necessarily need to get close enough to take a good picture, when you arrive at the water's edge in the town of Río Lagartos take your binoculars and look across the water, far to the east. On a mudflat at the edge of a mangrove swamp, in early morning sunlight you just might see pinkish birds with long necks and legs, and if you study the birds long enough you'll observe that the pink extends up their very slender necks. This last observation separates flamingos from rosette spoonbills, which is the only other large, pink bird it possibly could be.

In late morning a through-bus leaves Río Lagartos's Plaza for Mérida, passing through Valladolid.

Chichén Itzá

Archeological orientation

The tourist hordes visit Chichén Itzá' to see "Maya archeology's 1,000 hectares (four square miles) of classic splendor" or simply to have something to do that's an easy day-trip from Mérida and Cancún. Even for misanthropes, at least once in a lifetime it's worth enduring the crush of humanity to be in the presence of the Pyramid of Kukulcán, the temple of the Warriors, the Caracol and the Sacred Cenote.

In a way, Chichén Itzá is a kind of opposite to Uxmal. At Uxmal, you feel that the entire site is a single, coherent expression of ancient Maya sensibilities; the character of each building stands in harmony with each structure around it. In contrast, Chichén Itzá's architecture

The Itzá and Mayapán

Maya chronicles speak of the Itzá as lewd tricksters and rascals, and "people without fathers or mothers." About 1200 AD they were expelled from their home of Chakunputun, which may have been Champoton on the coast of Campeche. After leaving Chakunputun they migrated through present-day northern Guatemala, visiting Lago Petén Itzá where today Flores is located, then northeast along the Caribbean coast, and finally inland to the ruins that now we call Chichén Itzá, which by the time of the Itzá's arrival already had seen its glory days, and was neglected. The Itzá more or less encamped among the ruins. Their leader took the name of Kukulcan II — Kukulcan I being the former Toltec man-god.

In the late 1200s the Itzás founded Mayapán about 50km (30 miles) south of Mérida's present location. Soon it became Yucatán's capital and its population grew to about 12,000 people occupying some 2,000 dwellings. Attesting to the time's unrest, a defensive wall completely surrounded the 6,500ha (2½-square-mile) site.

Though this description of Mayapán makes it sound like a major Ruta-Maya destination, the Itzá did not leave much behind to inspire modern visitors. Mayapán's buildings were laid out haphazardly, without a hint of streets, and workmanship on buildings was shoddy. Mayapán's Temple of Kukulcan is a rather pitiful imitation of Chichén Itzá's Castillo. People's religious beliefs seem to have been as anarchic as their urban planning; excavators at Mayapán have found incense burners representing Mexican gods such as Quetzalcóatl, Xipe Totec (the God of Spring) and the Old Fire God, side-by-side with Maya deities such as Chac the Rain God, the Corn God, and Itzamná.

In the mid-1400's revolt broke out in Mayapán, the Itzá rulers were put to death, and the great city was destroyed and abandoned for all time. At Chichén Itzá the Itzá were expelled, and once again went looking for a new home. Eventually they wandered back to Lago Petén Itzá in northern Guatemala, where on an island they established a new capital called Tayasal — where modern-day Flores now stands.

In splendid isolation at Tayasal the Itzá Maya survived until 1697 — over two centuries after Columbus's maiden voyage into the New World!

represents a melding of disparate influences.

In Early Classic times Chichén Itzá was founded according to normal Maya procedures; then came Toltec influence. The story of what's implied by the words "Toltec influence" has recently changed. Most popular books on the market (by Coe and Thompson, for instance) explain that at the beginning of the Postclassic period (10th century) a people from central Mexico called the Toltec invaded, initiating a period in which Maya and Toltec society, beliefs and architecture amalgamated into a completely new, hybrid thing; Maya hands built magnificent buildings for Toltec overlords.

However, recent work suggests that "Toltec influences" may be manifestations of local Maya development, colored by increased traffic with the people of central Mexico. Though the "Toltec invasion" is a good story enshrined in many books, archeologists are still working on the question of why so much at Chichén Itzá shows central-Mexican style.

Chichén Itzá's story doesn't end with Toltec influences. In the Middle Postclassic (the 13th century), the Itzá, possibly Mexicanized Maya from the Gulf Coast, more or less became squatters among Chichén Itzá's neglected buildings (see page 85). As explained in the "Maya art" section (Chapter 11), one of the more enjoyable pastimes at Chichén Itzá is to see if you can figure out what's "pure Maya," what's "Toltec/Maya" and what's "Itzá/Maya."

Chichén Itzá's history is atypical in Maya chronology not only because of its Toltec and Itzá periods, but also because the site's most impressive buildings (especially El Castillo or the "Pyramid of Kukulcán") are Postclassic. Grand, Postclassic buildings are the exception in Maya archeology. In general, the Maya Postclassic was a time of greatly reduced building activity and diminished creative energy. Chichén Itzá's wonderful postclassic buildings reflect the fact that the infiltration of Toltec ideas resulted in a kind of rebirth for the site.

Once again I'll let traditional guidebooks (and abundant literature at the ruin itself) lead you around Chichén Itzá and tell you about the Nunnery Annex's eastern façade, the Caracol, the Sacred Cenote and the rest. Also, other books have plenty to say about traditional lodging, eating and coming and going. Here I'll supplement their remarks with info for the independent traveler arriving at Chichén Itzá by bus.

Logistics

Most second-class buses pull right up to the ticket area at the ruin's entrance, and these buses are frequently packed. If you want to try to avoid some of the crush inside the ruin you might try this strategy: Around mid-day when there's a good chance to find a hotel room, arrive in Pisté, the town about a kilometer west of the ruins. After arranging for a room, hang around town all day, doing your postcard-writing, hammock buying and other shopping in the area's many stores and roadside tourist-stalls. Then the next morning, using the sidewalk built between town and the ruins, walk down to the entrance gate and be on hand when the ruin opens. If you have a car, you might consider a similar strategy, taking an overnight room in Libre Unión or Valladolid, towns farther afield. Several campgrounds along the road announce themselves with signs.

BALANKANCHE CAVE

Balankanche Cave lies about five kilometers (three miles) east of Chichén Itzá. Discovered in 1959 holding a large cache of Toltec-Maya artifacts, today the lighted caverns are standard fare for the Mérida/Chichén Itzá/Cancún tourist route and are covered in standard guides.

QUINTANA ROO STATE

PUNTA LAGUNA

General information

At Punta Laguna, a village of about 50 Yucatec Maya, you can hike, go birding, stand a good chance of spotting some spider monkeys (they've been protected and sometimes feed right above the village's huts...), get to know some Maya folks, and visit some small Maya ruins.

In recent years Punta Laguna's citizens have suffered from droughts that burned up their corn and beans, and from Hurricane *Gilbert*, which came through in 1988. Outsiders have offered them money for baby monkeys, toucans and exotic plants but, so far, they've resisted these temptations. They've resisted because they hoped that someday — now — people like us would visit them and pay for their eco-touristic services. Mainly this includes our using the trails they've cleared to visit their nearby ruins and some good monkey-watching spots. Lots of people give eco-tourism "lip-service" but the 50 souls of Punta Laguna have put their lives on the line for the concept...

At this time of writing the Punta Laguna Project is still evolving; when a visitor arrives, nothing is assumed about the services being offered. It's all spontaneous: eco-tourism the way it's meant to be. Count yourself lucky if you get to be guided by Sr Serafio Canul, who discovered the ruins, became their custodian, and knows all about our interest in getting to chew *chicozapote* sap, hear about medicinal plants and poisonous snakes, etc.

Logistics

Punta Laguna lies on the road between Cobá and Hwy 180 (the road between Chichén Itzá and Cancún). Punta Laguna's road is paved. Currently buses from Valladolid pass around 0530 and 1430 heading for Cobá, Tulum and Playa del Carmen; at about 0630 and 1230, buses from Playa del Carmen pass, heading for Valladolid.

CANCÚN

At this writing Cancún is home to about 150 hotels; capacity is expanding at a rate of 25% annually; about a million tourists visit each year. Though the resort area, which was opened by the Mexican government only in 1974, does provide jobs for local people, it's estimated that 70 to 90% of profits leave the area. Cancún is not exactly what we're talking about when we speak of eco-tourism and its sustainable, nondestructive philosophy.

One way to escape from high-priced, ultra-touristic, beach-and-sun-

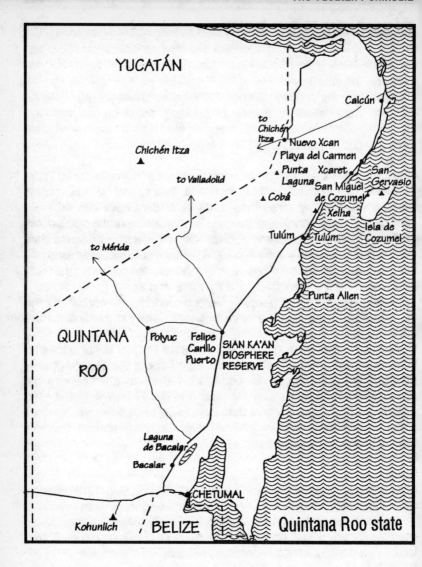

and-restaurants-and-hotels Cancún is by way of the bus station. Go to Terminal Cancún and buy a ticket either westward toward Chichén Itzá and Mérida, or southward to Cozumel, Chetumal and Belize. If you land at Cancún's airport and want to escape as soon as possible to someplace nearby where you can decompress, possibly after a trans-Atlantic flight, Playa del Carmen may be the best place to shoot for.

PLAYA DEL CARMEN

Most buses plying Hwy 307 between Cancún and Chetumal pull into Playa del Carmen; not only is the main ferry crossing to Cozumel Island here, but also Playa del Carmen is a fine destination itself. Its beaches aren't as spectacular as Cancún's, snorkelling isn't as good as around Cozumel Island, you won't find as many jet-setters at Playa del Carmen as at either Cancún or on Cozumel Island, but you *will* find a decent little Mexican town with a sunny, breezy beach populated by enough colorful characters to give you some fun.

Most backpackers arriving in Playa del Carmen abandon all ideas about camping on the beach when they walk down to the water, turn left to stroll up the beach, and almost immediately spot a place called **Campamento "La Ruina"**. Yes, here's a campground built around a tiny, authentic Maya ruin. Here either you can rent a hammock in a long wall-less building (US$1.00/night), or peg a tent in the grassy area (US$1.65/night for a small tent); the bathrooms and showers aren't bad and if you camp here and you are a fast runner you can make it to the water's edge in less than ten seconds. Gaining membership in this laid-back society requires a deposit of about US$8.00, which is refunded upon departure. If you want to store your backpack while out wandering, you can rent a locker for about 65¢/day. *Cabañas* are available for about US$6.00; you can park your small or medium-sized camper on the premises for about US$6.00.

Another camping area is available about 500 meters up the beach (north), beside Restaurant Narayan; here tenting costs about US$2.75/person. Dozens of hotels line Playa del Carmen's beach. The **Blue Parrot Inn**, a typical-looking, middle-range hotel toward the northern end of the beach, offers rooms for US$40/night — about one-third cheaper during off-season. A private bungalow costs US$65.

Yax-Ha Divers, next to the Blue Parrot Inn, rents snorkelling equipment — mask, fins and snorkel — for US$5.00/day. You can arrange diving instruction, with boat and transportation to a good spot, for US$60/day. Certified divers can rent one tank of air for US$35; two tanks cost US$50.

COZUMEL ISLAND

Archeological orientation

The Spanish first set foot on Cozumel Island in 1518 when a small flotilla captained by Joan de Grijalva was sent by Diego Velázquez, the Governor of Cuba, to explore the Yucatán area; Yucatán had been discovered the year before by Francisco Hernández de Córdoba and his crew, who had been searching for slaves for Cuba's plantations.

In Chapter 8 of Bernal Díaz's *True History of the Conquest of New Spain,,* Bernal tells us that when he and his fellow conquistadors waded onto Cozumel's shore, Maya villagers ran into the forests. Exploring the island, the conquistadors found an abundance of beehives and *patatas*, which probably were cultivated sweet potatoes. Bernal speaks of wild pigs, which he insists bore their navels over their backbones (probably collared peccaries with musk glands on their rumps). He reports three towns on Cozumel in those days.

The next year, in 1519, Bernal returned to Cozumel a second time, this time in the accompaniment of Captain Hernán Cortés; this was the beginning of the expedition that eventually took Cortés and his men on a gold-robbing mission all the way to Tenochtitlán, the capital of the Aztecs where Mexico City now stands, resulting in the collapse of the Aztec Empire. In Bernal's Chapter 25 we read how on this second visit some soldiers went into Cozumel's Maya temples and found chests filled with idols and gold jewellery.

In Chapter 27 we read the story of Gerónimo de Aguilar who in 1511, off the coast of Jamaica, survived a shipwreck and for 13 days drifted in a small boat until washing ashore on Cozumel Island, where he was enslaved by the Maya. Gerónimo rejoined his compatriots during Bernal's second visit to Cozumel. His Maya-speaking talents proved to be of immense importance to the conquistadors, for later the Spanish discovered a woman, Malinche, who spoke both Aztec and Maya. During subsequent days of the conquest, when Cortés needed to talk to the Aztecs, he'd first direct his remarks in Spanish to Gerónimo, then in Maya Gerónimo would speak to Malinche, and finally Malinche would translate the words into Aztec.

Of course, I'm repeating only a tiny part of the whole story; really you should read Bernal's own words in his *True History* while sitting on a Cozumel beach. Surely that experience qualifies as a true Ruta-Maya high! By the way, if you can't find Bernal's book, Fray Diego de Landa's *Relación de las Cosas de Yucatán*, penned in 1560, describes the Cozumel happenings in Chapters 3 and 4. Landa calls Cozumel "Cuzmil."

Biological significance

As often is the case with sizable islands that for millennia have been separated from the mainland, on Cozumel Island you find organisms that have evolved into unique forms — they're found no place else on earth. For instance, among the endemic birds are the Cozumel thrasher, *Toxostoma guttatum*, and the Cozumel vireo, *Vireo bairdi*, both of which are confined to Cozumel Island. Throughout southeastern Mexico, the bananaquit has a gray throat, but the race on Cozumel Island has a white throat.

All three of these species are fairly common on the island. I easily found the Cozumel vireo; it was particularly susceptible to the *shhh-shhh-shhh* sound that birders often make to coax curious birds closer for a good look. Its voice is rather like

Cozumel Vireo
Vireo bairdi

the white-eyed vireo's and, at least to me, seems ventriloquial — the bird is in one place, but its voice seems to be in another! The Cozumel thrasher looks remarkably like a small edition of the long-billed thrasher of northeastern and central Mexico.

Several of Cozumel Island's birds are more typically thought of as Caribbean species than mainland Mexican ones. For instance, the gray kingbird, *Tyrannus dominicensis*, resides mostly in the West Indies and southern Florida; the stripe-headed tanager, *Spindalis zena*, is found mainly in the Bahamas and Greater Antilles, but in Mexico lives only on Cozumel; the white-crowned pigeon, *Columba flavirostris*, lives in the Florida Keys, West Indies the Caribbean islands, and here; the Caribbean dove, *Leptotila jamaicensis*, is on Jamaica, Grand Cayman, St. Andrew and here and there in the northern Yucatán Peninsula; the Caribbean elaenia, *Elaenia martinica*, is in the Lesser Antilles and islands off Yucatán; and there are others.

Logistics

When you walk down to Playa del Carmen's beach, you'll see a long pier jutting into the sea, probably with one or more ferries moored at it. These ferries shuttle passengers between Playa del Carmen and Cozumel Island. If you cross on the old ferry called Barco Xel-Ha, one-way passage costs about US$3.15. If you travel in the fancier and wee-bit-faster Barco Cozumeleño, the ticket costs about US$7.00. A ride over takes a little less than an hour. If you want to take your car to Cozumel, you need to take the ferry from Puerto Juárez, just north of Cancún; a one-way ticket costs about US$30.00.

If you suffer from motion sickness, take dramamine half an hour before your trip starts because these ferries do bob around. Nonetheless, the trip over is quite pleasant, especially if you enjoy watching flying-fish. Flying-fish-watching connoisseurs know to choose a seat on the shaded side of the boat and to keep watching for slender, stiff-looking, silvery items launching from the water as if they were shot from below, and then apparently flying just above the higher waves for remarkable distances. I saw some that stayed airborne for seven seconds. Actually, ichthyologists insist that flying-fish don't really fly, but rather that upon leaving the water they *taxi* along the surface vibrating their tails in the water; once they build up momentum they use their wing-like fins to *glide* a bit farther. But, they look like they're *flying*.

On Cozumel Island you come ashore at the island's only town, formally called San Miguel, but referred to by most tourists simply as Cozumel. Cozumel's official information office lies not far from the pier. To find it, just turn right after disembarking and for a couple of blocks walk down Avenida Rafael Melgar, the street paralleling the beach; the office is a tiny one, adjoining the Mexicana Airlines office. Here you can acquire a city/island map, hotel information, current details on the best snorkelling areas, night-life, etc.

Though the friendly people here are wonderfully helpful, they may supply you with the famous "blue map" of Cozumel, with one side showing San Miguel's streets and the other side the entire island. Though the map's San-Miguel side can be helpful, the island side of this map is outrageously out of date in nearly every detail dealing with the roads and trails in which an eco-tourist especially would be interested. The "blue map" shows backroads wandering all over the island. However, most of these haven't existed since Hurricane *Gilbert* devastated the island's forests in September of 1988. This is a shame, because if these roads were open they'd make perfect roaming grounds for folks like us.

Cozumel Island's businesses specialize in offering bicycle and motorized scooter rentals; just walk down Avenida Rafael Melgar next to the beach and you'll find hotels, restaurants — everyone and his brother — ready to rent them. A bicycle costs about US$7.25/day; a scooter goes for about US$18.00. You can find cheaper offerings, but be careful. Though you'll see city buses in San Miguel's streets, theoretically these are for locals only, especially hotel workers travelling back and forth along the strip; tourists are supposed to use taxis, a tourist official told me, though surely if a backpacker jumped onto a bus he or she wouldn't be kicked off. A taxi from one side of the island to the other (San Miguel to Mescalito) costs about US$6.75.

Here are some typical lodging prices: An average double room in an average hotel (among dozens) along the strip costs about US$95 per night. Away from the beach, in downtown San Miguel, the rather modest-looking **Hotel "Yoli"** at Calle 1ª Sur 17, with hot water and a fan on the ceiling, costs US$11.75 for a double room. If you fall in love with Cozumel and want to live in a furnished apartment kept well scrubbed by a German owner, the monthly price is US$1200 at Hotel Villas Las Anclas, at 5ª Av. Sur 325.

If you're coming off the mainland and you've become used to living cheaply by camping, renting hammocks, and eating lots of beans, tortillas and bananas, Cozumel can be hard on you; it's clear that the city fathers expect you to spend money if you visit there. The only formal campground lies at the southernmost point of the island, near the Celarain Lighthouse. Though the camping there might be fine, there are no buses to drop you off, and you'll need to carry all your food and water there, for no services are available; you must walk, hire a taxi or rent a bike or scooter. I saw no tent-campers near San Miguel, and was told that the police don't tolerate campers on the beach. However, the island's eastern coast is almost unpopulated and offers practically unlimited primitive camping opportunities. Campers should get permission to camp from SEDUE, Mexico's environmental protection ministry, which is located on the second floor of the main street in front of the pier.

Before wandering off to peg a tent, you need to stock up; don't expect the usual little Mexican markets and eateries so typical everyplace on the mainland. One place with a good supply of bottled water and a few fruits is El Paso The Onyx Place two blocks northeast of the pier, along the beach road. A Conasupo store with cans of refried beans, animal crackers, etc is located at the corner of Calle 2 Nte and 10ª Ave Nte.

Probably Cozumel's most spectacular offering is its fine snorkelling and scuba diving. Along San Miguel's waterfront you'll find several diving shops. For instance, at Main Avenue and Calle 5 Sur 22 stands Discover Cozumel Diving. Among their packages is a "Deluxe Fast Trip," which includes transportation to a good diving spot in a 55-foot fast-boat, accompaniment by a dive master, two tanks of air, a box lunch and refreshments, weight belt and weights, and a one-night dive with hyperbaric insurance; this costs US$38.40. If you can't dive, they'll provide lessons leading to open-water certification for US$300.00; you can rent a scuba tank for US$6.00. A full day of snorkelling, including transportation, guide, equipment, lunch on board and beer costs US$28.00. These folks even have a toll-free number for callers in the US; it's 1-800-942-8591.

One way to escape the hotel zone is to travel north from the pier for about eight kilometers (five miles). Stay on the main beachside highway that passes the hotels, condominiums, yacht clubs and such. Finally the broad avenue abruptly ends at a turnaround, and a dirt road continues north for about another four km (2.5 miles). This dirt road makes a fine morning walk; endemic Cozumel vireos are rather common in the scrubby, hurricane-ravaged forest along it. After four more kilometers the road passes a stinking sewage treatment plant, then veers to the left. Soon it leads through an extensive field of an interesting, two-meter-tall species of fan palm, and finally through a mangrove swamp, before coming to the beach of a large bay, in the middle of which lies the Isla de Pasión. This is an excellent spot in which to examine mangrove biota, take a dip in the ocean, or simply enjoy an extended goof-off at the water's edge.

Another good way to escape the tourist area is to travel to the other side of the island, for the island's ocean-side is undeveloped. Here you find plenty of beach to walk along; but if you plan to stay long, stock up before going. A dirt road leads northwest from Mezcalito, paralleling the beach, toward Castillo Rey; southeast, a road follows the coast back to San Miguel.

San Gervasio
Archeological orientation
San Gervasio is the most accessible of Cozumel's several ruins. Though rather modest by Yucatán standards, once it was the Cozumel Maya's administrative center, and as such was the largest of more than 30 Cozumel sites. At San Gervasio you can walk down a *sacbe* — one of the Maya's famous paved causeways — watching for birds and iguanas; big iguanas are a specialty here, especially a half-meter-long, spectacularly orange-colored one that loves to sun on horizontal tree limbs.

Logistics
San Gervasio is reached by taking the cross-island road about six kilometers (3.7 miles) to the middle of the island, where a booth stands collecting a 65¢ user-fee for the ruin's entrance road. Walkers really won't find much inspiration hiking the cross-island road. San Miguel's suburbs extend along the road for a fair distance, and at this time the hurricane-ravaged vegetation is scrubby and kept cleared from near the highway; the pavement is straight as an arrow and dominated by fast-moving taxis; the usual Mexican roadside footpath is nonexistent. A taxi from San Miguel to the booth costs about US$3.25, and US$5.00 all the way to the ruin. Early-morning birders might enjoy being deposited at the booth in order to hike the gravel road from the booth to the ruins — about an hour walk.

The gravel road to San Gervasio goes straight to a crossroad. Here take a left and walk briefly to a 130° turn to the right, which carries you to the ruins where you pay the usual entrance fee. By the way, the large tree just beyond the fence and to the left, with small, roundish fruits and ash-like leaves is the *cedro* or "cedar," *Cedrela mexicana*, which, after mahogany, is this region's most important timber tree. Its lightweight wood is fragrant, durable, easily worked, pinkish to reddish brown, and famed for its great strength.

XCARET

Back on the mainland, about six kilometers (3.7 miles) south of Playa del Carmen, a sign points down an unpaved but passable 1.8km (1.1 mile) road leading to the little ruin of Xcaret (ish-kah-RET). Most visitors come here less for visiting the ruins, which are small and hardly mentioned in the literature, than for enjoying the general ambience. Beside the oceanside ruin, at Xcaret you find an eminently swimmable pool with very clear water, shaded by a rocky ledge. A path climbs up a ridge atop which you can gain a view of several emerald-colored, freshwater basins, crossed by a little wooden bridge leading to a cove filled with turquoise water which also yields fine swimming. A tiny restaurant on the ridge provides outdoor tables overlooking the scene.

Xelha (also spelled Xel-Há)

Xelha (shell-HA), the Maya ruin, was considered by Thompson to have been an important Classic city. Along with Tulum, Xelha is unusual among Maya ruins in that it was defended by stout walls. However, today most travelers don't visit Xelha to look at the wall. As one fellow explained, "The thing that everyone refers to as Xelha actually is a tourist trap of remarkably good taste."

Lying 116km (72 miles) south of Cancún and six kilometers (four miles) south of Akumal, between Playa del Carmen and Tulum, Xelha is touted in the tourist literature as "the most popular scenic place along the Turquoise Coast." In other words, during peak season Xelha can be incredibly crowded. Entering the park (entrance fee), you pass a large underwater preserve; when the water is clear you can see nurse sharks and stingrays. Xelha's coastal lagoons are extensive enough to enable snorkelers to swim out and more or less feel alone. The ruins lie about a kilometer across the highway from the lagoons. If you can arrange it, dedicate the morning to fish-watching; in the afternoon when tourists get too thick, head for the ruins, which most visitors completely ignore.

Five kilometers north of Xelha lie the X-Cacel and Chemuyil campgrounds, well identified with signs. Both campgrounds cost about 75¢ (entrance fee includes camping), offer cabaña rentals, provide clean showers, have expensive bars and restaurants, and plenty of camping area by the sea.

Tulum

Archeological orientation

In 1518 Juan de Grijalva captained the second expedition of Spaniards to Mexico; the first had been commanded by slave-hunting Hernández de Córdoba the year before. As Grijalva's fleet of four ships sailed along the Yucatán coast south of Cozumel Island, they took note of "a city or town so large that Seville would not have seemed more considerable." Actually they were seeing four Maya towns — Tulum, Xelha, Soliman and Tancah, clustered so close together that they looked like one population. In those days Tulum was a small trading port and ceremonial center probably holding no more than five or six hundred people; it belonged to the Maya province of Ecab.

Despite this first awe-inspiring impression, and the fact that today Tulum is the Maya world's *most visited ruin*, today archeologists think of Tulum's ruins as "nice, but not great." The problem is that Tulum blossomed quite late in Maya history, mostly during the degenerate Late Postclassic between 1200 AD and 1500; here we just don't see "Classic grandeur" of the kind gracing earlier sites. In fact, archeologists look at Tulum's shoddy handiwork and just shake their heads. Michael Coe refers to the principal temple, the Castillo, as "a miserable structure" and characterizes the ruin's other buildings as "dwarfish." He bemoans the "strikingly slipshod workmanship" of the buildings' upper façades.

Nonetheless, Tulum is "young" enough to have some richly detailed murals with patches of original paint still showing. In the Temple of the Frescoes it's interesting to note that though the *style* of the murals is considered Mixtec, a people from Oaxaca, their *content* is native Maya. In one mural the Rain God sits astride a four-legged beast; apparently the artists had seen, or heard of, Spaniards riding horses. Tulum is one of the few Maya ruins surrounded by a stone wall — a feature reminding us of the strife of Postclassic times, when war gods had supplanted the gods of rain and corn.

At the sea's edge, take a look at Coe's "miserable structure," the Castillo. Once this temple served as a lighthouse. Recently it's been discovered that if lanterns have been placed on shelves behind each of two windows located high on the Castillo's face, and you're in a canoe at sea, you can find your way through a natural opening in the reef by navigating where both beams can be seen at once.

Logistics

The reason that Tulum is the Maya world's most visited ruin is that it lies just 130km (80 miles) south of Cancún on an easy-to-travel road, and its oceanside setting is so spectacular that you don't really mind the site's "dwarfishness." At Tulum you climb a cliff and there before you lie the ruins with the blue ocean behind them; the ruin's buildings shine dazzlingly white in the sunshine; stiff sea-breezes whistle around dozens of stone building corners; though you might wander to the cliffs beyond the ruin and muse, "Just what might the ancient Greeks have done with a site like this — or even the Classic Maya?" you have to admit that the setting is spectacular.

Anyway, let's say that a Mexican bus just has deposited you along the road. *"Quiero bajar en la entrada a la ruina de Tulum,"* you've told the bus's ticket-taker — "I want to exit at the entrance to Tulum Ruins." You find yourself standing at a crossroads; a true sufficiency of signs point to the ruins, down the crossroad's eastern arm.

Commencing toward the ruins, to the right you soon spot a weather-beaten sign announcing "Tulum National Park." Immediately you realize that this park, which looks impressive and full of potential on some maps, is completely undeveloped, with only a few short trails used by toilet-minded locals and possibly a few die-hard birders. Sadly, 1988's Hurricane *Gilbert* and a later fire have wreaked havoc on the park's forest. You continue on the paved road about one kilometer (⅗ mile) before coming to the ruins; you know you're there when confronted with multitudinous tour buses parked everywhere belching black diesel fumes. The ruins are clearly visible on the rise beyond the buses.

If you're interested in staying in a standard hotel, at Tulum you're in a position to pick and choose. Just turn right at the ruins, continue down the road, and every kind of hotel (except the super-big ones typical of Cancún) offer their services. If you want to camp, here's how.

About 500m after turning right at the ruins you pass a modern lighthouse — a squarish, white building on the left, atop the ridge. Though some confusing signs suggest that a campground and *cabañas* lie toward the lighthouse, this information is wrong; just continue past the lighthouse's access road. About another 500m down the road you come to a restaurant called **El Mirador** where you can pitch a tent for US$2.65, rent a hammock for US$1.00 or spend the night in a *cabaña* for US$5.85. Typical of the more upscale accommodations available along this strip is the nearby **El Paraíso**, which charges US$33.00 for a double room with a private bath and hot water; a fine restaurant adjoins the lodging area. If you do check into a regular hotel, keep in mind that all along this strip, unless your hotel has a generator, electricity is available only between 0530 and 2230.

If you travel far enough down this road you'll come to spots between hotels that are fairly secluded; frequently in such niches, naked humans are spotted frolicking in the foam. At one spot, four or five kilometers down the road, there's even a small, semi-permanent camp of hut-dwelling European and North American hippy-types, living lives as disengaged from the world's problems as you can imagine.

On the main highway, a bit south of the main entrance road to Tulum, stands the town of Tulum, sometimes referred to as Tulum Pueblo. Here several hotels offer rates that are lower, and vistas that are less spectacular, than those found along the strip near the ruins. In Tulum Pueblo buses stop downtown along the main highway; just ask anyone to point out the tree to stand beneath to wait for one. If you catch a bus at the crossroad from which the ruin road departs, wait at the yellow, concrete *parada* about 50m south of the entrance; buses don't like to stop at the crossroad itself.

SIAN KA'AN

General information

Sian Ka'an is a biosphere reserve embracing 518,000 hectares (2000 sq miles) of marshes, mangrove forests and estuaries; it stretches from just south of Tulum to about 110km (68 miles) farther south, and up to 50km (31 miles) inland. It's home to some 350 species of birds and 30 known Maya sites. Among the reserve's threatened species of wildlife are spider monkeys, crocodiles and five species of cat. Green, loggerhead, hawksbill and leatherback turtles lay their eggs on Sian Ka'an's beaches. These turtles' populations are declining because of illegal hunting and the shortage of undisturbed beaches. Aggravating the situation is the belief that turtle eggs are an aphrodisiac. At Rancho Tancah just north of Sian Ka'an, the Research Center of Quintana Roo gathers turtle eggs for reburial in chain-link fence enclosures.

Logistics

Fortunately for Sian Ka'an's natural inhabitants, most of the reserve is hard to get to. If you continue down the road onto which you turned right when you reached the ruins of Tulum, if you're in a car, in about fifteen minutes you'll come to the Sian Ka'an Information Station. No literature is available here, but the guard will gladly explain in Spanish the following points: the fishing town of Punta Allen lies 57km (35 miles) farther down the road; the road soon becomes quite bad but pickups and microbuses usually can make it if they go slowly; in Punta Allen there are some restaurants, and fishermen will be more than eager to carry you to a certain island where you can see beautiful birds.

At this writing there's no bus service to Punta Allen, though recently a fellow in a white microbus made daily trips and maybe he'll start that again. If you don't have your own vehicle, you'll just have to hitch. I hitched for three hours before a white microbus came down the road and, mistakenly thinking the daily shuttle service had been reestablished, I flagged down a family from Michigan. Quickly our road became profoundly potholed — too bumpy for anything but strenuous driving, yet not really swampy enough to constitute high adventure.

It was kilometer after kilometer of coconut palms with their tops broken off by Gilbert, and dense, weedy understorey. Occasionally the road veered close to the sea, an expanse of ocean vista opened up, and briefly the bumpiness became endurable. Unfortunately, the best camping spots were all posted as private property (*propiedad particular*). However, just enough non-posted spots were available to suggest the possibility of finding one's own little tent spot or RV parking area. Halfway to Puerto Allen we had to turn back; the big potholes had become too much for my hosts. Finishing this trip requires an almost fanatical dedication to the principle that all exotic-sounding destinations at the end of dotted lines on maps merit a visit. And maybe that's the way any destination inside a biosphere reserve should be.

Cobá

Archeological significance

Cobá is a huge (6,500 mapped structures) Classic Period ruin composed not of a single tight cluster of buildings, but rather of several sites linked to a central complex by long, perfectly straight causeways, or *sacbes*. Here more than 16 *sacbes* have been recorded and no one is sure why this site has so many; several run for long distances only to reach what appear to be very insignificant endpoints. *Sacbe* #1 shoots from Cobá all the way to the site of Yaxuná 100km (62 miles) to the west. Michael Coe suggests that the most plausible use of these roads was for ceremonial functions, not commercial ones. Interestingly, several causeways are under water. This indicates that at one time the water table was lower than now, which supports growing evidence that during Maya civilization's history the climate has alternated drastically between hot, dry periods and cool, wet ones.

Though most of Cobá is in a sorry state of preservation, two major pyramids have been excavated. One of them, Nohoch Mul, 42m (138 feet) high, is the tallest in the entire Yucatán Peninsula; from atop it you gain an impressive view of the area's lakes and forest. During Cobá's main period of influence in the 8th century (mid-Classic), it was home to about 55,000 people, and served as an important trade center, especially for Guatemalan jade.

Logistics

On Hwy 307 between Mérida and Chetumal, the intersection with the well paved side-road to Cobá is clearly marked; it lies 1.9km (1.2 miles) south of the Tulum crossroad. After traveling toward Cobá for about 24km (15 miles), a well marked access road leading toward the ruins appears. After about three kilometers (1.9 miles) this road ends at a small settlement with some rustic restaurants sporting signs written in English, a couple of general stores, and some curio shops with at least one advertising, in English, "The Lowest Prices in Town."

Visitors to Cobá can spend the night in at least four different places. The first, at the town's entrance, is a small hotel called the **Bocadito** offering rooms with private baths and ceiling fans for US$8.35 per room; on down the road, lodging at the **Restaurant Isabel** cost US$3.25 for two people. For downright elegant accommodations, at the lake turn right for **Villas Arqueológicas**, where a double room costs about US$55.00. The fourth place to spend the night is the grassy area next to the ruin's parking lot. It's free. No hook-ups.

The bus from Valladolid passes the entrance to Cobá's three-kilometer-long entrance road at 0600 and 1500, heading to Playa del Carmen (thus also passing Tulum); at 0600 and 1200, buses from Playa del Carmen pass, heading for Valladolid (thus also passing the little Maya village of Punta Laguna, where you can hike looking for spider monkeys, and get to know some fine Maya folks).

General information

Cobá feels as though it's designed for eco-tourists. Its various temple-connecting paths and *sacbes* coursing through the forest are simply perfect for birding, looking at low-hanging epiphytes, tree-identification, etc. If you also explore some of the many footpaths leading off the main routes you can wander for hours. Though on the road between Tulum and Cobá the forest has been devastated by Hurricane Gilbert and subsequent fires, the forest around Tulum's ruins is in fair shape. Spanish moss dangles abundantly from tree limbs, much in contrast to Chichén Itzá, which lies only 90km to the west and not much farther north. If you like using the word "jungle," then you can say that at Cobá we're at least getting close to a jungly environment.

Emphasizing the wonderful biological diversity of this place is the fact that it's possible to spot all three species of Mexico's toucans — the keel-billed toucan, the collared araçari and the emerald toucanet. The gravel road leading from the ruin's parking lot to the little Indian village across the lake should be walked at dusk and dawn by anyone interested in spotting marsh birds.

During the winter, or dry season, two trees are especially conspicuous and easy to identify along Cobá's trails. Just past the entrance gate and to your left stands a large tree that looks like a tall locust with dangling clusters of yellowish-pink flowers. Actually the clusters are conglomerations of numerous winged fruits. In Spanish this tree is called *camarón*, or "shrimp," because of the fruits' shrimpy color. In English the tree is called pinkwing; it is *Alvaradoa amorphoides*, a member of the simaruba or quassia family. If you're familiar with temperate trees, probably another tree you know in this family is the tree-of-heaven, *Ailanthus altissima*. Also common along the main walkway is a small tree with elm-like leaves, and abundant, spherical, very bumpy, green or black fruits. This is "pricklenut," *Guazuma ulmifolia*, a typical tree of regenerating forests, and a member of the cacao or chocolate family.

From atop Nohoch Mul, the big pyramid, the lakes will look awfully inviting. To reach a lake, just after you enter the reserve, take the first right. Continue straight past the pyramid and follow the trail as it passes over an unreconstructed ruin and eventually descends to the water's edge. If you're lucky, here you'll discover a large tree trunk growing horizontally above the water's surface; at *siesta* time you can lie on the trunk, caressed by cool breezes, lulled by the sounds of waves lapping the shore beneath you, occasionally raising your binoculars to spot interesting birds in the canopy above...

CHETUMAL

Chetumal (pop. ±190,000), capital of the state of Quintana Roo, lies on Chetumal Bay, near the mouth of the Río Hondo, which forms the boundary between Mexico and northern Belize. Because Chetumal stands on a bay and not the ocean it doesn't possess the kind of beaches that would guarantee its becoming another Cancún, thank goodness. Chetumal is simply a very pleasant town with a Caribbean flavor, offering enough tourist infrastructure to make you comfortable, and serving admirably as a base for exploring surrounding areas. Evening strolls along the waterfront's Boulevard Bahía are fine; Avenida Héroes is famous for its duty-free shops; calypso is the town's favorite music. Seafood and "rice and beans" are Chetumal's soul-foods. One fancy local dish is *tikinchic*, which is fish grilled and seasoned with sour orange and natural spices. Several restaurants offer Lebanese fare, such as kivi ball, made of ground meat and wheat.

Any serious, Spanish-speaking, archeology and anthropology buff visiting Chetumal would do well to visit the Instituto Quintanaroense at the corner of Av Efrain Aquilar and Andres Quintana Roo. Enter the building on the Andres Quintana Roo side by walking across an area on which restaurant tables are set up; once inside the building bear left, looking for the door labeled Depto. de Promoción.

Here, if you express a more-than-average interest in things Quintana-Roo-ish, they well may give you for free such excellent reading material as issues of the monthly cultural magazine *Cultura Sur*, a 600-page book entitled *Cultura del Caribe*, and such pamphlets as *Cultivos del Caribe* and *Geografía General del Estado de Quintana Roo*. I asked specifically if they'll remain disposed to supplying *hundreds* of this book's readers with such literature, and they insisted that they shall. These folks are proud of their culture and they want to share it; and they see the wisdom in encouraging our kind of eco-tourism.

A booth supplying current tourist info lies a brief stroll east of Avenida Belice's southern terminus, on Francisco Primo de Verdad. The smoothly functioning Autotransportes del Caribe bus station on the northern side of town provides easy access to several nice spots around Chetumal, and Belize.

A coastal beach perfect for primitive camping (no services) and famous for its fishing parallels the last 40 or so kilometers of dry-

Bacalar and the Cruzob Cult

From 1847 to 1855 the Maya rose in rebellion against the Europeans. During this conflict, referred to as the Caste War, both sides massacred entire towns of the opposite camp.

After the Caste War the Mexican Constitution of 1857 instituted many liberal reforms, including the freedom of worship. The constitution deinstitutionalized Catholicism as the state religion, established secular education and abolished clerical immunities. To the Yucatán's Maya, who by this time were devoutly Catholic, this went too far. Pope Pius IX didn't like it either. Though his right to do so was questionable, he declared null and void "...everything the said decrees and everything else that the civil authority has done in scorn of ecclesiastical authority..."

Into this soup of history stepped José María Barrera and a Maya ventriloquist named Manuel Nahuat. Together they created the "talking cross," around which thousands of Maya followers flocked. These people became known as the Cruzob cult. The word "Cruzob" is derived from the Spanish word *cruz*, for cross, and the Maya plural suffix *ob*.

In 1858 the Cruzob sect captured Bacalar. They demanded, and then refused, a 4,000-peso ransom for the lives of Bacalar's citizens. James Blake, a gunrunner based in Belize, arrived with the ransom money, only to stand by as hundreds of men, women and children were chopped to death with machetes. The Cruzob ruled the area as the Empire of the Cross until dislodged by the Mexican Army in 1901.

weather road between the villages of Ubero and Xcalak; to get there you must travel north around the bay, then to the coast, and then south. At Xcalak, divers might consider hiring a boat to the 42-km long, 16-km wide (26- by 10-mile) coral bank known as Banco Chinchorro, famous for its shipwrecks.

About 40km (25 miles) north of Chetumal, Hwy 307 runs along a 56-km long (35-mile), narrow lake called Laguna de Bacalar, along which stand several hotels in restful, colorful settings. Regular buses serve the town of Bacalar, which lies about midway the lake. The most popular spot along Laguna de Bacalar is Cenote Azul, an intensely blue, 200-meter wide, 80-meter deep (125 x 50 feet), flooded sinkhole.

Southwest of Chetumal, paralleling the Río Hondo, which forms the border with Belize, the "road to La Unión" is home to several *instalaciones rústicas*. Especially pleasant are some springs in the town of Alvaro Obregón, 52km (32 miles) down the road.

CROSSING TO BELIZE

If you're traveling toward Chetumal with the idea of catching a bus from Chetumal into Belize, right before you enter Chetumal you'll pass *el crucero*, where the road to Belize connects from the south. From this intersection it's only three kilometers (1.9 miles) to the border, so you might be tempted to leave the bus here and walk to Belize, especially if busy bus stations don't appeal to you.

The walk to Belize is neither inspiring nor unpleasant. Just before arriving at customs you enter the small town of Subteniente Lopez, which is large enough to have a couple of stores — handy if you want to stock up on any item you've grown accustomed to in Mexico, but which you suspect may not be available in Belize. For example, in Belize animal crackers won't be as ubiquitous, cheap and good-tasting as they are in Mexico; purified water also is harder to find. If you've grown fond of Mexico's cans of refried beans, you should know that in Belize you may have to content yourself with baked beans imported from England.

Before the bridge crossing the Rio Hondo into Belize, for customs purposes you must enter the last building on the left, adorned with the words "Secretaría de Gobernación/Servicios Migratorios." After having your documents examined, proceed behind the document-checking official, to the left, exit to the left, and finally pass across the bridge into Belize. Mexico exacts no exit charges.

Kohunlich

Archeological orientation
Kohunlich's structures are older than those found farther north — they

are Late Preclassic. This ruin is most famous for its Pyramid of the Masks, equipped with steep steps flanked by some well preserved and thoroughly menacing-looking face-masks about 1.2 meters (47 inches) high. There are also a small ball-court and more than 200 unexcavated mounds in the forest surrounding the main ruin area.

Logistics

This site lies on the road between Chetumal and Escárcega, about 55km (35 miles) west of Chetumal. First-class buses plying the road between Chetumal and Escárcega stop at Xpuhil, but they do not stop at the nine-kilometer (5.6-mile) access road leading to Kohunlich. However, in Chetumal's Autotransportes del Caribe bus station you can buy a second-class ticket to the town of Francisco Villa, which lies about a kilometer west of Kohunlich's entrance road. "*Me voy a la ruina de Kohunlich y quiero salir en el crucero*," you can say to the bus's ticket-taker. "*¿Puede usted decirme cuando necesito salir?*" — "I'm going to Kohunlich ruin and I want to get out at the intersection; can you tell me when I need to exit the bus?"

Arriving at *el crucero*, you find yourself facing a well maintained, paved road shooting across a low, rolling landscape mantled with chopped-over forests, weedy pastures and abandoned fields, and there's no regular bus service to the ruin, and precious little traffic providing hitching services. If you do get a ride, probably it'll be with another traveler who has rented a car. Walking these nine kilometers in the hot afternoon sun is daunting. On the other hand, on a cool morning it might make a rather enjoyable two-hour stroll. Farmers and children from Francisco Villa bike the distance. I couldn't find anyone willing to rent a bike in Francisco Villa, but maybe you can.

Other information

Conspicuously and significantly, all around the ruins cohune palms (sometimes called corozo palms), *Orbignya cohune*, grow in abundance. These trees look like gigantic, green feather-dusters with their handles stuck in the ground. Their presence is significant because in a roundabout way they gave Kohunlich its name. Earlier the ruin was referred to by an English name, which was "Cohune Ridge." The local Spanish speakers couldn't pronounce that, so over the years "Cohune Ridge" evolved into "Kohunlich."

If you're a camper, you'll certainly enjoy Kohunlich's peaceful isolation and the surrounding forest's easy access. (Watch out for the locals who from time to time come barrelling down the trails on bicycles!) A well maintained grassy area right beside the ground's entrance is big enough to accommodate about five motorhomes and maybe 20 tents; most nights absolutely no one stays here. As with other Mexican ruins, camping is free but a *gratificación* to the lonely custodian is appropriate.

In fact, during my visit the ruin's custodian was as entertaining as the ruins themselves. Sr Francisco Ek Gorocica says that his father, Sr Ignacio Ek Dzul, discovered Kohunlich in 1971, and was its caretaker until he, Francisco, took over in the mid 80s. Moreover, Francisco says that his family is of an ancient Maya line of *brujos* (witchdoctors), and that he and his father can heal. Francisco's specialty is "problems of the mind — hysteria, demons, sexual perversions, etc," he says. His methods depend upon understanding relationships between planets, wild plants, and parts of the human body. Some nights, he says, looking you straight into the eyes, he enters the ruins and there among the ancient temples of his ancestors, he learns the most profound secrets...

Cohune Palm
Orbignya cohune

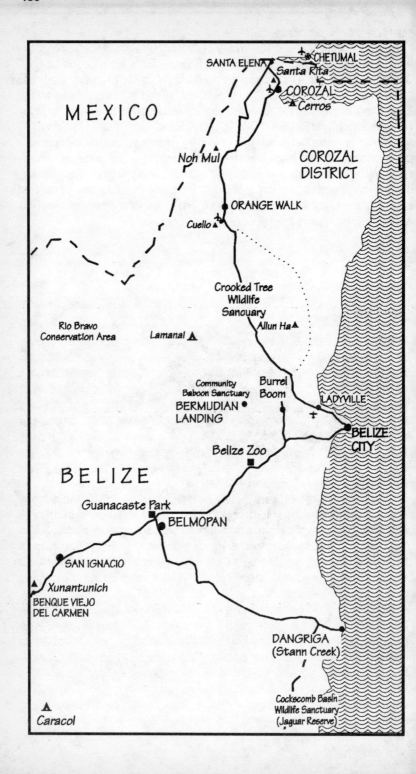

Chapter 13

Belize

THE SETTING

Geography

Like Guatemala, Belize's northern lowlands are level to gently rolling, but its southern highlands are rugged and mountainous. If you enter Belize from the north after being in Mexico's Yucatán Peninsula for a while, as soon as you cross the border formed by the Rio Hondo you'll see that Belize's landscape is different. The Rio Hondo itself points to the main difference. On the Yucatán Peninsula's limestone bedrock no real rivers are to be found; up there, most water flows underground. But little Belize accommodates not only the Rio Hondo, but also the Belize River, Sibun River, North Stann Creek, Monkey River, Deep River, Moho River, Sarstoon River...

The bedrock of northern Belize continues to be limestone, largely composed of ancient, fossilized coral reefs. One reason that in northern Belize regular rivers can course across limestone while in the Yucatán Peninsula rivers run underground is that Belize's lowlands truly are low; acid, limestone-dissolving water percolating downward doesn't have far to go, and thus has less chance for dissolving underground caverns.

Though most of northern Belize is fairly level, if you pay close attention you'll notice that sometimes an area's natural vegetation drastically changes, even though no fluctuation in elevation is apparent. Maybe you'll be passing through a dense swamp, with blackish water pooled in ditches alongside the road, and then suddenly you'll be surrounded by widely spaced pine trees populating what appears to be a dry, grassy savannah. What's happened here is that you have indeed changed a little in elevation. The pines grow on "ridges" that once were the spines of coral reefs; swamps inhabit the

Belize: A Different History, a Different Language

While most of the Ruta Maya's history is based on Spanish conquest and exploitation, the roots of Belize's history draw from another source.

Shipwrecked British sailors established Belize's first European settlement in 1638. Later the community grew when disbanded British soldiers and sailors moved there after the capture of Jamaica from Spain in 1655. The settlement's main activity became logwood cutting; the logwood tree, a member of the bean family, is *Haematoxylon campechianum*. From logwood heartwood is derived a compound called haematoxylin, $C_{16}H_{14}O_6$, which is oxidizable to the reddish-brown dye called hematein, formerly much used for coloring textiles.

During the next 150 years the community was frequently attacked by neighboring Spanish settlements because Spain claimed sovereignty over the entire New World, except for Portugal's part of South America. The attacks continued until the Battle of St. George's Cay in 1789, when the British won a decisive victory. Thereafter, British control increased and in 1862 British Honduras was formally declared a British Colony.

Though in 1973 the country's name was changed to Belize, independence was achieved only in 1981. Guatemala claims Belize as one of its departments. If you buy a map made in Guatemala, notice Guatemala's enlarged northern region...

low lying "valleys" between the "ridges." Seeing this wonderfully subtle "ridge-and-valley" topography sometimes requires imagination.

In stark contrast to northern Belize, southern Belize's Maya Mountains are largely constituted of granite — a rock producing thin, infertile, low-calcium, acidic soil. Frequently these mountains are mantled with pure stands of pine; pines often grow in acidic soils. Victoria Peak, Belize's highest elevation, in the Coxcomb Range, rises to 1,120 meters (3,675 feet). Flanking the Maya Mountains is a limestone landscape exhibiting well developed karst topography (having many caves, sinkholes and other solution features). Sometimes this landscape is also referred to as "cone and tower" topography; elevations here reach about 457 meters (1,500 feet) — about half the height of the Maya Mountains.

Biology

For its size, Belize has a remarkable variety of flowering plants — about 3,500 species. Tropical rain forest is found in northwest Belize and in the south, but not along the Ruta Maya.

Belize's barrier reef is second in length only to Australia's Great Barrier Reef. A "reef" is a projection of the ocean floor rising near or to the water's surface; the "barrier" part of "barrier reef" simply refers to the fact that the reef rises so close to the surface that it forms a barrier to ocean-going vessels and water currents. Belize's reef is composed of coral skeletons that for millennia have accumulated there.

Coral reefs occur only in warm, shallow waters. Sometimes you hear about living coral. This means that the animals referred to as coral are still living there, anchoring themselves atop the skeletons of their dead ancestors; an added implication of the term "living coral" is that among the coral colonies multitudes of other plants and animals flourish in the fragile ecosystem created by the coral.

The coral organism itself belongs to the phylum of animals referred to as the coelenterates. Coelenterates are aquatic organisms with no circulatory system, and a digestive system consisting of a simple saclike cavity with one opening, serving both as mouth and anus; jellyfish and sea anemones accompany coral in its phylum and thus are closely related. The most conspicuous difference between coral and its cousins is the limy skeleton the coral secretes.

By the way, if after visiting Belize you feel like supporting efforts to protect some of Belize's relatively low-populated back-country areas, contact the following organization: Programme for Belize, P.O. Box 385 X, Vineyard Haven, MA 02568 USA.

The People

One reason that Belize's ecology hasn't collapsed as badly as might be expected is its relatively low population density. Though the country is a little larger than the US state of Massachusetts, it has only 3% of Massachusetts's population — about 183,000. Since about half of this small population lives in cities along the coast, clearly the Belizean countryside is not very crowded; about 70% of the country is still forested.

About half of Belize's population is all or partly of African ancestry, and these people (sometimes called Creoles) speak English. Most other Belizeans are descendants of Maya Indians, frequently mixed with Spanish blood. Usually these people speak Spanish in their homes, but often they understand English as a second language. Moreover, in urban areas it's not uncommon to meet Caucasian, East Indian, Chinese, Lebanese and many other kinds of people, all calling themselves Belizeans. Sometimes people of mixed African-Indian blood are referred to as *garifuna*; people of mixed Spanish and Indian blood are called *mestizos*. As of late 1989, nearly 5,000 Spanish-speaking refugees, mostly from El Salvador and Guatemala, were resettled in Belize. Belize enjoys a literacy rate of over 90%.

A few isolated Carib villages also can be found. Belize's Caribs are dark-skinned descendants of runaway African slaves who intermingled with Carib Indians on the Caribbean island of St. Vincent in the 17th century. At the end of the 18th century the British deported them to the western Caribbean island of Roatán; later they spread to the coast of Central America. In Belize they mostly settled in Dangriga (Stann Creek), Hopkins, Seine Bight Billage, Punta Gorda and Barranco — all along southern Belize's coast.

Belizean English is a curious and wonderful thing. It's called Creole and the English-speaking visitor needs a while to develop an ear for it. One Creole speaker explained to me the differences between standard English and Creole.

"Creole is kind of a shorthand variety of standard English," he said. "We don't pronounce all the letters in all the words, and we don't say all the words that a standard English sentence thinks it needs. Maybe we do this because it sounds so good. When you sing or talk to a good-looking woman in Creole, it's beautiful; you can express your feelings better in Creole. Sometimes we use English words a little different from standard English speakers, and that makes the language more interesting!"

One morning I met a fellow walking down the road to Altun Ha and he told me that was "goin' a tap d'bush." I assumed that he meant that he was going to tap a chicozapote tree for its latex, but that wasn't his meaning at all. By "tap the bush" he meant that he was going to cut weeds with his machete! I have such difficulty with Creole that when I need to ask information in the streets, I look for Indians with whom, hopefully, I can speak standard Spanish.

By the way, the word "Creole" is a slippery, generic term. When applied to languages, it refers to a kind of hybrid speech composed of two or more other languages. Belize's Creole is English greatly influenced by African languages; Surinam's Creole is Dutch, similarly altered. In the U.S. the term Creole applies to the French patois spoken in parts of Louisiana. Moreover, in Belize, black folks refer to themselves — not just their language — as Creole, so sometimes the word implies a whole lifestyle.

The Maya have lived in the area now known as Belize since the Early Preclassic around 2000 BC — in other words, during nearly all the Maya civilization's history. Today three distinct Maya groups live in Belize, each speaking its own language. The Yucatec Maya inhabit the north, around Corozal and Orange Walk; during the mid-1800s many of these people's ancestors immigrated from the Yucatán because of conflict between the pure-blooded Maya who worked the land, and the mestizos (mixed Indian and Spanish) who owned it. Also in the mid-1800's the Kekchi Maya from Honduras and Guatemala moved into southern Belize, escaping from high taxes, forced labor and military conscription. In Succotz, near Benque Viejo on the Guatemalan border, live Mopán Maya.

PLACES TO VISIT

North of Belize City

SANTA ELENA: BORDER TOWN

In the north, Belize is entered by crossing a bridge over the Rio Hondo, from the Mexican state of Quintana Roo. Coming off the bridge, follow the road into the fenced-off area to the right. People in cars keep to the right and stop at the customs booth; walkers and bus riders must enter the first building on the left, which is the customs building, though it bears no signs or instructions to that effect. Inside, behind a bar-like desk stand two officials, who must examine your documents. Once you have your visa, go to the opposite side of the building to have your luggage checked.

As soon as you step outside the customs building you're promptly accosted by friendly young men proudly flashing wads of Belizean dollars and identifying themselves as the black market. They are indeed the black market, working in full view of all officials and obviously with permission to do so. They give better rates for your dollars than do banks. During my last crossing I saw a US businessman arrive from his base in Corozal to change several hundred dollars. On the Mexican side no similar money exchange operates.

If you enter Belize on foot, once you've finished your border-crossing tasks and find yourself in the tiny community of Santa Elena, you'll realize that there's not much to see or do there except continue heading south. The first-asked price for a taxi to Corozal, 8.5km away (five miles), is US$10.00.

If you prefer to forgo the taxi, hitching is fairly well institutionalized between the border and Corozal. If you prefer buses, walk across the customs station's wide, variously muddy or dusty driveway, make yourself at home in one of the very humble restaurants there, and wait for the next bus; outside the restaurants there's not much shade and in the sun it's usually oppressively hot and humid. Most of the time buses running between Chetumal and Belize City pass every hour or two, from 0400 to 2200, so you'll never really be stranded.

One final note before diving into Belize: If you come across a mostly green, glossy map of Belize entitled "Belize: The Adventure Coast Map," you are advised to burn the damned thing. Though it's available at every half-way touristy place in the country, it's grossly and dangerously inaccurate for anyone who might actually try to use it. The most accessible, fairly accurate map is called the "Maps & Visitor Guide of Belize," printed on cheap paper, in green and red inks, and sold in some hotels and stores for two or three dollars. Though its pages predominantly hold advertising, its city maps are very useful.

COROZAL

Corozal was settled in 1849 by refugees fleeing Yucatán's War of Races. It's a perfect place to settle for a day or two to begin absorbing what Belize is all about, and to train your ear for Creole. Situated on the shores of Chetumal Bay, Corozal nearly always is blessed with a fresh ocean breeze. Evening walks along the town's beach-side streets are simply delicious. And Corozal even has its share of Maya ruins!

If you want to camp in Corozal, follow the main thoroughfare, 7th Avenue, southward until you arrive at the beach, and then continue 1½ blocks along the beach road to Jo's Caribbean Restaurant, sometimes known as the **Caribbean Motel & Trailer Park**. The wry-humored Jo, a lady from the US, will let you tent-camp on the breezy, grassy area beneath her palm trees for US$2.00; an RV with one or two people pays US$4.00 for all hook-ups. I've heard it said that Jo's Restaurant offers the best food in Corozal. Jo has rooms, too, but I was so distracted by her wisecracking, obviously-feeling-at-home guests that I forgot to ask their price.

The cheapest rooms in town surely are found at the purple- and green-painted **Hotel Capri**, located back toward town, where 7th Avenue meets the beach. A room without a bathroom costs US$4.25; with a bathroom it's US$6.25. For this price you get to be in close proximity to a bar, too. About half a block down the street, across from the beach, stands the **Hotel Maya**, with modest but clean double rooms costing US$21.00; a pleasant restaurant operates downstairs. Rosita, the Hotel Maya's owner, is *the* person in Corozal to contact if you're interested in hiring a boat to the ruin of Cerros across the bay, or if you have any other special eco-touristic need or interest.

If a little luxury appeals to you, check out **Tony's Inn & Resort** even farther down the beach road; if you're interested in plenty of luxury, with cottages by the sea, water sports, day-tours, and all the rest, go to Corozal's plaza area and follow signs to the *Adventure Inn*, at Consejo Shores about 14km (nine miles) northeast of town. Near the town plaza you find both Barclays Bank and the Bank of Nova Scotia.

At Corozal's bus station, about every 60 to 90 minutes throughout the day the Venus Bus Line and Batty Bros send buses south. A ticket to the next large town, Orange Walk, costs only US$1.25. In other words, in Belize bus tickets are as much a bargain as elsewhere along the Ruta Maya.

Traveling between Corozal and Orange Walk from December to June, you'll likely witness sugar-cane harvest — *la zafra*, as it's called in Spanish. During *la zafra* you see men with machetes cutting tall sugar-cane stems and loading them in the backs of big trucks. Notice that the cane's leafless stems are charred black in places. Before being harvested, a controlled fire is set in the sugar-cane fields. The fire burns off some of the leaves and, more importantly, heats the stems enough to cause the plants' sugars to liquify and become more available for later extraction. It also causes an all-pervading, unforgettable, sweet-molasses smell to ooze across the landscape. Just south of Corozal, sometimes 200 or more big trucks loaded with sugar cane can be spotted waiting to enter a huge mill with black smoke pouring from its chimneys. Many truck drivers spend all night in this line, waiting, talking, pulling their trucks ever closer, foot-by-foot. Getting the cane to the mill is a major cultural event in this area, and of profound economic importance.

Santa Rita

Archeological orientation
Though now most of the former Maya city of Santa Rita lies beneath the modern town of Corozal, during Postclassic times Santa Rita was an important center; it was still occupied when the Spanish arrived. In archeological literature Santa Rita is famous for its murals. However, if you visit the ruin to see them you'll be disappointed, for they were destroyed by Indians almost as soon as they were uncovered — even before they had been completely copied by archeologists. Sir Eric Thompson suggests that the destruction may have been something other than mere vandalism. He believes that the superstitious Indians destroyed the murals because they held images of what seemed to be demons or maybe malevolent gods; they feared the murals.

Whatever the reason for their destruction, they're said to have been spectacular. Apparently they showed a sequence of gods (many of them very Mexicanized) ruling over the Maya years (years of 360 days, called tuns). Also present was a fragment of mural showing what must have been the "counting of katuns" (a katun being a period of 20 Maya years). Page 199 of Thompson's *The Rise and Fall of Maya Civilization* bears a drawing of a detail from the mural, showing the god of merchants holding a rattle and beating a drum.

In the old conquistador writings, whenever mention was made of the Maya village of Chetumal, they were referring not to a location coinciding with present-day Chetumal, Mexico, but to Belize's Santa Rita, or a site very nearby.

Logistics
The ruin of Santa Rita is so modest that, though it's within walking distance of downtown Corozal, you might not consider going there just for the ruin itself. However, there are other reasons, the main one being Pedro the custodian. Such articulate, friendly, well-informed, English-speaking guides are simply a pleasure to find; he gives

meaning to the hardly noticeable grassy mounds rising before the single, partially restored building.

To reach Santa Rita, follow the main road toward Mexico (the Santa Rita Road) until on the outskirts of town the highway bends sharply to the right, and a side road continues straight up a small hill. At this intersection stands a tiny, rectangular garden sprouting a conspicuous religious sign proclaiming in English that "Jesus said if man thurst... "

Take the side road up the hill, past the hospital for about half a kilometer (⅛ mile). Immediately past the conspicuous "New 10,000 gallons steel elevated storage tank" (It's square instead of round, and it'll be on your left) take the first right onto a gravel road, and then the next right onto another gravel road and, finally, on your left, the ruin will rise before you.

After hearing what Pedro has to say climb atop the building and try to spot the ruin of Cerros, barely visible across the bay; you'll want your binoculars here. Before leaving Santa Rita be sure to notice two very important tree species growing next to the ruin. Viewing the structure from the front, the eight-meter-tall (25-foot) trees to the building's left, with wild-fig-like leaves, and chestnut-like fruits lying on the ground, are *ramón*, or breadnut trees, *Brosimum alicastrum*, of the fig family.

Ramóns are common all through the Ruta Maya's humid-forest zones. Its seeds are nutritious and, when ripe, not bad tasting raw; when boiled they taste like bland chestnuts, maybe, or potatoes. The seeds can be ground into meal for making bread and tortillas. Leaves and young branches are cut for animal fodder; the tree's milky sap has been diluted and used as a substitute for cow's milk.

The ruin's other tree species worth noticing is one that Pedro planted because it's one of Belize's most famous organisms. It's the ziricote tree, *Cordia sebestena*, a member of the heliotrope family. After you're in Belize a while you'll notice that one item sold at every tourist-frequented place is ziricote wood-carvings. Ziricote is a swamp-growing tree and most carvers use the part of its trunk connecting to the tree's subterranean roots. The wood is heavy, dark and beautifully grained. Some ziricote carvings are wonderful works of art, unmistakably showing African influence. The ziricote's leaves are so rough that sometimes the tree is referred to by the name of sandpaper tree.

Cerros

Cerros was a fishing village during its first 300 years, in the late Preclassic. Toward the end of the Preclassic it developed into an important stop on the coastal trade route. It was inhabited by about

400 people who built two ball courts and some stucco-covered pyramids. Studies have shown that on 37ha (91 acres) of land the villagers planted corn, squash, beans and cotton. Around this land they dug a 1,100-meter (3,600-foot) canal 5.5 meters wide and 1.8 meters deep (18 feet wide and six feet deep). During the Classic period the coastal route was abandoned — possibly because it became too swampy as a result of a wetter climate and rising sea level — and Cerros's importance waned.

Even people not impressed with fairly modest ruins usually enjoy visiting Cerros because the boat trip over is fun, the site itself is pretty, surrounded by tall trees, and the boatman will probably include a heron rookery or two, just to make the trip more interesting. To make arrangements for the trip, talk to Pedro at Santa Rita, or Rosita at the Hotel Maya. Or just hang around the pier looking as though you want something, and certainly you'll be approached with various offers. The starting price for a day-trip to Cerros is US$50.00 per boatload.

ORANGE WALK

Buses stop in the center of Orange Walk, across the street from the town park and next to a government building with a sign on it saying "Orange Walk Branch Office." Besides Orange Walk being a pleasant place with a small-town flavor, Ruta Maya travelers have two good reasons for pausing here: First, five kilometers (three miles) west of Orange Walk lies the fairly modest but interesting and very important ruin of Cuello. Second, Antoñio and Herminio Novelo operate an eco-tourism agency called Jungle River Tours out of a little restaurant across the town park.

Unfortunately, at this writing, in Orange Walk there's no place to camp. **Camie's**, next to the park, has rooms with hot water and private bath; singles cost US$12.50 and doubles are US$20.00. For other hotels, some of them rather swanky looking, just tour the main road in and out of town.

Orange Walk was the scene of the last battle on Belizean soil. In 1872 the Icaiche Maya attacked a British garrison after soldiers had burned their village. The Maya leader was killed and the Maya retreated.

Cuello
Archeological orientation
Before Cuello was discovered, Maya civilization was thought to have begun around 900 BC. However, Maya artifacts unearthed at Cuello have been dated back to 2500 BC. Among archeologists, Cuello is a favorite because of its clear stratigraphic sequences — layer upon

layer of material has been laid down and not later disturbed. A platform at Cuello exhibits what may be the earliest known example of stucco used in the Maya area. In fact, information developed at Cuello supports the school of thought that Classic Maya civilization may have begun here in the lowlands rather than in Mexico or the highlands.

Cuello consists of two adjacent plazas with pyramids and platforms. However, despite its importance to Maya archeology, Cuello is not visually uninspiring; most of us will go there for only two reasons: for the pleasure of being in a place so important in archeological literature, and; simply to have someplace to go involving exploring and meeting people. Walking there through swamps and sugar-cane fields, on what's called the Yo Creek Road, makes an interesting early-morning birding experience, though later in the day it becomes very hot and humid.

Logistics
Cuello lies 6.5km (four miles) west of Orange Walk, on the grounds of the rather famous Caribbean Rum Distillery. Starting from the town park, for two short blocks continue south on Victoria Avenue (Northern Highway) toward Belize City; turn right at the fire station; this road continues all the way to Cuello. At the fire station's corner usually some kiosks and an informal market do brisk business, so if you have no car, before you begin walking or hitching you should ask when the next bus service is available to the Caribbean Rum distillery; in Orange Walk the distillery is better known than the ruins. If you do hitch, do it from the edge of town to avoid the considerable local traffic. Hitching usually is easy, especially during the sugar-cane-harvesting season from December to June, when big cane-carrying trucks ply the gravel road.

You'll know you've arrived at the ruins when a small, metal windmill appears on your right, across from a gravel road on the left leading to buildings about 150 meters away. Take the lane toward the buildings until you come to a gate on which a sign is mounted reading, "Permission To Enter Site Must Be Obtained From The Management Next Bldg. This Site Is Closed Monday To Saturday From 5:00 PM to 9:30 AM And All Day Sunday."

It's not clear which building is the "next building" referred to in the sign; it's the one at the end of the middle road, beside a tall, rectangular water tower; this is the rum distillery. Usually several people are working outside the building. Just walk up to anyone and ask whom you should ask for permission to visit the ruins, which lie behind the distillery. Don't feel awkward about asking to see the ruin; the ruin belongs to the Belizean government, not the distillery, and the government encourages visits to its attractions; the distillery's owners are used to people asking to see the ruins.

Nohmul

Archeological orientation

During the Late Preclassic and Late Classic, Nohmul was a major ceremonial center. It consists of twin ceremonial sites connected by a raised causeway, or *sacbe*. The tallest structure at Nohmul is also the highest point in northern Belize. Other than these prominences on the landscape, there's not much to see here.

Logistics

Nohmul lies in the village of San Pablo, north of Orange Walk; bus connections connect Orange Walk with Nohmul, but you'll have to ask around for the current schedule. To find Nohmul on your own, go to the restaurant eight or nine kilometers (five or six miles) north of Orange Walk and take a left, then go about 1.5km (about one mile) across a sugar-cane field. If you become disoriented, someone at the restaurant will gladly set you straight.

Lamanai

Archeological orientation

Having been occupied from Preclassic times (around 300 B.C.) until well past the Conquest, Lamanai is one of Belize's oldest and largest ceremonial centers. Though at the end of the Classic period Lamanai didn't suffer the precipitous population collapse seen at many other sites, apparently the population did gradually diminish. Very different from other Maya sites, where usually one or more ceremonial plazas are encircled by residential clusters, the ruins at Lamanai stretch along New River Lagoon's west bank.

The ruins, which include about seven major structures, cover 4.5 square kilometers (1¾ square miles). The structure known as N9-56, rising 17 meters (56 feet) high, is exceptionally well-preserved; it's unusual because of its corner stairs — not up the middle, as is typical. A small ball court, now in poor condition, was built during the late Classic. Though little of the site has been excavated, already dozens of burials have been found in which, in typical Postclassic fashion, one or more ceramic vessels had been smashed and strewn over the graves. In one burial an adult male with a pyrite mirror and a copper bell was found seated in a pit. Generally the grounds are uncleared, and only a few trails exist. Visitors can climb to the top of the main temple.

Logistics

Unless seeing unreconstructed ruins (mounds in the jungle) is of uncommon pleasure to you, probably Lamanai's main attraction will be the excellent adventure of getting there, and the interesting landscape seen along the way. During the drier parts of the dry season (the northern winter), four-wheel drives with a winch will probably be able to make it all the way.

Maps of the area generally contradict one another on how roads interconnect. If you want to try this trip in your own 4 x 4, at least you should study the topographic map on the wall of the Novelo Brother's restaurant at 20 Lovers Lane in Orange Walk (next to the town park). However, Herminio Novelo tells me that even this map is wrong in a few details. If you do try to get there on your own, but midway decide that the road is just too bad, at both Guinea Grass and Shipyard — settlements on the New River between Orange Walk and Lamanai — you can hire boats for the remainder of the trip. Shipyard is a Mennonite community. I'd hesitate to wander around too much in this area; I've heard about some marijuana fields here.

Certainly the most elegant and interesting way to visit Lamanai is to work something up with the English-speaking Novelo Brothers mentioned above. To find their restaurant at 20 Lovers Lane, from in front of the Orange Walk Branch Office (where the buses stop), head across the park to the corner on the far right and go right across the street. The Novelo Brothers will guide you on a one-day boat-trip up the New River to Lamanai, looking at crocodiles, turtles, four species of hawk, orchids and bromeliads, and a sugar factory for US$200 per group.

The brothers will also talk to you about a one-day, whirlwind tour taking in Cuello, the ruin of Nohmul, and the Indian village of San Jose. You might also ask about the possibility of becoming the guest of a family in one of the region's isolated Carib communities.

Castor bean
Ricinus communis

CROOKED TREE WILDLIFE SANCTUARY

Located 53km (33 miles) northwest of Belize City and just two miles off the Northern Highway, this easily accessible destination provides a look at Belizean biota. It's a fine place for birding, especially for those wanting to spot the jabiru stork which, with a wingspan of up to 3.7 meters (12 feet), is one of the earth's largest birds. (The Andean condor's wingspread is 3.1 meters (10 feet) and the wandering albatross's is around 3.4 meters (11 feet). At Crooked Tree you'll see the usual birds of lakes and marshes — herons, grebes, pelicans, ducks, kites, ospreys, sandpipers, kingfishers, gulls, terns, etc. Also you might hear, or much more rarely see, the black howler monkey, as well as crocodiles, turtles, iguanas, and maybe even a wandering coatimundi.

While Crooked Tree's proximity to Belize City and the Northern Highway causes it to be an easy place to drive to or take a bus to (exiting the bus, you can walk or hitch the last couple of miles), here's one way to get to the sanctuary in a more interesting manner. In Belize City, contact the Belize River Lodge (phone #52002) next to the Airport on the northern edge of town, and check out chartering a boat for a voyage up the Belize River, into Black Creek, and finally into Crooked Tree Lagoon — a trip of about two hours. Fishermen looking for "dream spots" do this, paying about US$75.00 per trip, depending on what kind of deal is struck. Tell whomever you talk to that Philip Andrewin, one of their guides, said that a boat might be available.

Altun Ha

Archeological orientation

At this writing, Altun Ha is Belize's most extensively excavated Maya ruin, though Caracol may soon snatch this distinction. Despite Altun Ha having been settled over 2,000 years ago, during the Late Preclassic, most of its major buildings are of Classic age. Altun Ha was a major ceremonial center as well as a center for trade, serving as a link between the coast and settlements farther inland. Situated just ten kilometers (six miles) from the sea, it supplied marine materials to inland Maya — shells, coral, pearls — and in return received such items as jade and obsidian, which aren't found locally.

In Altun Ha's Temple of the Masonry Altars was found the famous, ornately carved head of the Mayan Sun God, Kinisch Ahau, weighing 4.4kg (9¾ pounds) and measuring about 15.25cm (six inches) from base to crown; it's believed to be the largest existing Maya carving in jade. The Temple of the Masonry Altars is also interesting for another reason: It was found inside six layers of limestone construction. After it had been finished, every 50 years or so a new building had been built around it. Later the outer layers were removed; the structure we see today is from around 600 AD. Altun Ha's Temple of the Green Tomb was discovered to be a burial chamber holding human remains and a treasure of pendants, beads, figures and jewellery, all crafted of jade. One unusual feature of Altun Ha is that here you *don't* find carved stone stelae.

In addition to the main buildings, around 275 unexcavated ceremonial structures girdle the precinct, and hundreds of other mounds indicate that once approximately 10,000 people lived in an area around 500ha (two square miles) large; this gave Altun Ha a population density 85% greater than that of residential Tikal. Though today the area is considered far too swampy for decent farming, the ancient Maya were obviously able to support a very high population level. Several causeways cross the swampy ground.

Logistics

At the Belizean ruins mentioned so far, chances are that you will be the only visitor while you are there. That's not so at Altun Ha. At this writing, Altun Ha, along with Xunantunich on the Guatemala frontier, are the only frequently visited Belizean Maya ruins. There are several ways to get to Altun Ha.

For instance, if you're walking down a street in San Pedro on Ambergris Cay (Belize's answer to Cancún), maybe you'll succumb to a poster in a travel agency's window offering a quick day-trip to Altun Ha — fly to Belize City, then take a short drive north.

In Belize City itself, Altun Ha is one of the town's prime tourist-industry destinations; any travel agency can help you get there. For instance, Mayaland Tours at No. 10 "A" Street, will ship two to four persons not only to Altun Ha but also to the Crooked Tree Wildlife Sanctuary for US$55.00. The more persons going along, the cheaper the ticket.

Independent, bus-riding backpackers also can get to Altun Ha. Just take any bus between Orange Walk and Belize City and disembark at the road to Altun Ha, just north of the village of Sand Hill. From this point, the ruins lie 24km (15 miles) up the rather narrow but paved road. At this time, a bus from Belize City to points north of Altun Ha passes this junction in the afternoon, usually around 1600, except on Sundays; the return bus to Belize City passes around 0530 the next morning. Clearly, this bus schedule is designed for people on the Altun Ha Road who want to visit Belize City early in the morning, do their business, and return home before sunset — and not for anyone wanting to take an early bus to the ruins and return to Belize City the same day. Since no hotels are available in the area, the situation is even more interesting. If you arrive at the intersection too early to wait for the afternoon bus, you'll probably be able to hitch, though during the hottest part of the day it'll be slow. Altun Ha's gravel entrance-road lies up the highway at Mile 30½.

Along the three-kilometer-long (two-mile) gravel road leading from the paved road to the ruin stand several thatch-roof kiosks at which ziricote carvings are sold. Sometimes the artists are working in the kiosks; occasionally you find some masterfully done works. After about 2.5km (1½ miles) the road forks; keep to the right. You've arrived when you come to a nice picnicking shelter, beyond which stands a partially restored pyramid rising a good bit above the treetops. If you talk sweetly to the ruin's custodian you'll be welcome to camp in the general area around the shelter, off the ruin's grounds. The settlement next to the ruin is called Rock Stone Pond.

My main fun in this area was not at the ruin itself. One early morning I hiked back to the paved road and instead of waiting for a ride, began sauntering south, birding and frequently taking the time to chat with whomever looked like they wanted to chat. And most of the people I met could talk your leg off. One fellow in a pickup truck did stop, without my signaling, but I was having such a good time that I asked him to continue without me... Over the course of two days I strolled the entire 24 km (15 miles) back to the Northern Highway.

The long, narrow, potholed but paved road between Altun Ha and the Northern Highway doesn't see enough traffic to bother a walking birdwatcher. Most of the road passes through swampy forest so waterlogged that at the pavement's edge shallow trenches stand full of black water. (Yes, mosquitoes are bad, especially around dusk, and malaria is common here, so don't forget mosquito repellant.) Occasionally the road passes through extensive tracts of less soggy, interestingly intact forest, but nearly all of this acreage is staked out with "Private Property No Trespassing" signs. Sometimes the road courses through tiny hamlets such as Baton Rouge and other gatherings of houses known more by their mile number than any formal name.

Along this road you see such common "weed-birds" as tropical kingbird, barred antshrike and yellow-faced grassquit, as well as some real Christmas-candy species such as the green-breasted mango, citreoline trogon, red-capped manakin and rose-throated tanager; this latter species is endemic to the Yucatán Peninsula, this part of Belize, and northern Guatemala. During the northern winter, a goodly number of songbirds escaping North America's cold weather also can be spotted: The white-eyed vireo, yellow-throated warbler and the yellowthroat, for instance.

In the winter the walk is worthwhile if only to see the gorgeous flowers of the Guiana chestnut tree, *Pachira aquatica*, which grow up to 35cm (14 inches) long! Despite having such large flowers, this tree seldom stands over four or five meters tall (15 feet); usually it grows in shallow water or at pond edges. The flowers have gracefully recurved petals and dense clusters of stiff, pale-pink stamens. Occasionally in nature things are encountered that are so stunning that they seem unreal and unnatural; that's the case with *Pachira aquatica*, which grows rather commonly in swamps along this road. It's a member of the pantropical bombax family.

During the last couple of miles before the road ends at Sand Hill, suddenly — and I mean suddenly — the vegetation transforms from dense swamp-forest to open, dry-smelling woods of slash pine, *Pinus caribæa*, and some rather scrubby, thirsty-looking species of oak. This sharply defined vegetative frontier announces the fact that you've "climbed" atop one of northern Belize's famous ridges. And, indeed, if you use your imagination, you may even be able to see a slight rise in the landscape, over toward Sand Hill. (Sand *Hill*... ! Why, it's flatter'n a fritter there!) Anyway, the local biota seems to appreciate the acclivity. This oak/pine forest, despite its tenuous credentials to be anything but a swamp, is home to a whole oak/pine biota, including acorn woodpeckers.

If you want an excuse to strike up a conversation with the Creole- and Spanish-speaking folks along the road to Altun Ha, ask them if they'll sell you a coconut or some bananas. If you're hungry and you see a lady in her kitchen (frequently kitchens are in outside, unwalled sheds or beneath houses raised on stilts), don't hesitate to ask her how much she'd charge to fix you a piping hot meal — tortillas, beans and fried eggs if the conversation is in Spanish, beans and rice if in English. If it's late in the day and you don't cherish the idea of arriving in Belize City at night, ask anyone how much they'd charge to let you

Acorn Woodpeckers (*Melanerpes formicivorus*)

Acorn woodpeckers have a passion for acorns. Other woodpecker species have been spotted storing acorns in cavities in old tree-trunks, cracks in fence-posts, between shingles on rooftops, etc., but acorn woodpeckers make an art of it.

They choose a tree — usually an oak but a sycamore, pine or telephone pole will do — and methodically drill row after row of closely spaced holes large enough to store an acorn in. One large pine in California was found to have 50,000 acorns imbedded in its bark.

Of course, this acorn-storing behavior provides the acorn woodpecker with food during that part of the year when acorns aren't available. However, before attributing uncommon wisdom or foresight to this bird, we should take into account these observations: Sometimes pebbles are discovered lodged in the woodpecker's holes; occasionally so many acorns are stored that most of them are never eaten; and frequently the birds store their acorns in locations that are obviously vulnerable to marauding rodents, who eat them.

Apparently acorn woodpeckers don't think anything out; they just yield to a genetically fixed urge to drill holes, and stuff them. However, it's marvelous to reflect that nature can "program" a being with innate behavior that is this complex. Besides, maybe acorn woodpeckers sometime leave pebbles in their holes just to give us birdwatchers something to think about...

throw a tent beneath their lemon tree, or beside their pond.

The people along this road have seen thousands of tourists pass but you might be the first they've had a chance to talk with. Usually their curiosity is matched only by their hospitality. By the way, all along the road to Altun Ha stand long-handled, public water-pumps from which cool, clean-looking (but use your pills) water can be taken at any time. Finally, this re-reminder: Especially at dusk, take extreme precautions against malaria-carrying mosquitoes!

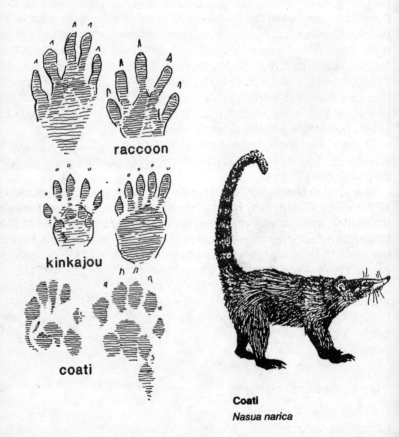

raccoon

kinkajou

coati

Coati
Nasua narica

Belize City and Surrounding Area

BELIZE CITY

Little Belize City (population about 45,000) is home to at least 18 tour operators, mostly having offices downtown. To give you an idea of lodging prices here, the **Isabel Guest House**, a take-stairs-between-the-hardware-store kind of place, located near the east end of Orange Street, offers single rooms for US$16 per night. **Glenthorne Manor**, a really fine bed & breakfast at 27 Barracks Road (easy walking distance from downtown), costs US$30.00 per night for a single room, US$45.00 for a double. The average resort-type, double hotel room goes for US$80 to US$120.

Whatever bus you take into town, when you disembark, "downtown" lies generally to the east. Have someone point you to Cemetery Road, which runs east and west, and just follow it eastward until it turns into Orange Street; continue your eastward trek until you meet the river, called Haulover Creek. Standing at the east end of Orange Street, the Post Office lies just at the foot and to the right of the swing bridge to your left. Banks of various kinds and several travel agencies lie to your right, down Albert Street. You can pick up the latest brochures at the Belize Tourist Board at 83 North Front Street, Belize City, Tel: 02 77213, Fax: 02 77490. You may be handicapped using this literature because hardly any of Belize City's streets are marked. To get around effectively you really need a map, a compass, and someone upon your arrival to show you your starting point.

Don't look for swimming beaches anywhere in town, for there aren't any. Besides, those open canals with raw sewage floating in them are emptying into the sea.

Bus service on the Northern Highway (to Mexico) and the Western Highway (to Guatemala) is so frequent, and conducted with such informality, that the way you leave town is simply to go to one of the "stations" (which may be just a place on a street), and buy a ticket for the next bus to your destination. Batty Bros and Novelo's Bus Stations are on Collet Canal St and the Venus Station is on Magazine Rd.

Belize City was built on a mangrove swamp only 45cm (18 inches) above sea level. When in 1961 Hurricane *Hattie* blew ashore with 257-kph (160-mph) winds, dragging a three-meter (ten-foot) tide behind her, she badly mauled three-quarters of town and left more than 260 people dead.

THE BARRIER REEF/CAYE SCENE

Offshore Belize is simply glorious fun. Brain coral, purple sea-fans, elkhorn coral, star coral, sponges, seafans, parrotfish, snappers, angelfish, moray eels and stingrays... sand, wind, sunshine... all are fair game for the eco-tourist. However, since offshore tourism as it's practised on Ambergris Caye, Caye Caulker and other such spots is the mainstay of Belize's traditional tourism industry, other guidebooks do a wonderful job leading you through that world. Here I'll just outline the situation, and tell you that "caye" is pronounced "key" and spelt Cay on some maps!.

On Ambergris Caye the average resort hotel room goes for US$100-US$150, with modest double rooms available for between US$35 and US$50. On Caye Caulker (also known as Caye Corker), clean budget rooms are available for around US$25. Backpackers generally gravitate to Caye Caulker. You might be interested in knowing that in 1869 the same gun-running James Black who tried to ransom the citizens of Bacalar from the Cruzob fanatics (see page 146) bought Ambergris Caye for US$625. Today, three nights in an ocean-front suite at Ambergris Caye's Ramon Reef Resort costs more than Blake paid for the entire island...

The good ship *Andera* leaves the docks of the Bellevue Hotel at 16.00, Monday through Friday, and 13.00 on Saturday, for San Pedro (Ambergris Caye), and returns to Belize City at 19.00. The boat for Caye Caulker leaves from A & R Service Station on North Front Street every hour on the hour.

THE COMMUNITY BABOON SANCTUARY AT BERMUDIAN LANDING

General Information

"I've never seen a place where people were happier to see you, and so friendly. After one day there it seemed that everybody in town knew our names and wanted to say hello!" That's what one US traveler told me upon leaving Belize's baboon sanctuary, which lies about 1½ hours northwest of Belize City, at Bermudian Landing. Moreover, though during our conversation the visitor roundly praised his hosts, and detailed several experiences he'd enjoyed, he never even mentioned "baboons" (see box on page 171). Clearly, at Bermudian Landing something is going on transcending merely traveling into a backwoods area to see furry primates.

Among other things, while wilderness-area landowners such as the ones around Bermudian Landing are usually interested only in cutting trees and squeezing every drop of quick-term agricultural gain from the land, the humble farmers in this sanctuary's 4,662ha (18-square-mile) area have chosen the preservation option. They've signed pledges promising to manage their land in ways ensuring the long-term survival of the area's 120 to 150 monkeys, and other wildlife. They're gambling that they can make better livings from eco-tourism

Are There Really Baboons in Belize?

No, at least not technically speaking. Here's why not:

The earth's monkey-like mammals, its primates, are separated into four fairly distinct groups:

The Prosimians (pre-monkeys); this group includes such primitive "pro-simian" creatures as lemurs, bush babies, and tarsiers. These animals tend to look more like squirrels and raccoons than primates; they're all native to the Old World — Africa and Asia.

The Ape Group; the apes are some of the most highly evolved, sophisticated species on earth. They include gorillas, gibbons, humans, chimpanzees and orangutans, all of which evolved in the Old World.

The Old World Monkeys; this very large group includes colobus monkeys, macaques, baboons and many other monkeys that are typically characterized by having long noses, and rumps equipped with tough callous pads; these pads are adaptations enabling the monkey for long periods of time to sit or sleep in a sitting position on tree limbs.

The New World Monkeys; these monkeys mostly have prehensile tails (Old World species cannot grasp branches with their tails), and include such species such as spider monkeys, howler monkeys, marmosets and capuchin monkeys; usually they are flat-nosed; they are found in the Americas.

In other words, technically speaking, baboons are Old-World species, not naturally found in the Americas. Belize's baboons really are howler monkeys, *Alouatta pigra*. However, to Belize's pioneering Blacks with long memories of Old-World Africa, *Alouatta pigra's* resemblance to baboons was close enough.

than from slash-and-burn agriculture. These simple people have seen the wisdom in investing in biological diversity and ecological sustainability at a time when most of the world's conservative power-holders still sniff at the idea!

Therefore, because the people in Bermudian Landing recognize that their economic survival depends on tourism dollars, travelers wandering into town get royal treatment. Surely within a few years Bermudian Landingers will become as jaded as any desk clerk on Ambergris Caye; however, at least at this writing, and maybe still when you arrive there, if you go to Bermudian Landing looking for "baboons," you might well find that before you leave, a lot of local people will be calling you by your name...

Logistics

In Belize City, except on Sundays, you can catch buses to Bermudian Landing at three different places: 1) Between noon and 1230, at the corner of Orange Street and Mussel Street, behind the Pacific Store; 2) At the same time, at the corner of Orange Street and George Street, and; 3) at 1730, at Cemetery and George Street. This last bus arrives at Bermudian Landing so late that you won't want to take it unless you've arranged lodging beforehand, which almost any of Belize City's travel agencies will be happy to do — they'll call ahead.

The bus lines mentioned above give the impression of being rather informally managed. By the time you find yourself in Belize City, other lines may be in existence, and the ones mentioned above may be out of service. If you're not eager for surprises you should visit the bus-leaving place a day in advance and confirm with the bus driver that the next day he intends to make the trip at the specified time.

If you're driving, go to Mile 13.5 on the Northern Highway and at Burrell Boom Cutoff head west for 23km (14 miles), past Burrell Boom and Mussel Creek, to the Belize River. Take the right fork and cross the bridge into Bermudian Landing. Arriving in town, head for the visitor's center, which is easy to recognize because it's the only building in town looking like a visitor's center. Here someone will help you organize your visit.

Guides are available for about US$2.50 per hour. Campers can throw a tent for US$1.50. For many visitors the most interesting experience here is staying in the home of a Bermudian-Landing native for US$5.00 a night; cooked meals are provided for US$2.00 per meal. The food is very simple — a bit heavy on rice and beans — but this is what the Belizeans eat, and nothing else would be appropriate.

If you do spend the night with a Belizean, your host may offer to leave a kerosene lantern burning in your room (no electricity, and it keeps away mosquitoes). Frequently the oily vapor from these lanterns is irritating to eyes, nose and throats, so you may opt to forgo the lantern's service; but be sure to smear yourself with plenty of mosquito repellent; a mosquito net is recommended. Remember that the malaria mosquito is active mostly at dusk.

Most commonly the monkeys' lion-like roarings are heard in early morning; during the day troops of four to eight move through the trees feeding and resting. Though I've never been able to confirm that if you approach this species too closely you'll have feces thrown at you (something told around campfires), I can indeed confirm that when you're standing right beneath them they do frequently feel nature's call; and falling feces splattered and scattered by tree limbs, I'd say, is wonderfully effective against nosey people. This story should be enough to keep you a fair distance. Also, you should respect the monkeys' need for space; if people hound the monkeys they'll become nervous and secretive.

One final suggestion: Don't visit the sanctuary with the single goal of seeing howler monkeys. These monkeys are wild creatures with their own routines and cycles, completely independent of any human need to see them. The area's general ecological diversity and the relaxed and friendly nature of the people in the seven Creole villages in the sanctuary should make your visit worthwhile, even if no monkeys are spotted or heard. With the wide variety of habitats in this area, from cornfields to dense forest and regenerating slash-and-burn fields to riverine habitats along the nearby Belize River, it's excellent for birding, sketching flowers, and general walking around.

Howler monkey
Alouatta pigra

THE BELIZE ZOO

About 50km (32 miles) west of Belize City, on the Western Highway, the Belize Zoo is home to over a hundred native Belizean animals. Tourist literature speaks of "seeing unique animals in their natural habitat," which suggests the enlightened approach of lodging animals in spacious surroundings landscaped to approximate the animal's natural habitat. Well, at the Belize Zoo deer do run in large compounds and many of the pens are more commodious than those typically used to confine animals. But the zoo's ambience lies somewhere between seediness and soul; the animals there, including snakes and iguanas behind glass, fish in aquaria, crocodiles in pools, etc., certainly are interesting to see. When you arrive you pay US$5.00 for a ticket; then a guide takes you around explaining things.

Buses drop off zoo-bound passengers at Mile 32 on the Western Highway, leaving them with about a mile to walk up a sandy road. About midway up this road a small, hand-painted sign in English shows walkers a shortcut to the zoo. Though the area is surrounded by secondary pine woods, there's no formal campsite and no hotels in the immediate vicinity.

Other Information

The Belize Zoo stands at an important geographical milestone along the Ruta Maya. If you've been in the Yucatán and northern Belize, and now you're heading west toward Guatemala, for the first time during your trip south, you'll *see some real hills*. Almost mountains! In fact, these are foothills of the Maya Mountains and if you've been flat-landing for several weeks they'll offer welcome relief from the uneventful horizon you've grown accustomed to. On the other hand, if you're coming out of Guatemala or other parts south and east, just tip your hat to the foothills around the Belize Zoo and say good-by to vigorous slopes. Another interesting feature of the landscape is how frequently and quickly vegetation zones change between the zoo and Belize City. Marshes and swamps alternate with sandy-soiled rises populated by species of oak and pine.

GUANACASTE PARK

General Information

Guanacaste Park is a 20ha (50 acre) parcel of forest located where the Hummingbird Highway, which runs south to Blue Hole National Park and Dangriga (Stann Creek), meets the Western Highway; it's about three kilometers (two miles) north of Belmopan. If you're looking for an easily accessible spot perfect for birding along trails passing through a variety of habitats, including some riverine communities adjoining the park, this is it. Guanacaste Park is sponsored by the Belize

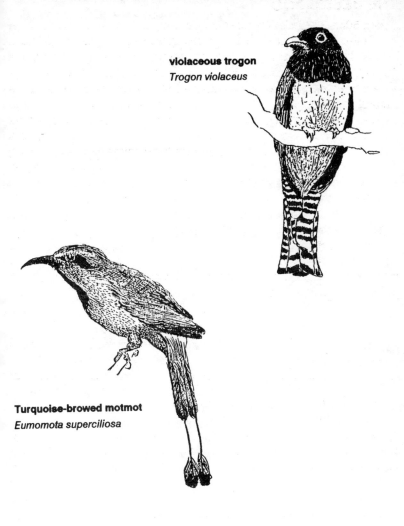

violaceous trogon
Trogon violaceus

Turquoise-browed motmot
Eumomota superciliosa

Turkey vulture

Black vulture

Audubon Society, the Government of Belize and the MacArthur Foundation. At this time there's no admission fee, though naturally monetary gifts are accepted.

The park takes its name from several magnificent guanacaste trees, *Enterolobium cyclocarpum*, growing there. Besides the trees' great size, you'll be astonished at how many different kinds of epiphytic plant grow on the big trees' branches — each guanacaste supports a veritable airborne garden!

Some of the more interesting birds to be spotted at Guanacaste Park include the blue-crowned motmot, black-faced antthrush, smoky-brown woodpecker, citreoline trogon, squirrel cuckoo, bright-rumped attila and white-breasted wood-wren. During my own birding walk I spotted an interesting mammal, a paca, *Agouti paca*, strolling down the path before me. Usually this species is both nocturnal and nervous; apparently animals in Guanacaste Park know that they're honored guests. Other mammals sometimes seen here include the jaguarundi, kinkajou, armadillo, agouti, white-tailed deer, opossum, and species of bat.

Tepescuintle or Paca
Cuniculus paca

How You can Help

During my visit Guanacaste Park's trails needed maintenance in some places, the trees were not adequately identified and no literature was available to help interpret the park's attractions. Since this park exists mainly because certain people volunteer money and work, I spoke with the warden, Martin Ack, and together we thought up an idea that extends eco-tourism into eco-activism.

In short, anyone traveling the Ruta Maya looking for a place to spend some time very cheaply while gaining experience with tropical ecosystems, who is really willing to work, and who possess one or more talents useful in maintaining and developing such parks, should contact the Belize Audubon Society's Wildlands Management Officer in Belize City, see if he or she can camp for a while at the park, and in return do some work.

Maintaining trails, using technical keys to identify and tag plants, building seats for trail-walkers, creating brochures with line drawings, putting together a list of birds, mapping the park's vegetation zones... who knows what talent you have that Guanacaste Park might need? The park already has tools such as shovels and saws. Here's your key to this interesting proposition: Wildlands Mgmt. Officer, Belize Audubon Society, P.O. Box 1001, Belize City, Belize, Central America, (tel. 02-77369)

Kinkajou
Potos flavus

Western Belize

SAN IGNACIO

San Ignacio is Belize's westernmost fair-sized town (population 2,750). Though there's no ocean here and traditional guidebooks don't treat San Ignacio with the enthusiasm they show for the cayes, it's astonishing how many travelers find their way here. "I was in Belize City and I just heard people saying good things about San Ignacio, so I came over to check it out," is how one Californian sporting a Hawaiian shirt and a handlebar mustache explained it. Since San Ignacio lies only three bus-hours west of Belize City, "checking out San Ignacio" makes a nice day-trip, and many who come for a day end up staying for several. Both Novelos and Batty Bus lines connect Belize City with San Ignacio.

Actually, San Ignacio's urban area consists of two towns, San Ignacio and Santa Elena, separated by the eastern branch of the Belize River, and a one-lane bridge; however, functionally, they're just one place.

Buses may stop at two or three places before finally crossing the bridge and pulling into San Ignacio's terminal area. If you haven't the foggiest notion what you're going to do during your stay, probably your first task upon arrival should be to walk around a bit (you can scan all the downtown area in about ten minutes) to acquire a general feeling for the place. The market with cheap, fresh fruit is less than a minute's walk from the bus station, next to the river and back toward the main road.

Once you start thinking about lodging and activities, then head over to Eva's Restaurant. If you didn't spot Eva's during your walk, anyone in town can point you in the right direction. Eva's Restaurant is the town's unofficial, general-tourist-information spot.

Inside Eva's, in addition to a healthy population of fellow foreigners, mostly sitting around sipping Cokes and watching CNN News on the TV behind the bar, you'll find stuck on the wall to the left of the entrance all kinds of leaflets, advertisements, maps and business cards. Cottages and cars for rent, interpreter services, horse trips, river trips and canoe rentals, a walk emphasizing medicinal plants, spelunking tours, day trips to Guatemala's Tikal... If you want something not mentioned on the wall, just ask for Bob Jones or his helper Wayne, behind the bar. I'm sure that some folks stay in San Ignacio mainly because of Eva's Restaurant, which is a little *Casablanca*-ish.

An example of a hotel price in San Ignacio is that of the **Central Hotel**, which on its sign out front offers "mosquito screening, hot showers, fans and budget rates"; it rents single rooms for US$9.00 and doubles for US$11.00. Several other places in town are more swanky or less swanky, and their rates reflect their swankiness.

Maya Mountain Lodge offers a beautiful, soothing, out-in-the-country environment. "Homestyle meals" are served in an open dining area from which sometimes you can watch keel-billed toucans feed in a banana tree an avocado-toss away. The lodge organizes several activities; you needn't be a guest to participate. A half-day river trip to see the Panti Trail (focusing on medicinal plants) costs US$30.00; a day's canoe rental costs US$30.00; one to three hours of horseback riding also costs US$30.00; a day's rental of a mountain bike takes US$15.00. Day-trips to Tikal are organized upon request.

Here cottages and rooms cost US$40.00 to US$70.00; but if you're an *independently* traveling backpacker and you show this book to the owners, Bart and Suzi Mickler, and *if* a room is available, you can have it for half price. By taxi the Lodge is five minutes from downtown San Ignacio; walking takes about half an hour. To get there, cross the river into Santa Elena, take the gravel road next to the Maya Mountain Lodge sign on the right, and go straight on the gravel road until signs tell you you're there. The Micklers are talking about opening a campground for tenters.

Cahal Pech

Archeological Orientation

Except for some mounds atop a hill in an extremely pleasant, park-like setting, there's not much to see at this modest ruin. Just because the ruin is within walking distance of San Ignacio and makes such a fine picnicking site, here's how to get there:

Logistics

From downtown San Ignacio follow the main road up the slope and out of town, toward Guatemala. When you come to the Y and the bust of Joseph S. Andrews, set on a red-painted, concrete pedestal, keep heading toward Guatemala, more or less westward, for about 300 meters (1/5 mile), until you come to a crossing of three paved roads and one gravel road. Take the gravel road, to the left, up the steep hill. At the top take the left descending through a gate; follow this gravel lane down slope about 50 meters and then take the first major right. Go up the rise to the point where cars can no longer continue; here you feel as if you're trespassing in someone's yard. However, everyone here knows what you're doing, for visitors come quite regularly. Continue in the same direction as before, briefly down-slope at first, but then upward toward the hilltop ruin. The trail up the hill branches again and again; just stay on the most-used path always leading uphill and eventually you'll arrive at the top, Cahal Pech.

Caracol

Archeological orientation

For a long time archeologists considered Caracol to be a large but inconsequential Maya ceremonial center. Then in 1986 excavations turned up a round, elaborately carved alter-stone describing a victory by Caracol's warriors over Tikal. Now the belief is growing that during the Middle Classic, for a period of about 140 years, Caracol eclipsed Tikal as the most important Maya city of the region. Caracol's largest pyramid, the Canaa, rises 43 meters high (140 feet), making it the tallest manmade structure in all of Belize. At this writing Caracol is still being excavated and the full extent of the site's greatness is yet to be determined. Discoveries being made here constitute some of the most exciting finds being made in Maya archeology today.

Logistics

During the preparation of this book, Caracol was closed to visitors so that excavation could proceed. However, it can be assumed that by the mid-1990s a visit to Caracol will become one of the most exciting possibilities along the entire Ruta Maya. Because the site lies about 40 air-km (25 miles) south of San Ignacio and is accessible only by very difficult roads, if accessible at all, it's hard to say whether this ruin will become a much-visited destination like Tikal, or a much-talked-about-but-seldom-visited ruin such as El Mirador and Bonampak. However it comes to be regarded, San Ignacio will remain the main entrance-town to it, the wall on Eva's Restaurant will continue to be the place to look if you want to try to get to the ruin, and the folks at Maya Mountain Lodge will certainly begin offering trips there as soon as they figure out a way to do it.

Xunantunich

Archeological orientation

Xunantunich is a major ceremonial center built atop a hill with a breathtaking view. "El Castillo," a 40-meter-high (130-foot) pyramid, is the most prominent structure. The pyramid has been partially excavated and can be climbed by a trail that winds back and forth across it, affording a fine view of Belize and Guatemala. El Castillo is a good place to observe the usual Maya method of construction, which entailed building new pyramids over old ones, causing the ruin to be layered onion-like.

Logistics

The entrance to Xunantunich lies across the road from San José Succotz, a brief ride down the road from San Ignacio, toward Guatemala, and less than five minutes from the Guatemalan border. San Ignacio's taxis gladly provide transportation; fares range from US$1.50 (if you squeeze in with a group of locals heading in the same direction) to astronomical sums. Buses heading toward Guatemala (Benque Viejo) will let you off right at the entrance. At the very beginning of Xunantunich's entrance road, you must cross the little Mopan River by human-powered ferry; this service is free. If you're walking, once you're across the river you're faced with a 25-minute climb up a gravel road to the ruins.

This walk is excellent for spotting birds early in the morning. However, though visiting the ruin is perfectly safe for visitors in vehicles and groups, sadly, the gravel lane climbing to Xunantunich has a history of robberies committed on hiking foreigners. Probably you shouldn't hike this road carrying anything of value, or alone. If you're traveling independently and you hang around the ferry for a while you'll probably be able to talk your way into a lift to the summit.

Across the road from Xunantunich's entrance, by San José Succotz, you can follow the signs to some fine cooking and lodging at **Rancho los Amigos**; a double room costs about US$12.50. This is run by some US folks; the woman is an acupuncturist.

BENQUE VIEJO: CROSSING POINT INTO GUATEMALA

At the frontier between Belize and Guatemala, the village on the Belizean side is called Benque Viejo del Carmen, or just Benque; the village right across the border, in Guatemala, is Melchor de Mencos. Both towns are large enough to have hotels. Though black-market money-changers are active on both sides of the border, they're most apparent on the Belizean side where they practically stampede new arrivals. Here the black market operates in full view of officials, and the exchange generally is better than that offered in official banks. Of course you should not deal with money-changers in a complete state of ignorance and trust; you should at least have a vague notion of what good rates are, and figure out before you deal with them what the minimum is you want. Unless you'll have use for your Belizean dollars later, it's best to exchange them here.

Approaching the frontier from the Belizean side, the Customs Building lies on the left side of the parking area. If you're driving, you'll stop on the building's right side; if you're walking, you can enter the buildings left side. After getting your papers straight, if you're walking, proceed through the door behind you and to your left as you stand before the customs official, and walk into Guatemala.

The frontier here is a surveyed one, paying no attention to the river flowing between Belizean customs and Guatemala's Melchor de Mencos on the other side. You cross the border at the barrier, not at the river. However, you don't *feel* as though you're in Guatemala until you cross the river.

Note: *Complete information on Belize is available in* Guide to Belize *from Bradt Publications (1993).*

Chapter 14

Guatemala

NORTHERN GUATEMALA (PETÉN)
The Setting
Geography
The northern third of Guatemala is made up of a hot, relatively low-populated lowland not unlike that of Mexico's contiguous Yucatán Peninsula. Guatemala's administrative divisions are referred to as departments; the entire northern lowland is incorporated into the single Department of the Petén, usually referred to simply as "El Petén."

Biology
Sometimes the impression is given that the Petén is mantled with "pure jungle." If we accept the term "jungle" as referring to tropical rain forest, then all of the Petén certainly is not jungle. The road between Flores and Sayaxché, especially around La Libertad, traverses extensive grassy areas populated by short, widely spaced trees. At one time investigators considered these savannahs the probable result of soil depletion caused by centuries of Maya slash-and-burn agriculture. However, paleoclimatological studies have revealed that nowadays the Petén is emerging from an extended period of drought in its history; as rains return, dense forests are invading the formerly more-extensive savannahs, not the other way around. At least, this was the trend before modern man began cutting the forests.

Even the well developed forests around Tikal and Seibal are not the kinds of rain forest visualized by viewers of TV nature-documentaries. In "story-book jungles" trees grow over 50 meters high (175 feet) and the forest is stratified with four distinct layers — 1) herbs and young trees; 2) medium-sized trees such as palms; 3) tall trees such as strangler figs; and 4) a few giants emerging through the tall-tree canopy.

Much of the Petén's forest, especially that along the Ruta Maya, stands considerably lower than 50 meters. Instead of the eerie twilight and sepulchral mood of the "real jungle's" floor, light sometimes penetrates all the way to the basement of the Petén's palm-rich forests. Nor do the Petén's forests enjoy as great a diversity of species as is found in more highly developed rain forests in Costa Rica, Brazil, and southeast Asia.

These are not words meant to disparage the Petén's native forests. On the contrary, here I'm emphasizing that the Petén's forests are unique. This is a forest in which abundant, graceful, frequently spiny palms characterize the forest, rather as proliferating species of bamboo typify many Asian forests. In the Petén's forests we find mahogany and tropical cedar, two of the world's most respected timber trees.

Moreover, food-producing trees such as the chicozapote, mamey and ramón emphasize the forest's incredible bounteousness and its potential for producing even more species that eventually might benefit mankind. Few sounds raise more goose flesh than the expressions of a troop of the Petén's howler monkeys roaring at dawn. In short, the Petén's forests, though frequently not fitting all the northern visitor's stereotypes, surpass our expectations.

The People

During Classic Maya times, the Petén was densely populated. However, by the end of the Classic nearly all the people there had disappeared; what caused this extinction or exodus is one of the most interesting mysteries in archeology today. Nowadays the Petén still is sparsely unpopulated, but new roads are being put in (such as the one between Flores and Cobán), and settlements are springing up everywhere along these roads.

Much in contrast to the southern lowlands, in the northern Petén you seldom hear Maya languages being spoken unless you wander into a newly established, isolated village whose population the government has transported en masse from the overpopulated uplands. Around Poptún in the southern Petén, Mopán is spoken, and farther west and south there's Kekchi.

In the lowlands the average country person wears factory-made clothes, instead of the colorful traditional dress typical of small Indian communities of the southern highlands.

PLACES TO VISIT

PETÉN

MELCHOR DE MENCOS: BORDER TOWN

Customs

On Belize's Western Highway the last town before Guatemala is Benque Viejo del Carmen; the town across the river in Guatemala is Melchor de Mencos. Both towns are large enough to have hotels. The frontier here is crossed at the barrier, not at the river. Though black-market money-changers work both sides of the border, they're most apparent on the Belizean side.

In Guatemala, cars stop at the obvious place near the barrier, and walkers enter the door on the Custom Building's Belize side, then proceed to the first room on the right. Though customs services in Belize and Mexico are free, in Guatemala you're obliged to pay. Entering without a visa, I had to pay US$5.00. Leaving is cheaper, costing only US$1.00. After getting your stamp, return through the door from which you entered.

Logistics

To find Melchor de Mencos's bus terminal, markets and hotels, as you come from Belize take the first right after crossing the bridge. At this intersection stands a sign declaring that the present altitude is 106.7 meters (350 feet), that Melchor's population is 13,000, and that from this spot it's 572km (355 miles) to Guatemala City, and 98km (61 miles) to Tikal. The right-hand turn puts you on a wide gravel road leading up a hill. Near the hill's crest a left turn leads into an open area where fruit stands do a brisk business and buses are usually loading. As you approach the buses, chances are that a bus attendant will call out, "*¿Flores?.*"

About half a dozen buses leave for Flores each day, costing approximately US$3.00. If you've arrived in Melchor heading for Belize, you'll be interested in the schedule painted on the side of the Batty's Bus Office at the plaza's edge: "*Sale de Belice a Melchor 6:00 y 6:30 horas AM; sale de Melchor a Belize 13:00 y 1330 horas PM*"; it says that the bus to Belize leaves around 1300. Upon leaving the plaza, some buses wander around Melchor looking for extra passengers, so if you're aboard and you realize that you're traveling in circles, stay cool.

If you've grown accustomed to Belize and this is your first time in Guatemala, arriving in Melchor may be a shock. Not only does English disappear and miles become kilometers, but also a whole new kind of living and thinking expresses itself. For me, Melchor (and all the rest

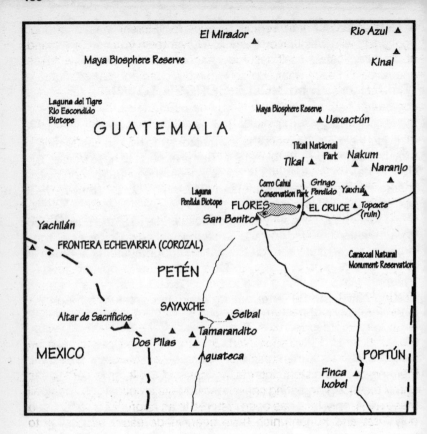

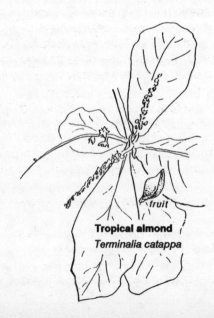

Tropical almond
Terminalia catappa

of Guatemala's Petén region, except for Flores) has a strong, frontierish, wild-west flavor about it. All over town you can feel a kind of uncomplicated, self-assured, almost primitive energy that's uncommon in easy-going Belize and more cosmopolitan Mexico.

In Melchor's *centro*, **Hotel Cony** offers a room with a fan and a communal bath for US$3.00; **Hospedaje Zaculeu** provides nothing but a bed and close proximity to a rambunctious bar for US$1.40. Several nice-looking restaurants are available, but my best down-home eating was found by wandering down the long line of *mercado*-style *comedores* beginning next to the bus plaza, opposite the point where one enters the plaza after coming up from the border. Here there's good, cheap soul-food of the *frijoles, tortillas y huevos* variety, and neighborly conversation, to boot. Remember, you want your food *hot*... At least in temperature.

Naranjo (Not *El* Naranjo)
Archeological orientation
In the Petén's northeastern corner lies an astonishing cluster of very large, very impressive, ruins. Tikal, Uaxactún, Nakbe, Nakum, Yaxhá, Río Azul, Kinal, El Mirador, Naranjo... In the same cluster can be included Belize's Xunantunich and Caracol and Mexico's Calakmul. Figuring out the historic interrelationships of these sites constitutes one of the most interesting challenges in Maya archeology. Among all these ruins, only Tikal has been restored to an appreciable extent and only Tikal and Xunantunich have been made easily accessible to travelers.

Little of the ruin of Naranjo has been excavated and not much can be said about it other than it was quite a large classic ruin at which frequently the emblem glyph for Tikal was found. The glyph's presence probably reflects Tikal's domination of Naranjo. At least half of the site's 40 known monuments have been ravaged by looters.

Logistics
Since Naranjo consists only of about ten widely dispersed, vegetation-covered mounds of fair size rising in the dense forest, (and many smaller mounds scattered about) for most of us the main fun in visiting this site will be in experiencing the trip itself. The trail to Naranjo passes through low hills frequently scarred by slash-and-burn agriculture, but also sometimes it leads through some fine stretches of fairly intact forest.

If you have a 4-wheel drive, you may be able to drive to Naranjo in April and May — the late dry season. It won't be an easy drive. When I hiked the distance in February, in three places large trees lay across the trail; in a 4 x 4 I wouldn't have been able to get through without a chainsaw or several hours of exercise with a machete.

If you do try to drive, consider taking along Sr Guillermo López, the *Inspector de la Zona*, who can keep you from taking some wrong turns; also, he possesses a single dog-eared map of all the ruin's identified buildings. Sr López's office stands next to the Biblioteca del Banco de Guatemala, surrounded by a high fence, in the shady little place called El Mangal, a couple of blocks from Melchor's bus-terminal

Road Conditions in the Petén District

In contrast to the rest of the figure-eight Ruta Maya, which is paved, most of the route in Guatemala's Petén region is gravel. At this writing only the road between Flores and Tikal is paved. During the rainy season — June through November, more or less — the Petén's part of the Ruta Maya occasionally becomes impassable. Especially between Flores and the Petén's southern boundary the road is sometimes closed by flooding and landslides. Between Flores and Belize, quagmires develop that even buses cannot negotiate; four-wheeled drives founder in them and usually along this road no big trees or rocks are available to winch from.

During the dry season roads become so dusty that bus passengers get heavily coated with choking dust; I travel with a bandanna over my nose and mouth to filter out the larger particles. The farther back in the bus you sit, the more dusty you'll get. If you're allowed to ride atop the bus on these roads you'll be much more comfortable and the dust won't be nearly as bad.

During my most recent trip through the Petén about a third of the scheduled buses simply didn't show up. I was told that a gasoline shortage was forcing cancellations; in one instance, bandits had just killed the driver of a night-bus, and other drivers had gone to his funeral. Once I was stranded for an entire day. Buses were mind-bogglingly full. I had to enter one bus via the back door because people were hanging out the front door by one arm; to close the back door behind me I had to shove on my neighbors awfully hard. Of course, when later even more people squeezed aboard, they had to shove me even harder.

Though by the time you travel these roads the gasoline shortage may be over, I'd guess that one or more other inconveniences or disasters will have taken its place. In general, travel in all frontier regions such as the Petén is usually tricky and uncomfortable. Of course, road experiences of the Petén type add to the color of travel, and increase one's store of character-building episodes; many of us regard traveling in the Petén as more fun than breezing along the usual tourist routes. Nevertheless, if you're trying to keep to a schedule (catching a jet in Guatemala City, perhaps) keep in mind that land travel in the Petén can be an iffy thing. Remember the problems of storing luggage atop Guatemalan buses. Don't ride the Petén's buses at night.

plaza. Upon arrival at El Mangal you'll just have to ask someone to lead you to Sr. López. The Inspector doesn't ask a fee for his services; however, a generous *gratificación* will open many doors. Sr López speaks no English.

Unless you have some experience as a jungle-walker, you shouldn't try this hike. Many times during the trip you'll need seasoned judgement when choosing between look-alike branches of the trail, and sometimes you may need to track yourself back to a Y where you've made a wrong decision... Otherwise, the hike isn't particularly dangerous. Here's one thing to keep in mind, though: Every person who sees you hiking to Naranjo will know that in the next day or so you'll be hiking back along the very same path. Though the folks around Melchor strike me as some of the most generous, harmless people in the world, I would advise hikers to avoid looking too affluent. It might even be a good idea to keep packed away all cameras, watches, jewellery and the like.

When you ask many people in Melchor for directions to the ruins of Naranjo, they try to send you all the way across Guatemala to the more famous ruins of *El* Naranjo, on the Río San Pedro, near the Mexican border; this gives you an idea of how frequently Naranjo is visited. At the beginning of the journey to Naranjo it's best to ask directions to the village of Bambunál, which is better known than the ruin, and which lies between Naranjo and Melchor. Even asking directions to Bambunál might cause some head-scratching, because this village is little more than a cluster of three or four huts.

Once you're on the trail you should begin asking directions to Naranjo itself because midway the trail splits and if you're following the main path you won't even pass through Bambunál. If you're driving, from downtown Melchor first head down the road to the sawmill, (*el aserradero*), and ask to be shown the gravel road leading toward Bambunál.

If you're hiking, before you set off, put plenty of insect repellent on your legs because along this trail chiggers are bad; then with compass in hand begin walking to the west side of town, to the dirt airstrip (*la pista*). About midway the airstrip, take the five-meter-wide dirt path leading west at 295°. Though this road soon splits, with the most-used arm leading to the right, continue straight on the lesser used, grassy path, passing to the left of the hill before you. After about a ten-minute climb to the top of the first slope, take the small trail leading off to the right, heading generally northwest. Descend to where black mud appears, then for three or four minutes walk generally west, until you hit a fairly nice gravel road (the one coming from the sawmill), and turn right, heading north. After about 20 minutes the gravel road drastically deteriorates.

More than any other trail profiled in this book, the Naranjo trail is

On the Art of Navigating Braided Trails

Sometimes trails passing through marshy areas such as those around the ruins of Guatemala's Naranjo and Nakum become so muddy that someone takes a machete and clears another trail bypassing the quagmire. Frequently it's not long until the second path similarly deteriorates, and a third trail is hacked out. After the third trail disintegrates, general trail usage possibly might again shift so that part of it follows the first trail, part follows the second, and part is cut through new territory — or some similar combination.

In other words, trails passing through low areas frequently are not simple footpaths, but rather interconnecting *networks* of trails. They're *braided* trails. Sometimes it's obvious that the various strands all lead to the same place, but other times it's not. Anyone unfamiliar with the trail won't know whether a departing footpath is simply a temporary strand skirting an upcoming morass, or an important bifurcation permanently leading off the main trail.

When a trail becomes braided, if you're unfamiliar with the route, you must ask yourself at least two questions. First, do you know the general direction you need to go? When I was hiking the braided trail to Naranjo, I knew from my maps that the ruin lay to the northwest. Therefore, as I hiked I watched my compass to be sure I never walked for more than half an hour in a contrary direction. Naranjo's part of the Petén is so empty that, basically, all footpaths heading northwest from Melchor eventually hit Naranjo, because that's the only destination to the northwest. At least, that was my theory.

Second, if you take a trail and it turns out to lead in the wrong direction, will you be able to find your way back to the point where the error was made? During my Naranjo trip I kept notes on every bifurcation, and the times spent walking between them. Also I made sure that at each intersection my footprints were clearly visible in the mud.

Beyond being able to reply in the affirmative to the above two questions, the main art in navigating braided trails is to stay alert (don't let a single strand of the trail wander away without recording it in the notebook) and to stay calm and think clearly when you start wondering whether you might be lost...

"braided"; it's easy to wander or drive off the main trail into a morass. If the trail branches, and both paths seem to wander in the same direction, just take the most recently used one. Usually this means taking the one adorned with the freshest deposits of horse manure. The main trail follows a generally northwest direction, but about midway it describes an S that isn't immediately apparent as you walk, so if your compass reports that you're heading the wrong way, don't get upset unless you continue in the wrong direction for over half an hour.

About four hours after meeting with the gravel road (rest periods subtracted, and walking at a rather unhurried pace), the trail splits, with the right arm climbing a hill to a cluster of thatch-roofed huts. This is Naranjo's guard station. Proceed up the hill and introduce yourself. If you wish, you can camp here overnight; there's even a hut available for you. No charge is demanded, but *gratificaciones* are always appreciated.

The ruin lies about a kilometer (half a mile) farther up the road, beyond the station. Though the guards are very friendly, they don't know much about the ruins themselves. As you wander among the ruins, check your compass from time to time, because the network of footpaths connecting the various temples create something of a labyrinth; high trees prevent navigating by the sun; getting lost is easy.

By the way, if you make this trip during the rainy season (lots of luck!) or even as late as February, you'll meet men leading horses on which portable-TV-sized masses are packed inside heavy plastic bags. These are blocks of chicle, the processed gum derived from the white latex, or milk, that issues from wounded chicozapote trees, *Achras zapote*. These men are *chicleros* and you'll probably never meet anyone more a part of real frontier life than them.

During my last trip into this area the *chicleros* told me that by using their trails it's possible to walk all the way from Melchor de Mencos, through Naranjo and Nakum, to Tikal. This is a backpacking trek to dream about, but it's a trip only for the kings and queens of jungle-walkers.

Yaxhá, Topoxte and Nakum (all on the same road)
Archeological orientation for Yaxhá
Yaxhá (also spelt Yaxja) is a tremendous site of over 500 mounds. Though little excavation has been done, it's considered the third-largest known Classic site in Guatemala. Yaxhá's Stela 11 shows influence of the central Mexican city-state of Teotihuacan.

Archeological orientation for Topoxte
Topoxte is a small site of about five unreconstructed mounds on an island in Lake Yaxhá. Its Postclassic architecture indicates that the island was occupied long after nearby Yaxhá, Uaxactún, Nakum and Tikal were abandoned.

Archeological orientation for Nakum
At the end of the trail, this enormous Classic ruin has more standing architecture than any Guatemalan ruin except Tikal. It's hard to get to but worth the effort.

Logistics for Yaxhá, Topoxte and Nakum

It's easy to drive to Yaxhá and easy to take a boat to Topoxte, but the best 4-wheel drive will have a hard time making it to Nakum, unless it's the very end of a truly dry dry-season. The road to Yaxhá, Topoxte and Nakum begins as a wide, well maintained gravel road leading north from the Flores/Belize road between El Cruce (where to road to Tikal begins) and the Belize border. The intersection is conspicuously announced by a large sign reading "Reserva Biosfera Maya." If you're on a bus, tell the ticket taker that you want off at *el cruce de Yaxhá.* From *el cruce* the road shoots north for about 8km (five miles), to the shores of Lake Yaxhá. At least during the week, local traffic eligible for hitching is almost nonexistent. If you're backpacking and think you might stay for a few days, take plenty of food unless you plan to eat at the tourist-oriented restaurant.

Approaching Lake Yaxhá you descend a steep hill, enjoying a fine view of the waters. At the bottom a side road leads to the left and a sign declares that down the lane lies **Campamento El Sombrero**. Taking this left, quickly you come to a pleasantly shaded, cool spot on Lake Yaxhá's shore where you can eat in the restaurant, pitch a tent for US$3.00, rent a hammock for US$5.00, or rent a room with an outside bath for US$8.00. For US$3.00 per person you can take a boat to the island on which is found Topoxte ruin.

Campamento El Sombrero serves as base for a man who guides horseback tours, using *chiclero* trails, all the way from here to Tikal! This is a major undertaking, of course, and probably the expense involved would require travelling in a group; I couldn't get a price from him he was willing to see printed in a book. For more information about this trip you can write to "Campamento El Sombrero Circus S.A.", Ave. Hincapié 3-81 Zona 13, Guatemala City, or call the Guatemala City number of 314051.

To continue to Yaxhá from Campamento El Sombrero, return to the main road and go down to the huts and barrier near the lake. You'll need to sign in here; no cost. By the way, in a hut adjoining the Administration Hut sometimes *chicleros* store large blocks of raw chicle for later shipment on trucks; you might ask if there's any for you to see. Into each heavy, slate-colored brick the owner's initials are carved.

Fifteen minutes of walking past the lake brings you to a road leading to the right, but this is just an access road entering a quarry; five minutes later the main road forks. Here the left arm parallels the lake's shore, so take the right. Ten minutes later there's another Y. The left arm goes to Yaxhá (about a kilometer down the road) and the right continues on to Nakum. A sign here declares that Nakum lies 17km (11 miles) away — about four hours of hiking.

The road to Nakum sometimes becomes braided (see page 188).

In places it's very easy and pleasant walking through lovely, interesting scenery; frequently laughing falcons can be heard guffawing from nearby perches. In other places the trail degenerates into an essay in mud, heat and weeds. Occasionally you pass morasses showing signs of past battles between man and mud that must have been of legendary proportions.

Horses frequently travel this road, keeping the muddy sections badly chopped. I'm not referring to minor irregularities in the mud, but rather to the kind of surface that forms when dozens of horses mire knee-deep. In places the chopped-up mud is dried hard into ankle-crunching obstacle courses; keeping your balance requires intense concentration — a hard task when the heat is bad. In fact, it's unwise to travel this road alone because you may need someone to go for a horse to carry you and your sprained ankle back.

Arriving in the vicinity of Nakum, the first thing you'll see is a *chiclero* camp containing one-man shelters with thatched roofs constructed of fan-palm fronds. Unless you've been masochistic enough to make this trip during the rainy season, the camp will probably be deserted. However, just looking at the roughly made shelters and smelling the charcoal from past campfires, as well as the mud and humid, moldy odor of the surrounding forest, you'll be able to picture how rough and primitive life must be for the *chicleros*.

To reach the ruins, continue straight through the camp, cross the bridge spanning a small stream, and when after a couple of minutes the road splits, take the path to the right. In a couple more minutes you'll enter a surprisingly large camp of well constructed, permanent buildings, standing ready for future archeologists and workers who will explore and reconstruct Nakum, making it into what possibly can be Guatemala's second-most important Maya-ruin attraction. If the ruin's custodians are out working, you can pass through the long, open-walled kitchen, walk down the alley between the buildings before you, and continue straight on the path to the ruin's central area. But don't forget to return later and sign in. In front of the long kitchen there's a spacious grassy area perfect for camping. No fee is asked, though the usual remarks about *gratificaciones* should be recalled.

This ruin makes the walk worthwhile, for I know of no other ruin along the Ruta Maya offering the combination of a good bit to see, a deep-jungle situation, and the strong likelihood that you'll be the only visitor in the park. When I was there, violaceous trogons flitted about like pigeons and howler monkeys roared not far away. It's simply a majestic place with plenty of trails to explore; but do bring copious quantities of mosquito repellent.

Once you've soaked up the ruin's ambience and taken leave of the custodians, who most likely will have enjoyed having their period of isolation interrupted, return to the *chiclero* camp and pass down the open way allowing access to the woods on the camp's western-most side. Here you should see a footpath entering the woods. That trail is the *chiclero* trail to Tikal...

Of course, when I learned of this trail, I immediately set off hiking it, planning to include it in this book. However, after a couple of hours I had to give up. Too many bifurcations. If you don't know the trail, you can simply get thoroughly lost, and if you look at this area on a map you'll see that you are far, far from help. If you get bitten by a snake or sprain an ankle, you're simply on your own. If you get lost and with your compass head south planning to hit the road, you'll surely first come to lakes, lagoons and marshes. The last wrong path I chose set

Handling Army Checkpoints

At this time army checkpoints are rare to nonexistent along the Ruta Maya in Mexico and Belize; however, in Guatemala they're fairly frequent. Here's what typically happens at a Guatemalan army checkpoint:

The bus stops and after some chatting between the driver and a soldier, the soldier enters and tells *everyone* to get off. Outside, all passengers are instructed to stand in a line while, one by one, their documents and possessions are checked.

While being frisked you must turn around, hold your arms out, and while a soldier sets his foot behind your right heel, he feels under your arms, in your chest and trouser pockets, inside your legs and around your ankles. During this time, plenty of other soldiers are standing around holding automatic weapons.

While passengers are outside, one or more soldiers enter the bus looking for contraband. I tend to carry my camera equipment and other valuables when I go outside; of course, everything brought outside is opened and examined. Soldiers also climb atop the bus to examine baggage; when I take my place in line I take a position far enough from the bus that I can watch the rooftop examination.

Sometimes, though the soldiers emphasize that *everyone* must leave the bus, women with children stay aboard and nothing is said to them; other times even they must leave and be frisked.

Once I was traveling with a young English woman who didn't fancy being frisked by the young men so when she was standing in line, right before it was her turn she slowly, adroitly, and very deliberately stepped forward, walked around the frisker and got in line on the other side, at the same time making a show of opening her document pouch for examination. Her message was clear: I'm willing to cooperate with document examination but I don't want to be frisked. Since she was wearing light clothing incapable of hiding weapons, the soldiers allowed her to forego the frisking.

me crashing through a marsh of three-meter-high reeds, and stinking mud that sucked off my boots; saw-toothed reed-blades cut my arms and face, spiders fell down my collar, snakes coiled defiantly in front of me and the intense heat caused me to be dizzy and confused. It was fun for half an hour or so, but I wouldn't want to do it if I were lost, hungry and injured. Someday, however, when use has caused the main trail to become more apparent, this just may qualify as one of the Ruta Maya's most interesting walks.

Chicleros

Victor W. von Hagen dedicates his book *World of the Maya* "To the great American chewing-gum chewer, whose insatiable demands sent the chicle-tree scouts into the jungles, where in the process of finding new gum sources they discovered, over the decades, uncounted Maya ruins."

Chicleros are the "chicle-tree scouts" Hagen refers to; chicle is the traditional base for chewing gum. The chicle-tree sometimes is known in books as sapodilla, and other times by its Spanish name of *chicozapote*; it is *Achras sapote* of the tropical sapodilla family.

During the rainy season a milky sap rises in the *chicozapote* tree and if the tree's trunk is wounded, sap flows out. Using techniques similar to those employed by Brazil's rubber tappers, *chicleros* go deep into the forest to collect this latex, boil it down until it's hardened and wax-like, and then mule-train it to civilization where it's sold to chewing-gum manufacturers. Nowadays most chewing gum is made with synthetic materials; however, Japan still imports a good bit of chicle and some local manufacturers use it.

A certain mystique has developed around the *chicleros*. They certainly have a lot in common with America's earliest frontiersmen such as Daniel Boone and Davy Crockett. They spend long periods "in deep jungle" where they survive tremendous hardships. They, more than anyone, know the jungle's secret trails and where "undiscovered" ancient Maya ruins lie.

Especially during hikes to some of the more isolated ruins in Guatemala's Petén District, unless it's well into the dry season when *chicozapote* latex isn't flowing, you stand a chance of meeting some *chicleros*. They are humble-looking men usually smelling strongly of wood smoke and sweat. But from those of us who admire folks whose heads are full of jungle lore and who are tough enough to survive long periods of demanding wilderness existence, they deserve a tip of the hat.

FLORES

For most travelers, Flores is the Petén's heart and soul; it's the base from which other trips are made, especially to Tikal, and it's the home people return to when they're aching for European/North-American comradeship, and hotels and restaurants familiar with European/North-American tastes. In short, it's full of tourists.

Buses don't leave Flores-bound passengers in Flores itself, but rather in the town of Santa Elena (see page 200); to reach Flores, you must cross a causeway, for Flores lies on a small island in Lago Petén Itzá. Naturally taxis are available to carry you there but it's a nice walk. If your bus drops you off in front of the Hotel San Juan just walk around the nearest corner and there to the right will be the causeway. By the way, inside the Hotel San Juan you'll find a very busy welcome desk changing money.

To reach Flores's excellent tourist-information office, coming off the causeway follow the main road to the left for two blocks, then turn right for one block, then right again, and walk until you reach, on the right side of the street, the Oficina de Información Turística El Tucan. Here, as with most of the plethora of travel agencies in Flores and Santa Elena, you can find out about such things as microbus tickets to Tikal, Belize and other destinations. If you're sick of bumpy roads and dust or mud, you may be interested in airplane tickets via Aviateca to Guatemala City or Aerovias Flores tickets to Belize City (both about US$50.00), or Aeroquetzal tickets to Cancún (US$112.00).

Frequently Flores's hotels and restaurants have walls on which you can find interesting offers, so always keep your eyes open. For example, if after changing money back at the Hotel San Juan you scan the wall behind you, you might find an announcement for the "new service by Belize Trans Air & Aerovías, S. A. of Guatemala offering a package between Miami and Tikal via Belize, US$109 on Tuesdays, Fridays, Saturdays and Sundays... " or maybe a hand-written note informing you of "Mule Trips to El Mirador/2 days in, 2 days out/Contact "Chepe" Krasborn in Carmelita, Petén."

In Flores hotel prices aren't as high as you might think they'd be. However, if you travel at peak times or arrive late, you may have problems finding a room; Flores's island status just doesn't allow its population of hotels to proliferate. Here are some sample prices: **Hotel El Itzá**, one of the first you spot as you come off the causeway, offers double rooms with private baths and cold water, and a community balcony with a splendid view of the lake, for US$5.00. The upscale-looking **Hotel Yum Kax** charges US$12.00 for a double room, US$16.00 with an air conditioner. If you can't find a place in Flores, you probably can in Santa Elena.

At both ends of the causeway you'll see boatmen waiting for customers. Mostly these men are offering the same two-hour package

— a visit to some ruins associated with Tayasal, the island called La Garucha, and the Petencito Zoo; the trip costs US$5.00 per person. About midway along the causeway, at El Relleno, you can rent Hawaianas (float boards) for 80¢ per hour, kayaks for US$1.60 per hour, and wind-surfers for US$3.60 per hour.

Walking around Flores, especially right after dawn while fog rises in billows off the lake, you can enjoy some very picturesque moments. Brightly painted boats and dugout canoes are frequently moored right at the road's edge.

Tayasal

Though there's not much to see of the old Tayasal — the city of Flores covers the site — Tayasal holds an honored position in Maya chronology. In the mid-1400's AD when the Itzá were driven from Chichén Itzá during ongoing conflict among Yucatán's city-states, some of their number migrated to this small island where in isolation they kept their traditional ways until 1697; the conquest of Mexico, under Hernán Cortés, had taken place 1¾ centuries earlier!

One ingredient in the final collapse of Maya society at Tayasal was nothing less than the erudition of a Franciscan priest, Andrés de Avendaño, who mastered the intricacies of Maya calendrics. In 1696, the year before the collapse, he visited Tayasal's chieftains and pointed out that, according to their own calendar, katun 8 Ahau, the katun of political change, was about to start. Avendaño suggested that during this new katun, destiny would oblige the Maya to accept Christianity. With their usual fatalistic outlook the Maya must have agreed, for four months before the start of the katun they and the Spanish fought a battle and though the Itzá had always enjoyed a reputation as furious warriors, this time they offered very little resistance. Maybe they figured that fighting against destiny was useless.

Thus the final manifestation of what we think of as Maya culture is considered to have been extinguished at Tayasal. You might wonder why the Lacandóns are not recognized as the final standard-bearers. Perhaps in some ways they are, for the Lacandóns have never "lost their independence" by officially being conquered. However, many view the Lacandóns' culture as having so degenerated during their centuries of isolation that in the context of Maya civilization's main traditions the Lacandóns are hardly relevant. Probably the most appropriate view is that one expression of Maya society certainly ended at Tayasal in 1697, but that other expressions live on today among the Lacandóns and, indeed, the millions of other people who are partially or totally descendants of the ancient Maya.

SANTA ELENA

If you can't find a place to stay in Flores, try across the causeway in Santa Elena. For example, the **Tziquina-há** has air-conditioned double rooms for US$14; also several basic pensions are available, such as the **San Juan III** near the bus terminal, the **Don Quijote** and **El Diplomático**.

In Flores you can look in vain for the sprawling, colorful, odoriferous, bustling *mercado* selling fruits, meats, handbags and saddles, machetes, inexpensive meals at *comedores*, etc. that in less tourist-oriented Ruta Maya towns we usually find; in island-bound Flores, real-estate is just too valuable to relegate to Indian markets. Happily, in Santa Elena, there's plenty of land.

To reach Santa Elena's Mercado Municipal, seldom visited by tourists, as you come off the causeway leading from Flores, turn right onto 2ª Calle (the first street paralleling shore), continue two blocks, turn left and proceed up slope for 1½ blocks, until everything starts looking markety.

In the market area we also find Santa Elena's Bus Terminal. Just continue on the street bringing you up the hill, through the market. The street will bend to the left, and then when it straightens out you'll see buses readying for departure. Here you can buy the cheapest tickets in town to Tikal (the Pinita line), passages to Sayaxché and points farther south (the Rocío line), and even to Belize (Fuente del Norte line). These buses' schedules strike me as rather tentative, so if you're considering using the Santa Elena terminal, the day before you travel you should visit there and ask questions. The Pinita and Rocío lines leave from inside the market area; the Fuente del Norte line lies on the same street, but a short distance beyond the market, where they're announced by a sign and, probably, some loading buses.

Santa Elena's bus terminal is simply an open place in the market where buses park side by side, so don't expect anything to be written on a big board. Most buses have destinations declared in their destination windows or written in soap on the windshield's lower, left corner. If you see a bus heading to your destination, hang around the back of the bus and try to meet the driver's assistant. Though to us anarchy seems to reign here, all the information you need is very securely locked in the heads of the drivers, their helpers and a surprising number of riders, who can be approached as they kill time in the shadows surrounding the terminal area.

THE SAYAXCHÉ AREA

General Information

Lying about 55km (34 miles) southwest of Flores, Sayaxché is a bit off the Ruta Maya as I define it. However, it's included here for two reasons: first, Sayaxché serves as the base for visits to the important ruins of Seibal, Dos Pilas, Aguateca, Altar de Sacrificios and Yaxchilán; second, Sayaxché itself is a true, wild and wooly frontier town just brimming with color, street-side drama and general other-worldliness.

Sayaxché stands on the banks of the Río Pasión, a fair-size river providing the only thoroughfare for many villages both upstream and downstream. It's fascinating simply to sit in the shade along Sayaxché's riverfront watching the endless comings and goings. You'll see ten-meter-long *lanchas* pulling ashore, riding low and full of sacks of beans and corn; later you may spot the villagers climbing back aboard, carrying newly purchased machetes, replacement parts for broken chainsaws, bolts of cloth for dress-making, cans filled with kerosene, candy for the kids...

Logistics

Throughout the day, every three or four hours, the Rocío Line in Santa Elena's terminal area provides service between Santa Elena and Sayaxché, and to points south of Sayaxché. The 55-km (34-mile) trip to Sayaxché takes about three hours on a wretchedly bumpy, dusty and/or muddy gravel road; a good deal of time is usually lost at an army checkpoint where all passengers must unload and be frisked. Some of the holes on this road are record-breakers. More than once I've been catapulted into the bus's baggage rack. Buses not continuing to destinations south of Sayaxché stop across the river from town, so passengers must descend to the river bank and board a motorized *lancha* for the quick trip over; it costs about 20¢ US.

In Sayaxché most foreigners stay in the **Hotel Guayacán**, which stands at the river's edge, on the left as you disembark. A double room with a private bath costs US$6.00; a room without its own bathroom goes for US$2.00. Probably the best thing about the Guayacán is its upstairs sun-deck, which offers hotel guests perches from which they can unobtrusively and comfortably spy on goings-on in the street below. If the street is quiet, it's interesting and restful just to watch the ferry shuttle traffic back and forth across the river. It's amazing how a single motorboat manipulates a barge large enough to carry semi-trucks and trailers on it!

If you habitually patronize the cheapest establishments, then **Hospedaje Sayaxché**'s rooms are available for US$1.00. If you're interested in staying at the home of a Sayaxchéan, ask directions to the well-known **residence of Carmen Kilkán**; being a guest in his home costs US$1.20. Sayaxché's electricity is available only for a few hours in the evening, and that's a bit irregular, so at the approach of dusk you'd do well to organize your flashlight and candles, especially if the next morning you plan activities beginning before dawn.

Overlooking the Pasión, to the right as you come off the ferry or exit the *lancha*, a sign announces the presence of *Viajes Don Pedro* — a travel agency specializing in river trips. Actually, in Don Pedro's office you'll find more boat motors and parts than tourist paraphernalia; in true Sayaxché fashion, Don Pedro is an eco-tourism pioneer.

Don Pedro's day-long river trips include the following: To the ruins of Dos Pilas, US$40.00 per boatload; to Seibal, US$60.00; to Aguateca, US$70.00, and; to Altar de Sacrificios, US$120. A two-day trip down the Usumacinta to Yaxchilán in Mexico costs US$300. A famous destination for fishermen is the pristine Laguna Petexbatún, made available for US$40.00 per day. Of course, these prices are vulnerable to seasonal changes, the availability of gasoline, how many motors are working, etc.

Anyone wanting to "escape to a deserted island," but in comfort, can approximate the situation at the **Posada de Mateo**, on an island in a lake 1½ hours by motorboat from Sayaxché; here there's a congenial scattering of bungalows surrounded by dense forest. The trip costs about US$40.00 and bungalows rent for US$80.00 per day; hammocks with mosquito nets go for US$40.00 per day. To arrange matters before arriving at Posada de Mateo, in Guatemala City contact: Izabal Adventure Tours; 7ª Avda. 14-44, Zona 9, tel. 502-234-0323.

Dos Pilas

Dos Pilas is a Classic ruin with some stelae and a staircase ornamented with hieroglyphics mentioning Tikal and other nearby city-states. Unreconstructed, mostly it's a collection of vegetation-covered mounds "deep in the jungle." In 1991 archeologists tunneling into a crypt deep inside the ruined structure behind Stela 8 discovered a well-preserved skeleton of a previous ruler. He was bedecked with a jade necklace, a headdress of cut shell and a jaguar skin. Despite such interesting discoveries, most of us visit Dos Pilas for the adventure, the beauty of the forest, or because we're serious Mayanists, not because we want to be overwhelmed by spectacularly reconstructed ruins. My most recent trip required a five-hour hike through some rather muddy, slippery terrain.

Aguateca

Aguateca is a seldom-visited, unreconstructed ruin discovered in 1957. Most people visit it just to have an easy, interesting walk through the forest. Access is by a wide trail leading half an hour from the shore of Laguna Petexbatún.

Altar de Sacrificios

This strategically located ruin lies on the banks of the Río Pasión, just before it joins with the Río Salinas (also called Chixoy) to form the Usumacinta. It's important to Mayanists because some of the earliest traces of lowland Maya habitation have been found here as well as postclassic material in the form of a layer of figurines and untempered pottery. However, other than its majestic setting, it's not exceptionally impressive. Probably you'll find it worth visiting only if you're already making the Pasión/Usumacinta trip between Sayaxché and Yaxchilán. If you do make a visit, notice that the site features sculptures made of sandstone instead of limestone, which is typical for the rest of this region. In this rather stoneless location some early structures are faced with mussel shells from the river so encrusted with natural lime that they're several times their natural size.

Yaxchilán

Archeological orientation

Yaxchilán, a very impressive ruin, is described on page 265.

Logistics

Yaxchilán can be reached by at least three different routes. Traveling the Río Pasión/Usumacinta route used by Don Pedro in Sayaxché (and others) is one. Also you can fly — a service gladly arranged by almost any travel agency in the Ruta Maya area. Probably the most popular approach is to enter from the Mexican side by taking a *lancha* down the Usumacinta from the town of Corozal, in Chiapas. This latter route is described in the Chiapas section.

Seibal (El Ceibal)

Archeological orientation

In the 9th century AD (Late Classic) stelae were erected at Seibal (called El Ceibal on some maps) bearing likenesses of people wearing Toltec Tlaloc masks and costumes, and some of the individuals wore beards and long hair — very un-Maya. Seibal is considered to have "collapsed" in 889 A.D. One interesting structure at large, rather impressive Seibal is a circular temple, one of only two known in the Maya world.

Logistics

Seibal, unlike most ruins in the Sayaxché area, can be driven to, at least during the dry season. The first part of the 17km (10-mile) trip from Sayaxché to Seibal is on the gravel road between Sayaxché and Cobán (not Honduras's Copán ruins); eventually this road passes the Quetzal Reserve and connects with busy Hwy CA 9, which runs between Guatemala City and Puerto Barrios, through the Motagua Valley. At the present writing this road is fairly new and both bus schedules and the road's condition constantly change, but it's fairly certain that during the next few years at least three or four buses a day will pass through Sayaxché, heading south and thus passing Seibal's entrance road. During my most recent visit a south-bound bus passed through Sayaxché at 0700, providing just the service needed.

From Sayaxché take the new gravel road south for 9km (5.5 miles), to Paraiso. Since this part of the trip is so short, and it passes through the Parque Nacional de El Rosario, you may be tempted to walk it. It's true that right at the road's edge very interesting vegetation, birds and butterflies can be seen. However, as usually is the case with gravel roads in rapidly evolving frontier situations, this thoroughfare is not very birdwatcher-friendly. Huge trucks pass frequently, either splashing hikers with mud or choking them with dust, and the roadside has been so broken up by trucks that have mired there that walking is slow and arduous. Hitching this nine-kilometer stretch is an option, especially if you look for a ride at the gas station about a kilometer south of Sayaxché's riverfront.

It's important to tell whomever supplies your transportation for this first leg of your trip that you want to get out at the entrance to Seibal *at El Paraiso*. Emphasize El Paraiso, and the fact that it lies nine kilometers south of Sayaxché because bus ticket-takers and truck drivers habitually think that instead of saying "Seibal" (seh-ee-BAHL), we're saying Sebol (seh-BOWL), which is a town far to the south of Sayaxché. "Quiero salir en el crucero de El Paraiso, que está nueve kilómetros al sur de Sayaxché," you can say — "I want to leave at the crossroad at El Paraiso, which is nine kilometers south of Sayaxché."

The eight-kilometer (five-mile) road from El Paraiso to the ruin is good for birding; it passes through relatively undisturbed forest in which it's possible to spot species restricted to dense forests. So little traffic plies this road that, unless you have your own vehicle, you might as well plan to walk the whole distance, though possibly a sympathetic tourist with a rented car might pick you up. Nonetheless, be prepared to get your shoes muddy. Though the Sayaxché to El Paraiso road can be traveled by any car, at least during the dry season, even in the middle of the dry season a four-wheel drive finds challenging mud-holes between El Paraiso and Seibal.

Tikal

General Information

For years Tikal has been regarded as the measuring stick against which all other Maya sites are compared. Tikal's reconstruction has produced a site in which you can wander for hours, always seeing new things. Other guidebooks and pamphlets, much of which is available in bookstores in Flores and at the ruins themselves, do a fine job leading you from temple to temple, explaining every little detail, and certainly Tikal's local guides are capable of doing the same; here I won't waste space repeating their copious information.

Before visiting Tikal you might want to review the excellent portfolio of paintings called "A Traveler's Tale of Ancient Tikal," beginning on page 799 of the December, 1975 issue of *National Geographic* magazine; this work portrays Tikal as it must have appeared around 800 AD (Late Classic).

One very revealing piece of information generated from work on which the paintings were based will surprise anyone who makes the trip between Flores and Tikal. Today the region is relatively unpopulated, giving us the impression that Tikal has always lain "deep in the trackless jungle." But studies show that 1,100 years ago, in a 13,000-ha (50-square-mile) area around Tikal, rarely were family compounds more than 450 meters (500 yards) apart; nowhere was there open space enough for slash-and-burn agriculture, much less trackless jungle. In the 8th century this was a very heavily populated zone, home to perhaps 55,000 people.

Logistics

Sometimes it seems that half the inhabitants of Flores somehow concern themselves with shuttling tourists to Tikal. Even the government makes it easy; at this writing the only paved highway in the whole of Petén lies between Flores and Tikal. If on any early morning you wander into Flores's streets you'll probably be approached by men offering microbus service to Tikal. Microbus services also may be offered when you check into your hotel, for your hotel clerk probably has a buddy who drives the circuit.

Prices for this service vary wildly, from US$20.00 and more, down to the average microbus asking-price of about US$5.00. With a little looking around, probably you can find someone willing to squeeze you in for US$3.00. During my most recent trip the cheapest ticket was with the Pinita Bus, which left two or three times a day from Santa Elena's terminal (see Santa Elena section); it cost less than a dollar. It's a slow, painfully crowded way of going, however.

At this writing, the entry ticket to Tikal costs US$6.00, and a spot in which to pitch your tent in the campground costs another US$6.00. To establish yourself in the campground, walk behind the Comedor Tikal and look for the attendant, who usually stays all the way to the back of the grassy area, in the small, white building behind the *palapas*. Within easy walking distance of the ruins, three places offer lodging. **The Jungle Lodge** has double rooms with private baths, cold water, and a fan above the bed for US$35.00; it also asks a US$20.00 deposit. The **Tikal Inn** rents rooms — breakfast and dinner included — for US$25.00. The **Jaguar Inn** has two double rooms, which go for US$30.00, and this price includes three meals.

Finally, you should know about Frank B. Smithe's fine little book *The Birds of Tikal*, which is available, among other places, at the Jungle Lodge. It's well illustrated and carries plenty of information on each of Tikal's 280 bird species; its appendices relate a lot of ornithological and ecological savvy.

Uaxactún

Archeological orientation
Uaxactún is major ceremonial center. Thompson considered a pyramid at Uaxactún, archeologically designated as E-VII sub, to be the finest surviving example of Late Preclassic architecture. During later times E-VII sub was completely covered by another pyramid; when the badly deteriorated outer pyramid was removed by archeologists, E-VII sub was found inside in almost mint condition. Also of interest is a two-story Classic building.

Logistics
Until fairly recently going to Uaxactún was a major undertaking. In her 1982 book *Backpacking in Mexico & Central America*, Hilary Bradt tells a story she heard in 1979 about a woman leaving Tikal with a day-pack, searching for Uaxactún, and becoming lost for eleven days. She survived by finding a logging camp, where she ate rotting oranges, snails, and other things! Nowadays getting to Uaxactún is a breeze. The easiest way is to hire a car and guide at your hotel, for US$20.00 to US$30.00. Here's how the independent traveler wanting to sniff flowers along the still-fairly-unused, 25-kilometer (15-mile) route can make a two- or three-day hiking trip out of it:

From the hotel zone walk toward Tikal's ruins. Just past the ticket-checking booth you'll see a large, hand-painted map of the ruins, with the road to Uaxactún shown leading off toward the map's top right corner. As you stand facing the map, the road to your right is the one you want to take; it travels about 50 meters before curving hard at another right. At this curve, a gate on the left permits entry to Tikal's Complex Q; for Uaxactún, continue on the main road to the right.

About two kilometers (1¼ mile) up the road there's a fork; the left branch is marked as leading toward the *Casas de descanso*; the right arm's sign reads, *Sitio Arqueologico Uaxactún a 23 km*. And this road to Uaxactún is a fine road; any VW bug can make it. You can camp at Uaxactún, with the usual remarks about *gratificaciones* applying.

THE GRINGO PERDIDO AND FAMILY

If you're strictly a camper or if you simply want to avoid the whole tourist scene at Flores — but you'd like to spend a while in the Tikal area — a spot at the eastern end of Lago Petén Itzá (the lake surrounding Flores) may be what you're looking for. Here's how you get there:

The road to Tikal joins the main highway between Flores and Belize at the town called El Cruce. The Gringo Perdido and neighboring destinations lie 1½ km (one mile) north of El Cruce (up the road toward Tikal) at the village of El Remate. If a bus lets you off at El Cruce, you can walk to El Remate in twenty minutes.

The **Gringo Perdido** is a lake-side campground. To get there, follow the only one-lane gravel road that leaves El Remate and hugs the lake's shore; it's about half an hour of walking. The road can be awfully muddy, and you may even have to wade through ankle-deep water. Camping overnight costs US$1.00 per person; the price of a bungalow, with two meals included, is US$15.00. This campground's location is such a pleasant spot that some folks stay a while. Not only is the lake right there, but also the campground lies at the foot of large hill. The nearby Cerro Cahui Biotope is available for exploring.

Moreover, about halfway down the muddy trail to the Gringo Perdido you pass a small pier to which some canoes are tied; right across the road stands a hut looking rather typical for the area, except that a garage-like shed is appended to its right side, sheltering a motorcycle. This is the establishment referred to as **Agua y Tierra**, run by a German woman. If you climb the slope and talk with the folks inside the house, you'll find that here you can rent a motorcycle (XT/TT 500 and KTM 250) for about US$16.00 per day; putting a passenger behind you costs another US$4.00. A guide can be arranged for about US$8.00 per day. Motorbiking to Uaxactún should be a fancy experience. At Agua y Tierra a canoe is yours for US$3.60 per day; a deposit of US$5.00 is required.

Back on the road between Tikal and El Remate, about half a kilometer south of the entrance to the road to El Gringo Perdido and Agua y Tierra, you'll see a place selling Maya-style clothing and other tourist items, called the Miscellania del Gringo Perdido. Exactly across the road from the Miscellania you can climb stairs carved into the dirt to **El Mirador de los Duendes**, which translates roughly to "The Elves's Lookout." During my visit this campground was just getting organized and the people didn't know what they'd be charging for camping, or what eventually they'd be offering other than camping. I wouldn't even mention this place if it didn't occupy the world's best view of Lago Petén Itzá.

If you talk to the owners of these three businesses about their ideas, motivations and plans, you start feeling that Lago Petén Itzá's eastern shore has a certain New-Age-Guatemalan feeling about it — one with heavy mystical-Maya overtones. Even if the businesses have collapsed by the time you get there the idealistic community will probably still be evolving, and I'll bet that other projects will be in the making. The Gringo Perdido seems so well rooted that you can be fairly well assured of having someplace to camp if you arrive there one late afternoon by bus.

POPTÚN'S FINCA IXOBEL

About midway Flores and the Petén's southern boundary, 100km (62 miles), or 4½ bumpy, dusty/muddy hours south of Flores, lies the town of Poptún. Poptún is a fine, frontier-flavored town worthy of spending a night in, if only to take a break from the bone-shaking gravel roads both north and south of it. For most international travelers, Poptún generally means one thing: Finca Ixobel (EESH-oh-bel).

The half-kilometer trail leading to Finca Ixobel leaves the Flores/Río Dulce road about three kilometers (1.8 miles) south of Poptún; a sign with a macaw painted on it plainly points the way. If you're coming from the south on a bus, you can ask to be let off here; if you're coming from Flores, your bus certainly will take a long meal-break in Poptún, so you might want to disembark in Poptún and walk the last three kilometers; it takes about 45 minutes and after the jarring ride you'll need a walk to work your bones back together.

Though Ixobel's meals are famous for being delicious and nutritious (for breakfast you can have granola (muesli) with fresh fruit and yogurt; two or three times a week the supper, always supplied with homemade wholewheat bread, is vegetarian) they're certainly more expensive than general Guatemalan fare; if you're on a strict budget, before heading for Ixobel you should avail yourself of the excellent *mercado* just a block northwest of where the bus leaves you in downtown Poptún.

To reach Finca Ixobel from downtown Poptún, if you're in a car, stay on the main road south for three kilometers until you see the sign. If you're walking, continue SSW from the gas station until you come to an earthen airport runway. Follow the footpath leading across the runway's grass, then continue walking SSW to the first right, take it, then the next left, and then walk the better part of a kilometer (⅔ mile), until the road ends. Turn right here, walk to the gate, go through the gate, and then simply follow the gravel road to the buildings.

At Ixobel you can rent a tree house or pitch a tent for US$1.00 per night. A bungalow costs US$2.00 per person, with private bath US$2.40. A bunk at the Multinational House costs US$1.60. A seven-kilometer horseride (four miles) costs US$5.00 per person. Also on Ixobel's grounds is a pond for swimming and a spring-fed shower.

The roof of Ixobel's main building is equipped with solar panels; the finca garden is as organic as possible. Also nice is the fact that the campground lies in a sandy-soiled area on which grow pines, *Pinus caribæa*, in stark contrast to the surrounding humid, ragged-looking, broadleaf forest. The pines' resin causes the air to smell clean and crisp, and breezes sighing through pine needles sound cool and restful.

At Ixobel you can take a three- or four-day horseriding trip, with an English-speaking guide, to Naj Tunich, the Cave of the Inscriptions, 28 kilometers (17 miles) east of Poptún and four kilometers (2½ miles) from the Belizean border; it costs US$16.00 per day. Naj Tunich Cave is a kilometer long and contains spectacular formations. More importantly, inside it you find what is generally regarded as the largest number of ancient Maya inscriptions and charcoal drawings found in any cave. Archeologist George Stuart of the National Geographic Society has characterized these writings as a "Maya equivalent of the Dead Sea Scrolls" because they "...put names, dates and cities together like a modern genealogy." Charcoal found in the cave has been dated from the Late Classic period (about 750 AD); ceramic analyses indicate that the cave was used as a shrine around 300 AD. Sadly, over 20 of the 90 known drawings have been vandalized.

While at Ixobel, watch out for extremely tiny, blood-sucking seed-ticks inhabiting the finca's grassy pastures and campground area. Ixobel's ticks are millimeter-sized creatures that climb up the legs, usually attaching themselves in the crotch area, beneath the belt, under arm-pits and in the hair. Use insect repellent, especially on the legs, avoiding lying and sitting on the grass, and consider stuffing your trouser legs into your socks.

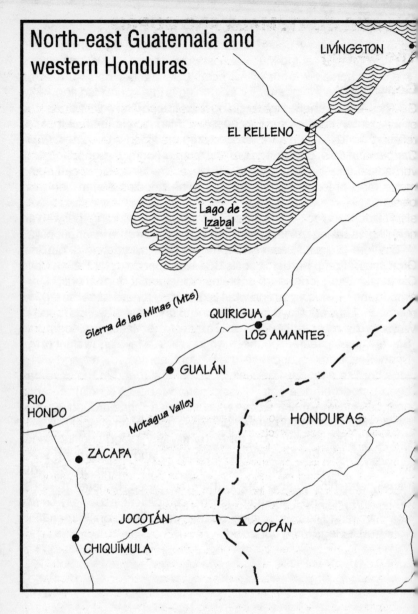

North-east Guatemala and western Honduras

LIVÍNGSTON

EL RELLENO

Lago de Izabal

Sierra de las Minas (Mts)

QUIRIGUA

LOS AMANTES

GUALÁN

RIO HONDO

Motagua Valley

HONDURAS

ZACAPA

JOCOTÁN

COPÁN

CHIQUIMULA

UPLAND GUATEMALA AND COPÁN

The Setting

Geography

Guatemala's southern highlands owe their character to the violence of vast tectonic plates scraping against one another in the process referred to as continental drift; along the line where the small Caribbean Plate grinds against the much larger American Plate, vulcanism resulting from the friction has resulted not only in the 4,000-meter (13,100-foot) volcano called Tajumulco, and the smaller but better known volcanos of Agua, Fuego, Pacaya and Acatenango, but also the range of young mountains known as the Sierra de las Minas, rich in gold, silver, jade and obsidian.

The Río Motagua, Guatemala's longest river, cuts across southern Guatemala, flows through the Motagua Valley and empties into the Caribbean Sea. Its headwaters lie far to the west of Guatemala City — even west of Chichicastenango, which has an elevation of 2,071 meters (6,790 feet). Any traveler passing from one end of the Motagua Valley to the other on Hwy CA 9 will be astonished by the profound

---

Is All Jade Green?

We're always hearing about the Maya's love for jade. Among the most famous Maya jade artifacts are the 8th-century mosaic funeral mask found at Tikal and the 4.4-kg (9¾-pound) carved head of Kinisch Ahau, the Mayan Sun God, unearthed at Altun Ha. Possibly only the ancient Chinese surpassed the Maya in their appreciation of jade, and their ability to work it. Despite its importance in many cultures, the exact definition of jade is sometimes hard to nail down.

In Chinese, the word *yu*, which we understand as meaning "jade," is used to designate any rock worthy of being carved. To complicate matters further, two chemically distinct materials are legally accepted in world trade as jade: One, a silicate of calcium and magnesium, coming in a variety of colors including white, is called nephrite; the other, a silicate of sodium and aluminum, mostly green but also black, white, lavender and other colors, is called jadeite. Nephrite is most plentifully scattered throughout the world, but jadeite is the form found in the Ruta Maya area, in Guatemala. Chemically, jadeite is $NaAlSi_2O_6$.

In Guatemala, the Motagua River Valley is the source of most of the ancient Maya's jadeite; it's still mined there today. But if you leave your bus at the bridge over the Río Motagua, on the road between Río Hondo and Chiquimula, and wander along the river bed looking for jadeite, remember that all jade *isn't* green. Moreover, all that's green isn't jade.

changes experienced in climate, vegetation, geology and kinds of people. The western end is high and cool; the eastern end is low and hot. The western end, sometimes rising into the clouds, can be moist, and it's certainly moist on the Caribbean end; however, in the Motagua Valley's middle elevations there is hot desert. In the uplands indigenous Maya traditions are evident; in the lowlands Spanish culture dominates.

Road-cuts in the Motagua Valley are very interesting, frequently being excavated through massive, horizontal layers of volcanic ash. Obsidian, the black, glass-like rock used by the ancient Maya for making razor-sharp blades, often can be nudged from the ash. Obsidian is formed when lava cools very quickly, as when it falls into water. When this happens the lava's atoms "freeze into place," not having the time to group themselves into crystalline configurations leading to minerals. Because obsidian is thus unstable, it's found only in areas of fairly recent volcanic activity. For instance, though once the geologically ancient Appalachians of Eastern North America were volcanic, today no obsidian is found in the eastern US; however in the western US, around the much younger Rocky Mountains, obsidian is locally common. Besides obsidian, sometimes jade can be picked up in the Motagua Valley's stream beds.

Biology

While in the Petén vegetational patterns have been most profoundly influenced by subtle interactions between local geology, the recent history of there having been a relatively hotter and drier climatological period, and perhaps even from the effects of ancient Maya agricultural practices, in the highlands natural ecological zones are most influenced by the mountains.

Many of Guatemala's peaks reach into the clouds, where often cloud forests form, as described in this chapter's section dealing with the quetzal reserve; on the leeward side of mountains, as in the Motagua Valley, rain-shadows produce deserts populated with giant cacti. On mountain slopes between moisture-saturated cloud forests and valley deserts we find several forest types. Usually pine or pine/oak forest is found below cloud forests; below the pine/oak, there are various kinds of broadleaf trees and bushes; gradually the height of this broadleaf forest diminishes as the desert valley is approached.

What's the difference between a rain forest and a cloud forest? In general, a rain forest occurs in the lowlands, is hot, and is sustained by abundant rain. Cloud forests occur in the highlands, are cool, and are wet not only from rain but also from cloud condensation.

Cloud forests of the kind found at the Quetzal Reserve occur where moist, warm air streams up a mountain's slope, trying to get to the

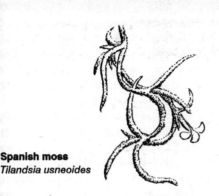

Spanish moss
Tilandsia usneoides

mountain's other side. As this air rises, it cools. Since a cubic meter of warm air has the capacity to hold much more moisture than a cubic meter of cold air, as moisture-laden air flows up a mountain's slope, eventually it cools to the point where it can hold no more moisture — it reaches its saturation point. As the air continues rising and cooling, the moisture must go someplace, so water molecules combine into droplets of fog or cloud. For this reason, whenever we find high mountain peaks with streams of air flowing over them, those peaks usually are mantled with clouds. Plants and animals inhabiting cloud forests are often unique and quite rare.

The People

In terms of traditional villages and language groups, Guatemala's densely populated highlands are much more diverse than the lowlands, being home to about 18 languages. In contrast to the lowlands, in most small upland villages today these languages are still being spoken. In upland villages, frequently women wear colorful traditional dress, and sometimes the men do, too. In Guatemala's southern highlands we need not be content with ancient Maya ruins; we can move among the Maya themselves, and in small villages we can see with our own eyes traces of ancient Maya traditions.

A Special Note for Guatemala's Uplands

Traditional guidebooks do a good job directing you to upland Guatemala's best "Indian markets," festivals and tourist-oriented towns. Moreover, upland Guatemala's touristic infrastructure (buses, hotels, restaurants) is so well developed that if you want something like a bus from Guatemala City to Xela, all you have to do is to go to the terminal and hop on it. If you want a hotel, just walk around a bit, and there one is. Guatemala City, the colorful and much visited towns of Chichicastenango, Quezaltenango (called Xela by the locals), Huehuetenango and Antigua Guatemala, as well as the picturesque Volcanos of Fire and Water, and the unbelievably beautiful country around Lago de Atitlán and the tourist town of Panajachel... They're written about everyplace and, even without any guidebook, getting to them is as simple as following everybody else.

I have yet another reason for treating the uplands superficially. Though I believe that if in the highlands you stay on the tourist circuit, look like a tourist and act like a tourist — if you never "go native" or wander around in non-standard places — you'll be safe, in my opinion, at this time the Guatemalan uplands are dangerous for independent travelers. Lone tourists or even small groups somewhat off the beaten path in Guatemala's uplands run an unacceptably high risk of being robbed and hurt. If you really want to visit some isolated highland Indian villages, do so in the accompaniment of an experienced guide. Travel agencies and hotel clerks can frequently put you into contact with one; freelance guides often hang around spots where buses discharge their passengers.

Your security may lie in being a member of the predictable, money-spending, staying-close-to-the-main-road tourist pack. Happily, upland Guatemala's landscape is so majestic, its people are so lovely, and its importance is so great to Maya archeology and tradition that even under these awkward conditions it's worthy of our attention.

The first of the following destinations are still in the lowlands; the cautions set out above should be considered as coming into force step-wise; in general, the higher in elevation you climb, the more you need to stick to the usual tourist circuits.

Publisher's note
The people running *The Shawcross Aid Programme for Highland Indians* (see box on page 213) disagree vehemently with Jim on the safety aspect. Mike Shawcross writes: "I am constantly telling people it is more dangerous walking home to one's pension in the town than it is walking for a week in the remote areas of the Ixil triangle." The decision is yours.   *Hilary Bradt*

At the close of 1992, 500 years after Columbus, the Mayan Indians' struggle against oppression in Guatemala gained the highest recognition when Rigoberta Menchu from Quiche province was awarded the Nobel Peace Prize.

AID FOR HIGHLAND INDIANS

Many Indian villages in the 'Ixil triangle', a remote area north of Nebaj in south west Guatemala, were totally destroyed by the Guatemalan army and their inhabitants forced to flee into the hills or seek refuge in other areas during the civil war of 1979-85. They are now gradually returning to their villages but the problems of resettling them and re-creating the infrastructures of village life have been considerable, and outside help has been necessary in a number of key areas, particularly the installation of potable water systems, the provision of seeds and medicines and the employment of Ixil-speaking teachers.

The Shawcross Aid Programme for Highland Indians is a non-profit making, non-religious and non-political organization. It was established by Mike Shawcross in 1986 to aid the victims of violence in the civil war. It doesn't actually *do* the work of reconstruction for the local people but is a technical assistance programme. Technically skilled jobs like the installation of potable water systems are carried out under the supervision of Aid Programme Volunteers, mostly young people from Europe, North America and Australasia with the necessary skills who spend on average about three months working on the programme. Other projects include setting up networks for the marketing of village weavings through alternative trading organizations and retail outlets in Europe, North America and Australasia — an important task since this has helped to augment the family incomes of the villagers. There are also plans to establish a preventive medicine programme in the area.

Since 1987 a new village has been re-settled monthly in the Ixil triangle and requests for help from other villages are flooding in. Funds for the Programme come from various supportive voluntary organizations and individuals and it is mainly by giving money that people can help this worthwhile programme. $100 a month for instance would pay the salary of an Ixil-speaking teacher for villages up to 10 hours walk away from the nearest gravel road. Anyone with the requisite skills, time and commitment, on the other hand, who is travelling in Central America and who might want to take part in the programme as a Volunteer should seek Mike out at Casa Andinista, 4 Calle Oriente No 5, Antigua to see whether he or she can be of help. *Don't* write to him as he is already seriously burdened down with correspondence from all over the world and time spent answering letters is at the expense of other things that need to be done on the programme.

Donations should be sent to: Shawcross Aid Programme, a/c 5595-8, c/o Margaret Myers, RD4 Box 10, 4043 State Route 39, SHELBY, Ohio 44875, USA.

Malcolm Keir
Globetrotters Club

PLACES TO VISIT

Eastern Guatemala

Río Dulce (El Relleno)

Most travelers stopping at Río Dulce have one thing on their mind: Taking a boat down the Río Dulce to Lívingston. Lívingston is inaccessible by land. Its fame as an easy-going town with some passable beaches and a delightful Caribbean flavor is especially attractive to those not going to Belize.

As soon as you exit the bus at Río Dulce young men approach you offering less-than-two-hour trips by *lancha* to Lívingston for US$10.00; some offer to throw in a quick trip to the Castillo de San Felipe for an extra US$2.00. This is a restored fortress built by the Spanish around the end of the 16th century mainly to defend against pirates sailing up the Río Dulce to Lake Izabal. Transportation prices during my visit seemed non-negotiable. The broad river between the town of Río Dulce and Lívingston and some of the surrounding forest are protected as part of the Chacón-Machaca Biotope.

Castillo de San Felipe

Camping is possible near the pool of the hotel called **Turicentro Marimonte**, on the Río Dulce's southern shore not far from the bridge; double rooms cost about US$10.00. Nearby, closer to the bridge, the **Pensión Izabal** has rooms for under US$5.00. More elegant accommodation can be had on a small island about ten minutes by boat down the river — at the **Hotel Catamarán** where double rooms cost about US$15.00 and bungalows cost US$25.00.

Quiriguá

Archeological orientation

Quiriguá is a Classic site situated in what once was "deep jungle" near the banks of the Río Motagua. Though its buildings are of little distinction, its enormous sandstone stelae are wonderful. Stela E, erected late in the 8th century (Late Classic), could be considered the most impressive ancient stone monument anywhere in the New World. Standing 11 meters (35 feet) high, it bears the carved figure of a bearded man holding a hand shield and a scepter; its sides are covered with texts containing Long-Count dates. Confirming the

Maya's obsession with calendrics, one stela at Quiriguá computes a date reaching back approximately 390,000,000 years.

Also noteworthy at Quiriguá are its strange altars, which are huge boulders shaped into monsters; sometimes they're referred to as zoomorphs. Aesthetically they are pleasing for the art with which such ponderous masses have been transformed by being adorned with graceful, intricate details. Though Quiriguá is a purely Maya site, some isolated sculptures have been found in Cotzumalhuapan style; Cotzumalhuapan sculpture is characterized by Coe as "hard, cruel and unsympathetic," and much more Mexican than Maya. The last monument erected at Quiriguá was in 810 AD. Sir Eric Thompson, refuting the theory that Classic Maya civilization collapsed because slash-and-burn agriculture depleted the soil, points out that the soil around Quiriguá, frequently fertilized by flooding of the Río Motagua, was one of the earlier cities to cease functioning.

Logistics

Quiriguá lies on the busy main road between Guatemala City and Puerto Barrios, so visiting it is easy. The gravel road connecting the main highway with the ruins — the intersection lies just east of the town of Los Amates — is about three kilometers (two miles) long, takes 40 minutes to walk, and is especially interesting because it passes right through a huge banana plantation owned by the company producing Del Monte foods. Buses ply the road from time to time and it's easy to hitch. However, if in your life you want to walk through at least one banana plantation, this certainly is the time to do it. Just hike straight through the plantation to the road's end, then cross the railroad tracks and a small bridge to the right, and you're at the ruin.

By the way, the white plastic bags covering the banana stalks encourage uniform maturation throughout the stalk and protect the bananas from sunburn. Also, about midway the plantation you'll come to a large barrier more or less of the type that drops across a road when a train is coming. Usually this barrier is raised, but sometimes it drops and then you can see that actually the barrier is part of a banana-transportation system. Suspended below the barrier's arm you'll see a "conductor" pass, riding in a seat, followed by about a hundred dangling stalks of banana covered with white plastic bags. This mini-rail system extends all over the plantation, freighting bananas to a central packing location.

Just outside the fenced-in ruin area lies a grassy area perfect for tent-camping, which is allowed, and free. Nearby stands a restaurant; at night a guard is on duty just on the other side of the fence. The park's bathroom and an outside spigot providing water lie inside the fenced-in area and thus are available only during the ruin's regular visiting hours.

Guatemala's Sweetgum Trees

In the high-elevation cloud-forest around Guatemala's quetzal reserve you'll see a broadleaf, deciduous tree with star-shaped leaves. Visitors familiar with the forests of the US southeast will recognize this tree as the sweetgum, *Liquidambar styraciflua*, of the witch hazel family.

The sweetgum tree is not distributed in one unbroken population all the way from Guatemala to the eastern US. Its US population extends into southeastern Texas, but then the next population to the south is found atop some mountains in central Mexico. The population around the quetzal reserve is one of the sweetgum's southernmost mountaintop populations, separated from other sweetgum communities by big valleys.

The sweetgum's strange distribution pattern has roots in the Ice Age. At that time, as the ice sheet moved southward, vegetation zones migrated before it. Thus eventually tundra migrated into areas previously mantled with oaks and hickories; and the US's Eastern Deciduous Forest shifted far southward, into regions now occupied by tropics — to Guatemala.

When the ice retreated, the Eastern Deciduous Forest retreated with it. However, some species retreated not only by migrating back north, but also by gradually ascending mountains. As the mountains warmed up, generation after generation of cool-weather organisms simply migrated up slope to where it wasn't so hot.

Another species that has maintained "outposts" at high elevations deep in the tropics is the blackgum, *Nyssa sylvatica*; its distribution extends into southern Mexico.

Guatemala's sweetgums are different in subtle ways from their northern comrades; for example, among Guatemala's sweetgums I've noticed a tendency for more of the star-shaped leaves to be three-pointed than in the north. My former ecology professor at Western Kentucky University, Dr. Joe Winstead, showed that when sweetgum seeds from North America and the tropics were grown under identical conditions in the lab, seedlings grown from seeds collected in the tropics had, among other differences, significantly longer growing seasons. Gradually, Latin America's sweetgums and blackgums are evolving into new species. Several taxa already have done this.

Sweetgum also is interesting because of the yellowish resin that oozes from injuries on its trunk. Traditionally Indians have burned hardened sweetgum resin as incense. Any child in an area where sweetgum grows is likely to use the resin as chewing gum. Most people in this area call sweetgum *liquidámbar*, which also is its scientific genus name.

Copán in Honduras

Archeological orientation

Located in Honduras near the border with Guatemala, Copán is one of the Ruta Maya's largest ruins; about 3,500 mounds are found in its 2,400-ha (9.25-square-mile) central ruin area, and another 1,000 mounds lie up and down the valley. At its peak, Copán's population must have stood between 18,000 and 20,000.

The main temple-pyramids rise on an artificial acropolis partly eroded away by the Río Copán. Among the most important structures is that of the Temple of the Hieroglyphic Stairway, completed in the 8th century A.D. Originally it consisted of 72 steps, each half a meter (a foot and a half) high, the risers of which were embellished with more than 1,250 hieroglyphs. Unfortunately, in the 1800s the Stairway collapsed so that today only 30 of its risers are in their original order. Copán's ball court is the most perfect Classic Period one known. Doorways, jambs and façades of the main temples are ornamented with figures of various gods. About 20 stelae from Early and Late Classic times are present, and about fourteen "altars" have been recorded. Sculpture at Copán is significant for its three-dimensional development. In 1990, archeologists tunneling into the heart of Structure 16 discovered a mint-condition 1,400-year old temple (Classic) entombed inside the outer pyramid — as well as the most spectacular ceremonial offering ever unearthed at Copán. The most interesting items accompanying the burial were nine intricately carved chert ceremonial pieces.

Probably I'm not the only one who wonders at the portraits on Copán's stelae, which look like Chinese in ancient Egyptian poses. All around this airy ruin stone faces peer out, exhibiting no obvious Indian characteristics. Also we find ape-headed humans and personages that seem more like caricatures than somebody real...

The great Mayanist Sir Eric Thompson rhapsodized that: "There is a peaceful splendor here, which, the wickedness of child sacrifice forgotten or forgiven, now evokes the incomparable third movement of Beethoven's Fifth Symphony." It seems that Copán affects different people in different ways, but always it produces a powerful effect.

At Copán began the Maya convention of calculating with the formula "149 moons = 4,400 days," which was eventually adopted by nearly all other Maya centers. This formula, which must have required centuries to develop from direct observation, figured the period of time between two successive new moons as averaging 29.53020 days, which is incredibly close to the actual value of 29.53059 days. When you consider that sometimes a moon "looks full" three nights in a row, it's easy to see that nailing down the actual length of a day with such precision is quite an accomplishment.

The October, 1989 issue of *National Geographic* magazine gives an in-depth look at Copán, especially focusing on the burial discovered inside the Temple of the Hieroglyphic Stairway.

Logistics

On Hwy CA 9 between Guatemala City and Puerto Barrios, near the town of Río Hondo, take CA 10 south to Chiquimula. If you're riding a bus continuing down CA 9, ask to be let off at *la entrada a Chiquimula*. *La entrada* is a large triangle with a busy roadside market inside the Guatemala-City-side corner. The best place to catch a bus to Chiquimula is across the road from the market. The road to Chiquimula is well paved and goes over a mountain; you'll see giant cacti along the way.

Chiquimula itself is large enough to offer the services a traveler needs, from banking to hotels, yet isolated enough to provide some interesting surprises. For example, in a *comedor* in Chiquimula's municipal market I enjoyed the largest, best-tasting, cheapest meal of scrambled eggs, black beans and tortillas found anyplace on the entire Ruta Maya! If you're coming from the humid lowlands, you'll also appreciate Chiquimula's low humidity. Though the town has plenty of hotels and pensions of different kinds, they do a bustling business, so late arrivers sometimes have problems finding lodging. A clean but unostentatious double room with bath costs about US$7.50.

To get to *el centro* and the municipal market and the general area of various hotels, from the bus terminal (just a large, open area with several buses parked on it) orient yourself by facing up-slope; then walk two blocks to the left and four blocks up-slope. While still at the terminal area, notice that to your right as you face up-slope, across the street stands the Transportes Vilma bus line; here you can buy your ticket to the Honduran frontier near Copán.

At this writing, Transportes Vilma's buses leave for the Honduras border seven times a day, from 0600 to 1630. If your ticket takes you all the way to the border, its destination will read "El Florido" and it'll cost US$1.00. About half of the "Copán buses" travel only halfway to the border, to the town of Jocotán (the ticket costs 50¢) where a bus, theoretically, waits so that you can immediately transfer to it and continue to the border. Unless someone tells you, the only way you'll know you're in Jocotán is if your bus stops next to a busy plaza area and everyone else gets off. If you're not sure, you should ask "*¿Es este pueblo Jocotán? ¿Donde está la camioneta que nos lleva a la frontera?*" — "Is this Jocotán? Where's the bus that takes us to the border?"

The bus carries you to the very border. You get out, pass to the left of the barrier, and stop at the window beneath a sign saying "Oficina de Migración". At the border you can ride to the ruins in pickup trucks or microbuses for about US$1.50. In the town of Copán Ruinas, in Honduras near the ruin, there's a healthy variety of lodging and literature about Copán available. Other guidebooks take you step by step through these deservedly famous, much-visited ruins. At this writing, six buses a day travel from the border back to Chiquimula, between 0700 and 1430.

Other Information

The passage between Chiquimula and the border is fascinating; usually the road climbs or descends steeply, providing excellent vistas of the countryside. If you see fields of plants about a meter tall, with very broad, light-green leaves, that's tobacco. When tobacco is cut, it must cure for a time before the leaves can be sold. During this curing process the leaves lose most of their moisture and turn brown. In temperate tobacco-growing countries the curing tobacco usually is hung in special barns, but here you may see tobacco plants hanging on special scaffolding set up in the fields, walled all around with fronds of the locally common fan-palm.

In the river valley you may see large fields of tomato. In other fields grow meter-tall plants with palmate (hand-shaped) leaves, large, yellow flowers, and green, carrot-shaped fruit-pods about 10cm long; this is okra, of African origin; nowadays okra finds itself in the vegetable soups of developed countries.

During the ride between Jocotán and the frontier, people enter the bus carrying palm-frond petioles (petioles are the stems of leaves), about half a meter long. The inside face of each petiole is concave, and inside this concavity is smeared a brown, very viscous goo. This goo is locally produced molasses. Here we may be seeing a goo-carrying technique used since the times of the ancient Maya — who probably carried honey this way instead of molasses.

Sometimes you see small, hillside orchards of a low, stout tree with small, roundish fruit clustered at the ends of its branches. This is the *jocote*, after which the town of Jocotán is named; in English the *jocote* is sometimes called hog plum. It's *Spondias* sp, of the cashew family. These trees produce juicy, slightly acidic, aromatic fruits vaguely similar to plums; tropical folks all over the world eat them raw and make sweet drinks from them, but they are not well known in the Temperate Zone; the trees don't survive cold weather.

Also common along this route are mango trees, *Mangifera indica*, likewise of the cashew family. Mango trees can grow quite tall. They possess slender, sharp-pointed, tongue-shaped leaves about 20cm (eight inches) long. Curiously, the cashew family to which both of these excellent fruits belong also holds North America's poison oak, poison ivy and poison sumac.

CENTRAL GUATEMALA

THE "MARIO DARY RIVERA" QUETZAL RESERVE
About Quetzals

The word quetzal is pronounced ket-ZAHL. Resplendent quetzals, *Pharomachrus mocinno*, belong to the trogon family of birds.

Among the differences between Quetzals and trogons is that trogons have square-ended tails while male quetzal tails are long-tapering and female quetzal tails are rounded. The male resplendent quetzal's meter-long (yard-long), shimmering, metallic-green tail feathers are so spectacular that they cause the bird to look artificial.

While about 36 species of trogon are found in the Americas, Africa and Asia, quetzals are restricted to the Americas, where there are only four species. Mexico is home to eight species of trogon (seven in Guatemala), but in both Mexico and Guatemala the resplendent quetzal is the only quetzal. The resplendent quetzal makes its home in cloud forests from Chiapas to western Panamá. The other three quetzal species are found in South America; one of them, the golden-headed quetzal, reaches into eastern Panamá. None are as spectacular as ours.

The resplendent quetzal is separated into two subspecies, or races. The Mexican/Guatemalan race is *P. mocinno mocinno*; the other subspecies, found in Costa Rica, *P. mocinno costaricensis*, is slightly smaller than ours. Over most of the quetzal's distribution it's been hunted to extinction and its cloud-forest habitat has been destroyed. Before I saw my first quetzals at this reserve, I had searched for years for them in likely places in Chiapas and elsewhere in Guatemala. Most birders agree that the resplendent quetzal is the New World's most gorgeous bird.

Resplendent Quetzal
Pharomachrus mocinno

Probably the best chance for seeing a quetzal is *not* by penetrating deep inside the reserve. Surprisingly, the ones I saw seemed to be attracted to busy CA 14 and were not disturbed at all by the obstreperous, diesel-fume-belching trucks and buses that were always passing. Between the reserve's entrance and the Hospedaje rises a terraced road-cut facing a small plateau across the road. The terraces make perfect platforms on which birders can perch, looking across the road to a particular tall tree for which the quetzals seem to have a special affinity. In fact, the quetzals I saw perched there in plain view for long periods! Another fairly common but spectacular bird frequenting the tall bushes along the highway is the emerald toucanet.

If the quetzals surprise you by being so conspicuous and incautious, then the reserve itself will fulfil your hopes for finding a majestic, other-worldly locale. Unfortunately, visitors sometimes enter the reserve so specifically looking for quetzals that they overlook the reserve's own special character. Ideally you should spot your first quetzal before entering onto the reserve's trails so that the cloud-forest experience won't be spoiled by single-mindedly "looking for quetzals."

About the Reserve

The reserve occupies a mountain's steep slope; two trails allow the visitor entry. The Fern Trail, *El Sendero de los Helechos*, is 1.8km (1.1 mile) long; the Moss Trail, *El Sendero de los Musgos*, is 3.6km (2.2 miles) in length. Since both trails are generally quite steep, usually slick with mud and — more importantly — one spends a lot of time gazing open-mouthed into treetops, it's impossible to estimate how much time you might spend on each.

Here horizontal branches of massive oaks carry whole gardens of epiphytes — tree-borne mosses, ferns, lichens, peperomia, bromeliads... (see page 218). Maybe the tree ferns, *Cyathea arborea*, are the reserve's most striking plant-form. They look like regular umbrella-shaped trees three meters tall (ten feet), but they are real ferns reproducing by means of microscopic spores, and their fronds unfurl fiddle-head-like, just like the most delicate of frilly, temperate-zone ferns.

When you come to especially wet, rocky places, as near waterfalls and boulders in stream-beds, take the time to look at the spongy covering of tiny plants mantling the rocks. A patch of cloud-forest turf the size of one's hand is no less than a lilliputian forest with its own ecology, aesthetics and remarkable diversity.

Around the quetzal reserve you'll see whole slopes cleared and covered with black canvas suspended on low scaffolding. The crop being grown below the canvas is *shate* (SHAH-teh), sometimes known in English as parlor palm or feather palm, *Chamaedorea elegans*;

shate is a dwarf palm usually growing less than knee high. In the Petén you often meet *shateros* who during a season roam *chiclero* trails collecting hundreds of kilos of *shate* frond. The cut fronds are exported to northern countries for placement in floral arrangements. At funerals in the US *shate* is everywhere... *Shate* fruits can be eaten, and *shate* shoots can be prepared like asparagus.

Also, at the higher elevations around the reserve, notice a deciduous tree with star-shaped leaves. North Americans familiar with trees of the southeastern US will recognize this species immediately, for it's common in their forests, as a pioneer species on cleared land, and even as a street tree. It's the sweetgum, *Liquidambar styraciflua*, of the witch hazel family.

Logistics

From CA 9 between Guatemala City and Puerto Barrios, take CA 14 (which is paved and well maintained) west and then north toward the town of Cobán (not Honduras's Copán). If you're riding a bus that

Upland Guatemala's Language Schools

Why not take advantage of one of the many Spanish-language schools in Antigua designed specifically for foreigners staying a short time in Latin America for weeks? Judging from the graduates I've met, many of these schools are good. Their teaching method generally emphasizes conversational skills instead of the memorization of grammatical rules. When learning any language, nothing beats being totally immersed in a culture, with a caring native teacher in the background.

On a bus recently I sat next to a Swiss woman who four weeks earlier hadn't spoken any Spanish at all. But now she could hold fairly complex conversations with those around us. Of course she made many grammatical errors, but her ear for the language was as good as mine had been after traveling in Latin America for years!

Most of these schools are in Antigua. To find a school, simply wander into Antigua and start looking at ads on hotel walls, in tourist agencies and on telephone poles, or, better, just talk with other foreigners who look settled-in enough to know the ropes.

In Quetzaltenango the Spanish School Juan Sisay has been particularly recommended. Profits go to community projects and students learn about current Guatemalan issues while lodging with local families. More information from 15 Avenida 8-38, Zona 1, Quetzaltenango, Guatemala or 3465 Cedar Valley Ct, Smyrna, GA 30080, USA. Tel: (404) 432-2396.

For more information on Antigua's language schools see the magazine South American Explorer *No 20, available from the S.A.E.C. (see advert) or Bradt publications.*

town of Cobán (not Honduras's Copán). If you're riding a bus that doesn't enter CA 9, tell the ticket-taker you want off at the road to Cobán, near El Rancho. Specify the road to Cobán and not El Rancho because the bus may stop several times in El Rancho before reaching the intersection — *"Quiero salir en el crucero de Cobán."*

As with the road to Chiquimula, CA 14 and CA 9 form a triangle when they join, with each side about a kilometer long. Buses heading north toward the reserve can be caught at a rather robust *mercado* along CA 9, in the triangle's Puerto Barrios corner. Before reaching the reserve CA 14 splits at Kilometer 132, with much of the traffic flowing left toward Salamá; the reserve lies to the right, toward Cobán. The Quetzal "Mario Dary Rivera" Biotope lies at approximately Kilometer 160.

The trip from El Rancho to the reserve is a trip *up*. No matter how hot and sunny it may be at El Rancho, you should know that 160 kilometers up the road it well may be cold and rainy. If you hitch in the back of a pickup truck or even if you're in a bus with your backpack on top, you may arrive at the reserve in a miserably cold state.

You can camp for free at the quetzal reserve. However, usually the weather here is so cold and rainy that even hardcore campers prefer having a bed off the ground. At Kilometer 156 the hotel called **Posada Montaña del Quetzal** has double rooms for about US$17.00. If you want a dry bunk in a communal log cabin perched on a mountain slope where you can sit on the porch and sometimes see quetzals, you can walk down the road about five minutes below the reserve office, and at the **Hospedaje Ranchito del Quetzal** pay US$1.75 per person. The blankets provided at the Hospedaje are completely ineffective against the night's coldness; take a sleeping bag. For groceries and other supplies, the village of Purulhá lies about four kilometers (2½ miles) down the road toward Copán.

Buses frequently pass the reserve, heading both directions. The Transportes Escobar line runs several times a day between Guatemala City and Copán. In Guatemala City this line operates from its own terminal at 8ª Av. 15-16, Zone 1. The "15-16" means "between Calle 15 and Calle 16."

Kaminaljuyú

Archeological orientation

Today so many of Kaminaljuyú's hundreds of temple mounds have been destroyed by Guatemala City's encroachment that there's not much to see. However, Kaminaljuyú is considered to be a very important site, and it's so accessible to Guatemala City, that you might enjoy visiting it.

Most of Kaminaljuyú's monumental sculptures are late Preclassic, of the Izapan art style, reflecting early communication with Pacific-coast peoples. Other finds of Early Classic age indicate strong links with the great city-state of Teotihuacan, 1060km (650 miles) to the northwest, near where Mexico City now stands. Starting on Page 63 in his *The Maya*, Michael Coe describes the contents of one of Kaminaljuyú's excavated tombs, even providing a tomb plan showing how items were arranged.

Logistics

Kaminaljuyú lies in the northwestern corner of Guatemala City, in Zone 7. Take the highway toward Mixco Viejo and San Juan Sacatepéquez (inside Guatemala City this highway is called Calzada San Juan, or the San Juan Highway) to 23ª Avenida, turn right and go six blocks. It's easy to get there using local buses. Guatemala City's buses are exceedingly simple for foreigners to use. Just stand at any bus stop, look pitiful, and ask whoever is standing beside you for instructions. Native Guatemalans carry an amazing store of bus-knowledge in their heads and usually they're delighted to share it and to debate with their neighbors which of them is correct... Keep a sense of humor.

Lago Atitlán's Flightless Grebe

Among birders, Lago Atitlán is most famous not for its exquisite scenery, but for *Podilymbus gigas*, the flightless Atitlán grebe. In 1969 only 130 members of this species survived and, in the whole world, were found only on Lago Atitlán. Despite heroic efforts by ecologist Anne LaBastille and others to educate the public, and to preserve the grebe's habitat, now the Atitlán grebe is extinct. Standing on Lago Atitlán's shore at the tourist-town of Panajachel, it's easy to see why. During the years since 1969 vacation homes along the lake have increased in number by over 1,600%; hotels and tour boats similarly have proliferated, sending their sewage into the lake. Wildlife habitat has diminished by 80%. This was just too much for a sensitive bird like *Podilymbus gigas*.

Lake Atitlan to
Huehuetenango

Iximché

Archeological orientation

In the 1400's AD, during the Late Postclassic period, the Cakchiquel Maya founded Iximché atop a hill, surrounded by deep ravines. The defensive position was important because, typical of Mayadom during the Late Postclassic, the Cakchiquel were not on the best of terms with their neighbors, especially the Quiché Maya. In early 1524 an army of Spanish conquistadors, under the leadership of Pedro de Alvarado, entered the area and cleverly allied themselves with Iximché's Cakchiquel to fight the Quiché. Alvarado and his men actually camped inside Iximché's fortifications. The Iximché people feared and revered the blond, blue-eyed Alvarado, calling him "Tonatiuh" — Son of the Sun. Of course, the Spaniards and Iximché's Cakchiquel handily beat the Quiché.

On July 25, 1524, the Spaniards founded their own settlement next to Iximché and for two months the two societies coexisted. Soon Alvarado decided to provoke his former allies into war. He set off for Mexico City to get more troops for the job, leaving his brother Jorge in command. Jorge immediately began making of the Indians outrageous demands for gold and other treasure. To the Spaniards' surprise, about half of what was demanded actually was delivered, but then the people of Iximché changed their minds and secretly escaped, climbing down walls of the ravines around their village. When Pedro returned he quickly realized that the Indians could put his army under siege, so in August of 1524 he moved his camp to another spot where now the town of Tecpán stands. Two years later other Spaniards came through and torched whatever was burnable of Iximché, and left the rest to the ravages of time.

Thus at Iximché we find the ruins of the last Cakchiquel capital as well as the site of Guatemala's first Spanish settlement. Now about all that's left at the site are foundations, a ball court, and the remains of some murals.

Logistics

The ruins lie at Kilometer 3.5 from Tecpán. Anyone in town can point you in the right direction; *taxistas* will carry you there gladly. In Tecpán, market days are Thursday and Sunday.

Zaculeu

Archeological orientation

Similar to the happenings at Iximché, Zaculeu was a functional Maya city when the conquistadors arrived; it served as the capital of the powerful Mam Maya. While the conquistadors, under Alvarado, were allied with the Cakchiquel (see above) the Cakchiquel encouraged the conquistadors to attack the Mam at Zaculeu, not only to settle old accounts but also to share in the booty. Pedro's brother Gonzalo led the fight. After four months of conflict, Zaculeu's Mam Maya fled into the mountains. Today you still find many Mam-speaking villages in the Sierra de los Cuchumatanes, which rise to the north of the ruins.

Logistics

Zaculeu lies about six kilometers (3¾ miles) from Huehuetenango's *centro* — a walk of about 1½ hours. Taxi drivers request about US$4.00 for round-trip service. At the city park, for 10¢, you can catch a bus to the ruins; a sign on front of the ruin bus says *"La Ruina."*

Pedro de Alvarado

What Hernán Cortés was to the Aztecs in central Mexico, Pedro de Alvarado was to Guatemala's highland Maya. In short, against the native peoples he effectively used superior Spanish warring technology, political intrigues, his own and others' avariciousness, and a capacity to rationalize unrestrained cruelty and genocide as consistent with his Christian faith.

Alvarado, under orders of Cortés, lead an expedition into Guatemala in 1523, systematically destroying Indian resistance as he went. Besides the Spanish using guns against spear-throwing Indians, the Indians had never seen a horse; they suspected that the man-horse thing was some kind of god, and how could they fight a god?

At that time the Quiché Maya dominated the Guatemalan uplands. This was hotly resented by the Cakchiquel Maya; the Cakchiquel managed to forge an alliance with Alvarado, and together they went after the Quiché. The last Quiché stand was at Utatlán, now Santa Cruz del Quiché, where the Quiché tried to trick Alvarado with friendliness. But Alvarado was trickier; in the end, he razed the whole city.

Once the Quiché were defeated, the Cakchiquel invited Alvarado's army to their capital, Iximché; Alvarado established there, in 1524, Spain's first military outpost in Guatemala. Of course, later Alvarado decided to betray the Cakchiquel, and the whole story ends in destruction of Iximché.

In 1541, while chasing some rebellious Indians up a steep slope, a horse fell onto Alvarado, crushing him. He died in great agony a couple of days later. When his second wife, 22-year old Doña Beatriz, got the news she behaved in a way of which her husband would have been proud: She proclaimed herself Captain General, thus becoming the first woman head of government on the American continent.

However, just one day after Doña Beatriz took charge, a deluge sent floodwater raging down the Volcán de Agua, completely destroying the capital city, and drowning Doña Beatriz.

Zaculeu was restored in 1946 by the United Fruit Company. The ruins are dazzling in bright sunshine as they stand in a wide, open area, with the Sierra de los Cuchumatanes in the background. However, there's little archeology to enjoy other than the general layout.

When buses arrive in Huehuetenango they unload their passengers in the streets, not at a central terminal. Disembarking tourists are frequently approached by freelance guides such as José Alfredo López who offers certain packaged tours. For instance, besides Zaculeu, Don José takes people on a five-hour hike to El Mirador from where, he says, you can see Guatemala City about 120km (75 miles) to the southeast, as well as Chichicastenango, Lago Atitlán, and the volcanos south of Antigua. Also he'll take you to the springs at which the Río San Juan originates, and some isolated Indian villages such as Todos Santos and San Martín.

Huehue is large enough to offer a variety of hotels. If you walk down the streets surrounding *el centro* you'll find tiny, cramped rooms for as little as US$1.50, and quite pleasant ones, such as at the **Hotel Zaculeu**, costing about US$10.50 for a double room. If you want to study Spanish someplace other than in Antigua, check out the Instituto El Portal at 1 Calle 1-64, Zona 3. By the way, in Huehue the main market is called La Plaza and it lies at the juncture of 3ª Ave. and 4ª Calle; every day is market day. The city park is called El Parque; to find it, just walk toward the town's highest buildings.

THE CROSSING BETWEEN GUATEMALA AND CHIAPAS, MEXICO

The most popular *gringo* bus in Huehuetenango is the Transportes El Condor bus that leaves at 1000 for the Mexican border. It loads across from the Hotel Zaculeu, near El Parque. Leaving Guatemala is very straightforward. Buses travel to the very frontier (the last half-kilometer or so passing by a bustling roadside market). One simply disembarks, walks into the customs building and pays the required fee; entering Guatemala without a visa cost me US$5.00; leaving cost US$1.00.

Young black-market money-changers swarm around the customs building; they're thicker on the Guatemalan side than the Mexican side, each changer dealing in pesos, quetzals and dollars. In my experience, of the various black markets found along the Ruta Maya, the money changers here offered the least favorable rates. However, at other markets the exchange rates seemed to be fixed; here, after lengthy haggling, I got a good rate. Always when dealing with black-market changers you should know beforehand the rate you are willing to change for. Upon leaving Guatemala you'd do well to change all your quetzals. They're very hard to change outside Guatemala.

Chiapas State, Mexico

Chapter 15

Chiapas

THE SETTING

Geography

Most of Chiapas is composed of chilly highlands; only at the two points where the Ruta Maya enters this southernmost Mexican state does it pass through lowlands. After crossing from Guatemala near the border town of Ciudad Cuauhtémoc, the first kilometers in Chiapas run across the floor of a broad valley referred to by physiographers as the Central Depression. As you climb from the Central Depression onto the plateau, at times you can look south across the valley and see the Sierra Madre mountains. By the time you reach La Trinitaria and Lagunas de Montebello, you're atop the plateau.

At the southern edge of Chiapas's northern lowlands, from atop the ruins at Palenque you can gaze north across lowlands extending all the way to the Gulf of Mexico; this northern lowland is called the Gulf Coastal Plain. The highlands between the northern and southern lowlands is referred to as the Central Plateau.

Biology

About 65% of Mexico's bird species can be found in Chiapas, as well as approximately 80% of the country's 1,200 species of butterfly. Over 40% of Mexico's plant species grow here. Plants and animals of Chiapas's southern highlands have a lot in common

Zebra Helicona
Heliconius charitonius

Swallowtail butterfly
Papilo thoasautocles

with those of upland Guatemala. In fact, Chiapas's ecological communities are more closely related to Guatemala's than to the communities of the highlands of the contiguous Mexican states of Oaxaca and Veracruz. This is because in Mexico's narrow isthmus between the Gulf of Mexico and the Pacific Ocean — the Isthmus of Tehuantepec — mountains disappear; it's just rolling hills and flatlands. A plant or animal with ecological requirements restricting it to the highlands cannot migrate from Oaxaca to Chiapas. No such ecological barrier exists between the highlands of Chiapas and Guatemala.

Lowland eastern Chiapas similarly is ecologically related with Guatemala's Petén region, as well as with the lowlands farther north on Mexico's Gulf Coast. However, Chiapas's lowland forests are much more devastated than similar forests across the Usumacinta River in Guatemala's Petén District. Not long ago Chiapas's Lacandón Jungle was the nearest major rainforest to the US. Today about half of it has been destroyed, mostly through legal, quasi-legal and outright illegal logging and oil exploration; now it's crisscrossed with primitive roads and settlers continue to flood in.

However, in 1977 part of this land was incorporated into the Montes Azules Biosphere Reserve. At this writing, the present Mexican administration, more than former ones, seems concerned about protecting natural areas. I was told by a politician in Palenque that timber cutters recently discovered illegally cutting trees in the Lacandón Jungle have gone to jail. Of course it's impossible to guess what the next administration's attitude to environmental protection will be.

Chiapas has the potential for being a world-class destination for serious naturalists, eco-tourers, and people who simply want to see good examples of profoundly diverse, luxurious and beautiful nature. But if the forests continue falling, it will only become a world-class theater of rank weediness, aching poverty and unbearable sadness.

The People

Two thirds of Chiapas's people live in rural areas, just the opposite to the rest of Mexico. In Chiapas's highlands most people are of Maya Indian stock; in isolated villages you'll hear people speaking Tzeltal and Tzotzil. In Chiapas's northern lowlands, if you walk to Naranjo behind the ruin of Palenque, you can hear Chol. A small number of

Zapotec live on Chiapas's Pacific coast. Zapotec are an independently developed people, separate from the Maya. The main Zapotec ruins are Mitla and Monte Albán in Oaxaca. Some Zoque villages are found in the Grijalva Basin; the Zoque people also have developed apart from the Maya. Nowadays thousands of Guatemalan refugees are found in camps and dispersed informally all through southern and eastern Chiapas, and among these folks you may hear anything from Quiché to Kekchi to Cakchiquel.

Iguana
Iguana iguana

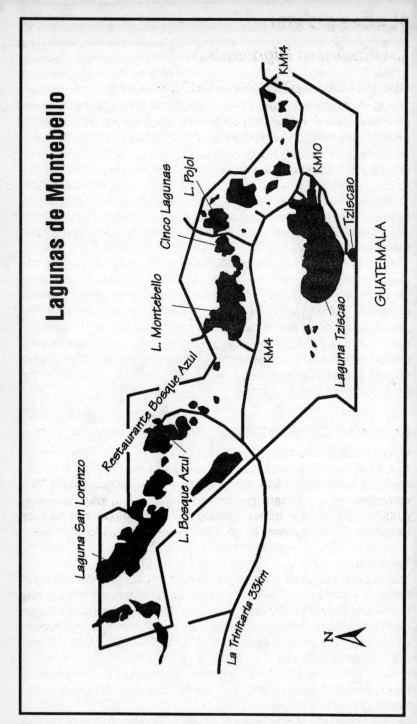

Lagunas de Montebello

PLACES TO VISIT

The Southern Highlands

CIUDAD CUAUHTÉMOC: BORDER TOWN

Though in Guatemala buses come right to the border, in Chiapas the main bus service on Hwy 190 begins in Ciudad Cuauhtémoc, 4km (2½ miles) inside Chiapas, at the Cristobal Colon terminal. Also, though a small Mexican customs booth does stand right at the border, the main office is in Ciudad Cuauhtémoc, across the highway from the Cristobal Colon station. The Mexican tourist card is available at the main office.

Taxis and passenger-ferrying pickup trucks do a brisk business between the border and Ciudad Cuauhtémoc. Taxis ask four or five dollars per trip. You can travel in the back of a very crowded pickup truck for about 30¢.

Cristobal Colon bus service is first-class; three or four times a day departures are made for San Cristóbal and Tuxtla Gutiérrez. If upon your arrival at this station you're heading into Mexico, but the next departure is several hours away, you should keep in mind that sometimes second-class buses running between here and Tuxtla, but not allowed to pull into the Cristobal Colon terminal, arrive in front of the terminal, turn around, and leave without much fanfare. If you're not making good Cristobal Colon connections, ask the locals when the next second-class bus arrives.

LAGUNAS DE MONTEBELLO NATIONAL PARK

General information

At Lagunas de Montebello you find high-elevation, cool, good-smelling, pine forests like those left behind in upland Guatemala; moreover, here you can "go native." This is a big park, covering 6,022ha (23 square miles) holding 68 lakes interconnected by footpaths... You can really let your hair down and stay for a while.

Logistics

The nearest fair-sized town large enough to offer a good variety of hotels is Comitán. In Comitán, every hour or so throughout the day microbuses leave for the park from the offices of Transportes Lagos de Montebello at 3ª Norte, Poniente. A one-way ticket from Comitán all the way to the park — a distance of about 58km (36 miles) — costs approximately US$1.20.

If you're coming from San Cristóbal or Guatemala, there's really no need to enter Comitán unless you want to stock up on food. If you're traveling by a bus plying Hwy 190, buy a ticket to La Trinitaria, which lies 16km (ten miles) southeast of Comitán, and ask to be let off at "*la entrada a Lagunas de Montebello*" — the entrance to Lagunas de Montebello. This access road to the park lies on the Comitán side of La Trinitaria. Once you're deposited at the intersection, probably at least within an hour a *cumbe* from Comitán will come; it costs about 80¢ for 42 km (26 miles) of service.

It's astonishing how you can leave Comitán or even La Trinitaria on a hot, sunny day with hardly a cloud in the sky, but arrive at the park — without changing elevation or crossing hills — in a cold drizzle, even during the dry season. Therefore, any trip to the park should begin with rain gear and warm clothing near at hand, no matter how absurd it seems at the trip's beginning. Nights in the park can be downright cold.

The park's "touristic heart" is **Restaurante Bosque Azul**, which lies right below the turnaround at the end of the *cumbe* route. Here you'll find the owner, María del Carmen al Boris, who will provide such services as sell you food, direct you toward horse and boat rentals, help you get a guide, and show you where to camp in a grassy area below the restaurant, right at the lake's edge, next to a workable toilet. Doña María refuses to establish a set price for her services. "*No es caro, es barato,*" is all she'll go on record as saying. If you're coming from Guatemala, you may find her price expectations too high, but if you've been in Mexico a while, probably she'll charge about what you expect. A visitor told me that US$3.30 per hour for horseback riding was about right.

You can spend days without going beyond the park's boundaries. Small boys greet new arrivals as they step from the *cumbes* at the turnaround, asking to serve as guides to *las grutas*. The *grutas* are a couple of natural bridges not a kilometer away. Though they're easy to find by asking directions at every corner, to get there you must pass across ground that feels like other peoples' private back yards, and go through at least one gate that seems to have been placed there to keep people out; paying a boy to go with you is worth the money, if only to keep from feeling like an intruder. Besides, it's good eco-touristic practice to hire local people. The boys also steadfastly refuse to quote a price for their services. However, I saw them turn away and look disgusted at a fellow traveler's offer of 35¢.

Backpacking to Bonampak

If you're interested in making the hike to Bonampak (see page 260) with a seasoned guide, then Roberto Castellanos is your man. Just ask for him at Doña María's, (neither he nor Doña María speak English) or when you go to *las grutas* up the road a little beyond the restaurant, look for him at the first house you come to. For US$100 per person Roberto will lead you through the rain forest to Bonampak, 100 air-kilometers (61 miles) to the northeast; this amounts to five days of hiking across the Montes Azules Biosphere Reserve. This is certainly one of the most interesting backpacking trips along the entire Ruta Maya. However, it's rugged. Hilary Bradt, this book's publisher, with much backpacking experience, says that this remains the toughest hike she's ever made.

Roberto *looks* like a jungle-savvy fellow who can sniff out trouble before it happens. I simply would not advise making the trip without him or another experienced local guide. Besides Bonampak, Roberto will take you on a two-day trip that includes a visit to the very nice cascades of Loma Bonita and the submerged Maya ruins in Lake Miramar (US$100 per person); a one-day trip to the Loma Bonita cascades costs US$50 per person.

Chinkultic

Archeological orientation
Chinkultic is a modest ruin from the 6th and 7th centuries, which places it in the Classic Period. On the grounds you can see a ball court, some temple platforms, a spring, and the principal pyramid with the remains of three altars.

Logistics
From the turn-around at Doña María's restaurant, the road to Chinkultic lies nine kilometers (5.6 miles) up the road toward La Trinitaria; the entrance road itself is about three kilometers (1.8 miles) long. Though it's easy to catch a *cumbe* to the ruin's entrance, if you don't have your own car, you'll probably end up walking the last three kilometers. Doña María's brothers work as custodians at Chinkultic so if you're patronizing her establishment, you'll find yourself especially welcome there. If you're interested in touring a 300-year-old colonial house you might ask the brothers about a visit. Part of Doña María's family lives in that house, which stands near the ruin. After being in this area for a while you feel that if you count Doña María among your friends, it's like having a "Key to the City."

SAN CRISTÓBAL DE LAS CASAS

General information
Throughout this book cities and "touristy places" are practically ignored. However, though San Cristóbal de las Casas (founded in 1528) falls squarely into both categories, at this writing it's managed to retain enough *soul*, and even a modicum of class, to receive honorable mention. Part of its attraction is the beautiful setting, with mountains all around; part is its being a place with real, back-country

Indian-folk constantly streaming into and out of town; part is the relatively high caliber of traveler who gravitates there, and part is the relative tranquillity with regard to political and social problems.

In San Cristóbal, I remember one chilly evening in the Zócalo huddling with a special friend, sitting, talking, watching the world *pasear* while from loudspeakers mounted on *flamboyán* trees at the park's corners Chopin was played from a scratchy record. We were nibbling steamy-hot, roasted *elotes* drenched in lemon juice and sprinkled with salt and chili, bought from an old Indian lady. Sparrows cavorted among the park's trees, and firecracker-rockets sent from atop El Mirador were exploding high in the sky... San Cristóbal is full of moments like this.

Logistics

San Cristóbal enjoys good connections with the outside world. The first-class bus line called Cristobal Colon provides service all the way from Mexico City's eastern terminal (the San Lázaro stop on the Observatorio/Zaragoza Metro run) to San Cristóbal. Notice that you do not leave from Mexico City's southern terminal, which seems most logical.

Frequently the direct bus from Mexico City to San Cristóbal is full so you must be content with a ticket to Tuxtla Gutiérrez, Chiapas's capital and largest city. Buses from Tuxtla to San Cristóbal always are crowded or even full, so in Tuxtla you may have to wait a few hours for the next empty seat. If you're able to take the night bus from Mexico City you'll arrive in Tuxtla late the next morning and probably get into San Cristóbal at about dusk after hours of waiting and aggravation in hot, dusty, industrialized Tuxtla. Among other key Cristobal Colon stations with good connections to San Cristóbal are one in Ciudad Cuauhtémoc on the Guatemalan border, in Comitán (located on the main highway), and in the town of Palenque.

Immediately upon your arrival in San Cristóbal young men may approach you offering free info about cheap pensions and hotels. Certainly they have some bargains. If you want to scout the town yourself, just step across the knee-high concrete barrier at the Cristobal Colon station, turn right onto Avenida Insurgentes, and walk north for about seven blocks until reaching the Zócalo (park). For a double room the fancy **Hotel de Ciudad Real** on the Zócalo charges about US$26.00. Four blocks away a really dingy room hardly bigger than a bed, with a communal bath, costs US$2.25. At this writing San Cristóbal is home to four four-star hotels, eleven three-star ones, five two-star ones, three that admit to being one-star, and several with no stars.

One aspect of San Cristóbal's traveler-friendly attitude is that though it's a smallish town, it has two laundromats — the Laundromat

Lava Sec at Crescencio Rosas #12, and the Lavorama at Guadalupe Victoria #20-A. In the one-star Hotel Real del Valle, ask about renting a bike.

Two places in town offer camping. The most accessible is **Rancho San Nicolas** about one kilometer (⅔-mile) east of town at the very end of the street called Francisco León (head two blocks south from the Zócalo, toward the Cristobal Colon station, and turn left). Here pitching a tent costs US$1.35 per person; cabañas on the hillside costs US$2.00 per person and rooms with private baths and hot water cost US$3.35. Here also you can rent horses for about US$5.00 per hour, or else rent them from 0800 to 1500 for about US$13.75.

The other campground, more oriented toward RV's needing hookups than tent-campers (but accepting tenters), is at **Restaurante el Campestre** three kilometers (two miles) west of town, beyond the Periférico Pte., on the road designated as Diag. R. Larrainzar, but frequently called *la carretera a Chamula*. *Cumbres* passing the campground originate at San Cristóbal's *mercado*; just ask for *los cumbres a San Juan Chamula*. At Restaurante el Campestre you can pitch a tent for US$1.00; with an RV it costs about US$2.70 per person, with hook-ups. One special attraction at Restaurante el Campestre is a steam bath.

About 1.5km (one mile) farther up the highway (thus also accessible by *los cumbres a San Juan Chamula*) lies one of the most interesting nature-oriented spots around San Cristóbal — the Reserva Ecológica PRONATURA. PRONATURA is Mexico's most successful environmental organization, frequently working on joint projects with the World Wildlife Fund, Nature Conservancy and Wildlife Conservation International. Here at Km 3.5 on *la carretera a Chamula* the mountain called Cerro de Huitepec is protected as a nature reserve and provided with an interpretive trail two kilometers (1¼ miles) long. Cassette tape players can be rented and carried along, describing what's what. Officially the reserve is open from 0900 to 1700. However, I arrived at 1000 on a Monday morning and it was closed; perhaps before your visit you should give them a call at 8-06-97.

Back in San Cristóbal, the Oficina de Turismo is located in the Palacio Municipal, on the Zócalo's west side. Here you may be able to pick up the free English/Spanish shopping guide called *Aquí San Cristóbal!* Though mostly it's filled with tourist-oriented advertisements for everything from pizzas to spirulina algae, and travel agencies to spiritual advisors, also it includes interesting historical information about the area, important telephone numbers and a map of San Cristóbal. Some of San Cristóbal's bookstores are good. The post office lies one block southwest of the Zócalo, at the corner of Cuauhtémoc and 16 de Septiembre. The public telephone, Casetas

A Visit to Reserva Ecológica PRONATURA

Oak trees (genus *Quercus*) predominate in Cerro de Huitepec's hillside forests; here are some of the oak species: *Q. peduncularis, Q. laurina, Q. candicans, Q. rugosa, Q. crassifolia* and *Q. crispipilis*.

A fine assortment of birds can be spotted here. For example, among the "exotics" are the mountain trogon, black-throated jay, blue-throated motmot, brown-backed solitaire, gray silky-flycatcher, crescent-chested warbler, ruddy-capped nightingale-thrush and green violet-ear. During the northern winter some overwintering species are familiar to North Americans, who know them as summer visitors. These include the Townsend's and Wilson's warbler. Other species are distributed from North American oak/pine zones to here. These include Steller's jay, Northern flicker (red-shafted form) and the acorn woodpecker.

Certain other bird species look familiar to northerners because their genus is represented farther north, but in reality San Cristóbal's birds are different species. For example, the rufous-collared robin looks, acts and sounds like the typical American robin, except that its red breast expands onto the nape, creating a necklace. The black robin similarly acts like the American robin, but it looks almost exactly like the European blackbird — except for its yellow legs.

Most of the reserve's mammals are nocturnal, so probably you won't see many. However, the diurnal Chiapas gray squirrel (*Sciurus griseoflavus*) frequently is seen among the oaks, and sometimes you can spook up the Chiapan race of the cottontail rabbit (*Sylvilagus floridanus*); other species that are more strictly nocturnal include the *tlacuache/* opossum (*Didelphis marsupialis*), *comadreja/* weasel (*Mustela frenata*), and various species of *musaraña/* shrews and *roedor/* mice and rats.

At the reserve's entrance gate stands a sign on which information is given in Tzotzil, the main indigenous language of the area. I can't translate what the words say, but I put them here just so you can see what a Maya language looks like:

> *A li te'etik xchi'uk li sat vo'etik li'e sk'an*
> *jtuk'ulantik ta jkotoltik*
> *A li te'etik xchi'uk li sat vo'etik li'e sk'an*
> *an me jk'eltik ta jkotoltik*

PRONATURA produces a quarterly newsletter, in English, called *Biodiversity*. If you are interested in becoming involved with PRONATURA's projects, contact:
PRONATURA
Joann M. Andrews
Calle 13 No. 203-A, Col. García Ginerés
Mérida, Yucatán

Tel. LADATEL, is in the Palacio Municipal. You can even fax something back home at the Telegraph Office about three blocks west of the Zócalo on Diego de Mazariegos.

Na-Bolom is a museum, open Tuesdays through Sundays, at Avenida Vicente Guerrero No. 33, a healthy hike to the northeastern corner of town. From the Zócalo walk north on Gral. Utrilla (toward the *mercado*) to the street called Chiapa de Corzo; turn right and walk to the end. Na-Bolom is the creation of Trudy Blom, Swiss wife of famed archeologist Frans Blom, and a photographer who has spent a long life photographing this part of the world, especially the Lacandón Indians. A few years ago a film about Trudy Blom's life and work made the rounds in Europe and North America so now Na-Bolom is something of a pilgrimage destination for her fans. In the museum tour you'll see many of her works and after the tour the film *La Reina de la Selva* is shown — "The Queen of the Jungle." For those involved in serious study of this part of the world and/or its people, Na-Bolom provides access to its Fray Bartolomé Library. For US$46/day, full board, you can stay in Na-Balom's guest house; prior reservations essential. Conversations around Trudy Blom's dining table can be nothing less than wonderful.

Other spots worth wandering to include the small museum and library called the Centro Cultural de los Altos de Chiapas about seven blocks north of the Zócalo, up 20 de Noviembre Street (toward the *mercado*). The museum of regional costumes (Museo de Trajes Regionales) lies about four blocks northwest of the Zócalo, on 16 de Septiembre Street. Especially at dawn and dusk, a climb up the *Mirador* — the church-topped hill southwest of the Zócalo — makes a fine walk. From the Zócalo, walk south on Insurgentes for three blocks, then right on Hnos. Domínguez. This street leads to a very long series of steps and resting spots; at the top you have a fine view.

San Cristóbal's *mercado*, about nine blocks north of the Zócalo on Gral. Utrilla, is cluttered, chaotic, odoriferous, and full of good-tasting fruits and vegetables, as well as all the other items good Latin *mercados* offer.

THE TZOTZIL HIGHLANDS AROUND SAN CRISTÓBAL

In this book's section on highland Guatemala I advise against going to where foreign visitors are uncommon. With this approach we avoid the problem of our presence having a negative impact on the indigenous culture around us. In some of the world's more remote destinations, this problem has developed into a dark side to eco-tourism. With regard to the Tzotzil Highlands around San Cristóbal we must address the issue.

On page 239 you see a map of the Tzotzil Highlands. It's a neat little

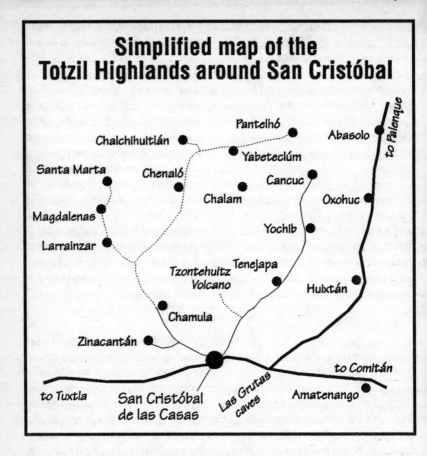

Simplified map of the Totzil Highlands around San Cristóbal

to Palenque

Pantelhó

Chalchihuitlán

Abasolo

Santa Marta   Chenaló

Yabeteclúm

Cancuc

Oxohuc

Magdalenas

Chalam

Larrainzar

Yochlb

Tzontehuitz
Volcano

Tenejapa

Huixtán

Chamula

Zinacantán

to Comitán

to Tuxtla   San Cristóbal
de las Casas

Las Grutas
caves

Amatenango

map that makes traveling into the highlands north of San Cristóbal *look* easy; early in the morning, just hike down to the second-class bus station near where Allende enters the main road, buy a ticket, and go... But, it's not that simple. Roads and connections to the more distant towns are not good and little "touristic infrastructure" is in place. More importantly, the towns on that map are not Disneyland representations of something, but rather the real things, where real Indian-folk struggle to survive, economically as well as spiritually, as Native Americans. Moreover, some Tzotzil speakers regard the outside world with resentment and fear — a mix of emotions that can cause volatile and dangerous conditions for travelers.

Generally the Tzotzil speakers are fervently religious, with beliefs manifesting strong influences of Catholicism upon their ancient doctrines; in 1869 they crucified a boy, desiring to have their own Christ. Nowadays when conservative priests try to "purify" the Tzotzil-speakers' rites, they meet with vigorous resistance and, sometimes, force. Tzotzil speakers who abandon the old ways are ostracized.

Hilary Bradt says that when she was there in 1969 a lone hiker was murdered; one popular guidebook repeats the story that I could not confirm that a while back two tourists were murdered for taking pictures in San Juan Chamula's church.

At this writing a permit for photography in this area is officially required. You can buy your permit, and get updated information on travel in the highlands, at the Tourism Office in San Cristóbal (in the Palacio Municipal next to the Zócalo). Don't let the Tourist Office's promotional, Chamber-of-Commerce attitudes lull you into believing that visiting these places is just "standard tourism." In the official little pamphlet issued by the Mexican Secretaría de Turismo, called *Estado de Chiapas*, some of these towns are described as if they were roadside tourist-traps.

If you do visit the more distant towns, before you leave, you should talk to other travelers to gather impressions and news from that area, and maybe you also need to do some "emotional engineering" inside yourself. Prepare yourself for a kind of spiritual journey and simply don't go if the root feeling causing your interest is anything other than respect for the people and land you are about to enter...

It should be clear that many people in this area resent picture-taking. My opinion is that enlightened eco-tourism in places like this is best realized without a camera. As you travel along, take mental pictures. In contrast to regular snapshots, the colors, clarity and significance of mental pictures only intensify with age.

Finally, I want to admit that I feel queasy encouraging people to go into this area, for I know that a certain percentage of visitors will always be rude and insensitive. Therefore, why do I even include this section? It's because tourists do spend money, and money is desperately needed in these little villages. Also, I know that among the readers of this book a much higher percentage of people will be of the compassionate and sympathetic kind than among the general tourist population. Perhaps, together, we can bring some light to this potentially dark face of eco-tourism that sometimes is labeled "cultural erosion."

ZINACANTÁN

Zinacantán can be visited in cumbes from San Cristóbal's market; if you have other means to get there you'll see that on the same road going to the PRONATURA reserve (Guadalupe Victoria), for Zinacantán when you come to the Y at Kilometer 7 you take the left; four more kilometers brings you to Zinacantán. Here the churches of San Lorenzo and San Sebastián constitute one of the town's attractions (not terribly special); otherwise the main reasons for visiting this town are to enjoy the scenery en route, and to meet the people, who are famous for their gaudy dress. "Meet the people." To be honest, though many tourists do make it to Zinacantán, most inhabitants of this town still haven't made peace with the fact; they don't seem terribly happy having their town invaded. Most tourists go there to see women and girls wearing pink shawls embroidered with floral patterns and tinsel, and men in pink ponchos adorned with tassels. But, going to Zinacantán just for this reason is like visiting Celestún just to see the flamingos. Go to Zinacantán because during the trip you pass through some beautiful countryside, and because when you get there you wish to rejoice in, among other things, a certain earth-rooted flamboyance you've not experienced in mankind before. Photography in Zinacantán is totally forbidden. Elevation 2,250 meters (7,380 feet).

SAN JUAN CHAMULA

You get to San Juan Chamula the same way you get to Zinacantán, except when the Y appears at Kilometer 7, you go right instead of left. As in Zinacantán, the Tzotzil-speakers are fairly accustomed to seeing foreigners wandering around, and neither are they exceedingly tickled about it. In Chamula, population about 400, the main thing to see is the church and the rituals performed inside; but do not take pictures inside the church. You'll probably need to pay admission to the church; a policeman either will accompany you inside or meet you there. Outside the church you may be accosted by young people wanting money for being photographed, which usually is permitted. Probably you'll also have a chance to buy some of the fine weavings and little *muñecos*, or stick-dolls, dressed in traditional Tzotzil costume, for which Chamula is famous.

During Easter ceremonies the Chamulans are especially sensitive about picture-taking. Photo-taking is not permitted during processions. Men carrying sticks see that the rules are enforced. In nearby San Andrés people have been arrested for disturbing the peace by photographing in the *mercado*; the fine can be pretty stiff; the jail is terrible. These rules, and the methods of enforcing them, change from time to time, so don't depend on what's written here or in other guidebooks to prepare you for your visit. Again, talk around, and at San Cristóbal's Tourist Office tell them what you want to do, where you're going, and ask what permits are required, and once you've done all this, even then know that during your upcoming trip you need to stay alert and exercise uncommonly good sense and sensitivity.

San Juan Chamula lies at about 2,200 meters (7,200 feet) above sea level.

MITONTIC

Lying 18km (11 miles) from San Cristóbal, on a dirt road beyond Chamula, this town is more conservative and traditional than most; weavings and pottery are produced.

CHENALHÓ

This is the region's administrative and ceremonial center where Tzotzil-speakers meet to elect their government. Market days are on Sunday. *Carnaval* is celebrated from February 20th to the 23rd.

CHENALÓ

Among all the towns off the main road, Chenaló may be the most congenial to outsiders; for about a dollar a night you can stay in the **Casa de Don Alberto Aguilar**, about two blocks north and one block east of the plaza; it's the pink house with green pillars. About 2km from town the Río San Pedro disappears into a cave inside which the water is knee-deep. At 0500 each morning, at Don Alberto's, the bus leaves for San Cristóbal.

CHALCHIHUITÁN

Lying 45 bumpy kilometers (28 miles) from San Cristóbal, Chalchihuitán is a town of farmers, weavers and pot-makers. Its market days are on Thursdays and Sundays and its main festival is *carnaval*, celebrated 15 days before Ash Wednesday. Elevation 1,760 meters (5,776 feet).

AMATENANGO DEL VALLE

On the main road to Comitán, 37 km (23 miles) east of San Cristóbal, Amatenango is more easily accessible than the above towns, and its inhabitants are fairly accustomed to visitors. If you visit there any way other than in a car probably you'll feel frustrated because the town's specialty is pottery — items not traveling well on crowded buses. Besides the usual pots and trays, also produced are animal figures colored ocher, brown and black.

GRUTAS DE SAN CRISTÓBAL

General information

Grutas are caves. Lying just ten kilometers (six miles) southeast of San Cristóbal, these *grutas* are accessible by numerous second-class buses traveling between Comitán and San Cristóbal. For the camper and amateur naturalist this spot provides more than just a well-lighted, walkway-equipped fifteen-minute stroll in a cave full of stalagmites, stalactites and other cave features; the park around the cave comprises a large pine forest crisscrossed with a network of trails good for hiking and horseback riding.

Though hiking in this forest is exceptionally pleasant, especially on sunny days when cool winds sigh through the pines, from the naturalist's point of view species diversity here is strikingly low; pines really dominate. Just enough oaks are present to support an occasional acorn woodpecker. Sometimes a raven or sparrow hawk soars overhead.

If you're looking for unguided, easy, beginner-level horseback riding, maybe there's no better spot on the Ruta Maya than here. To rent a horse, hang around the park's entrance at the edge of the meadow on the valley floor, in front of the barrier across the gravel road leading into the woods, toward the cave. The horse-renting man has no office; you just have to find him or be found according to standard hit-or-miss procedures. Thirty horses are available, each renting for about US$3.35 per hour. If you want a guide, you need to negotiate, for there's no standard fee. Remember that back at the campground in San Cristóbal horses cost US$5.00/hour.

Passing through the barrier to the park's wooded area costs, with a horse, about 70¢; on foot, it's free; a ticket for the cave costs only 35¢. Though over seven kilometers (4.3 miles) of the cave have been explored, at this writing only a small section at the mouth is open to the public because the boardwalk has collapsed.

Camping in the park is free. Simply take the gravel road to the cave and nearby restaurant, and then follow any access road or trail in any direction into the forest. During my visit I was the only camper in the park; literally thousands of excellent tent-pitching spots were available throughout the forest. A restaurant is available near the cave's entrance, maintaining the park's only bathroom; nearby no markets or *comedores* are handy.

If you do walk or ride a horse along the park's trails, make a special effort to keep yourself oriented; the network of look-alike trails is confusing. However, staying oriented is easy if from the first you take a fix on the tall mountain to the south; also, sometimes you can hear diesel trucks on the main highway to the north. At this writing the Mexican army is establishing a large camp two or three kilometers southeast of the park's entrance (toward Comitán) so it can be assumed that in the future security around the camp will be tight; also it can be imagined that sometimes off-duty soldiers will wander through the forest. You should keep these points in mind when choosing your camp's location, and leaving your camp unattended.

OCOSINGO

General Information

Ocosingo is the main town between San Cristóbal and Palenque; if you hear a Maya language in Ocosingo, probably it's Tzeltal. Cheese connoisseurs should know that Ocosingo is famous for its *quesos de bola* — its cheese balls. A surprising number of no-star lodging places are available, as well as bank services and average-class restaurants. There's nothing touristy and nothing similar to the awkward Indian-versus-tourist situation of the Tzotzil uplands; this is just a fine Mexican town where genuine hospitality is the rule. The town's main *fiesta* is La Fiesta de la Candelaria, from February 1st to the 5th, emphasizing cattle and agricultural products. La Fiesta del Patrono San Jacinto is from August 13th to the 15th. Ruta-Maya'ers mainly stop in Ocosingo because it's the entrance town to the ruin of Toniná.

TONINÁ

Archeological orientation
From atop Toniná's pyramid-top temples you can enjoy a tremendous view of the Ocosingo Valley; the whole site occupies seven terraces carved into the valley's northern slope. The buildings themselves are not spectacular; most interesting are the carved stones and stelae scattered here and there about the site, and in the little museum/office/ticket booth. The best carvings are crammed into the museum.

Logistics
At this writing no regular bus service is scheduled to anywhere near the ruin. Since a fair amount of traffic uses the road maybe by the time you get there buses will be available. Ask at Ocosingo's open-air terminal area, which lies on the main road skirting the up-slope part of town. One second-class bus, reading CENSO in its destination window, does travel about three kilometers (two miles) of the distance; however, this lets you off next to a left-pointing sign reading *"Ruinas de Toniná 11 Km"* Eleven kilometers amounts to almost seven miles; and for hikers, a hot, humid, weedy, uninspiring seven miles it is.

Taxi service between Ocosingo and Toniná can be arranged at the Zócalo for about US$7.00. Another option for getting to the ruins is to visit the *mercado* around mid-morning, when the area's produce trucks have finished unloading and visiting, and look for someone heading toward the ruins. *"¿Hay una camioneta aquí que esta mañana va rumbo a la ruina de Toniná?"* — "Is there a truck here that this morning is heading toward Toniná?" Curiously, though Toniná is on the itinerary of every tour-operating travel agency in San Cristóbal and Palenque, it's surprising how many Ocosingoans haven't the foggiest notion about anything called Toniná. If your question draws a blank look, just ask someone else.

THE CASCADES OF AGUA AZUL

General information

Between San Cristóbal and Agua Azul the Ruta Maya crosses the Central Plateau; Agua Azul lies along the Plateau's northern boundary. You can think of Agua Azul's cascades as representing the point at which streams placidly flowing northward across the level Central Plateau suddenly begin tumbling over the plateau's rim.

Agua Azul's cascades are truly cascades, not high waterfalls; nor are they particularly rambunctious cascades. However, that's one of the nice things about them. They're spectacular enough to be interesting, yet small and friendly enough to play with. Swim, wade, sit near them and read... When the sunshine mingles with their sparkling bluish waters (*agua azul* means blue water), it's almost hypnotically inviting. The most spectacular fall lies about four kilometers (2½ miles) below camp, accessible by a trail along the river.

Logistics

Agua Azul has become a real "destination"; walk into any travel agency in Palenque or San Cristóbal and they'll have ways to get you there in fancy buses at fancy prices. In Palenque, at the Chambalo *cumbe* service (see section on Palenque), at 1000 and 1300 *cumbes* leave for Agua Azul, costing about US$5.00. Most regular buses running between San Cristóbal and Palenque stop at Agua Azul; tickets on them cost about a dollar. The cascades are 56km (35 miles) from Ocosingo and about 62km (36 miles) from Palenque.

Since the trip from Palenque takes only about 1½ hours, on a regular bus you can leave Palenque early in the morning, spend the day at Agua Azul, and return the same day. Palenque's *Cumbes* carry their passengers all the way to the falls, but if you arrive on a regular bus you'll be deposited about four kilometers (2½ miles) short of your destination. The walk from the bus stop to the falls is entirely, and steeply, downhill; it takes about an hour to walk.

No hotels operate in Agua Azul at this time, but camping is excellent both for tenters and RV'ers (no hook-ups). The ticket to enter the area in a car costs US$1.65; by foot it costs about 65¢. Camping costs US$1.65 per person, and renting a hammock slung in a *palapa* costs the same, though if you want a mosquito net over your hammock it costs about US$3.35. The horse-renter said that his horses cost about US$10.00 per hour, which is far too expensive; maybe he was just joking; try negotiation. Two restaurants are available. A meal of scrambled eggs, beans, rice, tortillas and coffee costs about US$1.65; most of the time local folks are circulating, peddling bananas and other fruits.

MISOL-HA

General information
At about Km 46, a bit farther north on Hwy 190 toward Palenque, Misol-Ha is a natural swimming hole formed beneath a 30-meter (hundred-foot) cascade. At this writing it's very pretty and hardly developed at all, but they're building some bungalows right next to the pool, so who knows what it'll be like by the time you get there?

Palenque

Archeological orientation
Palenque is a Classic-Period ruin famous for its well-preserved buildings, carved stucco ornamentation, fine bas-reliefs and extensive hieroglyphic texts. In 1952, deep inside Palenque's Temple of the Inscriptions, one of Maya archeology's greatest discoveries was made when the tomb of Pacal the Great (died around 683 AD) was opened by its Mexican discoverer, archeologist Alberto Ruz.

Before you descend the Temple of the Inscriptions's interior steps to see the tomb yourself, you might want to read the riveting account of the tomb's exploration. The story is told in Thompson's *The Rise and Fall of Maya Civilization* (page 77, with drawings), Coe's *The Maya* (page 104), and on page 755 of the December, 1975 issue of *National Geographic* magazine. Accompanying Pacal the Great's corpse was a treasure-trove of jade, including a life-sized mosaic mask. Pieces of jade were held in each hand and another piece was placed in his mouth — a custom not only of the Yucatec Maya and the Aztec, but also of the ancient Chinese... Also found were pottery vessels and two sensitively modelled stucco heads. Five young victims had been slaughtered outside Pacal's door to serve him in the hereafter.

When you enter Pacal's tomb you'll see a great slab of carved limestone serving as the sarcophagus's lid. On this slab stands a portrait of Pacal himself, apparently descending into the jaws of an underworld monster. Notice that one of his toes has a nick in it. Supposedly this is no slip of the artist's chisel, but rather a real-life portrayal of Pacal's split toe — a congenital defect. Pacal also is depicted in two portraits as having a clubfoot. These deformities may have been caused by repeated inbreeding within the royal family. It's believed that Pacal continued the tradition by marrying his sister, Ahpo Hel.

An abundance of Maya-oriented literature is available next to Palenque's entrance gate, and fine English-speaking guides will lead you around.

Logistics

Both the town near the ruins and the ruins themselves are known as Palenque, though sometimes the town is referred to as Santo Domingo or Santo Domingo de Palenque. Several bus-lines serve the town so getting there is simple. If on your way to Palenque you must change buses in Villahermosa, remember that sometimes when you can't buy a first-class ticket to Palenque, you can walk a few blocks to the second-class station and immediately get what you want. To find the second-class station ask, *"¿Puede usted decirme donde está el caminero central de segunda clase?"*

Cross section of Palenque's Temple of the Cross showing a corbelled vault

The ruins of Palenque lie about eight kilometers (five miles) south of town. In and around town lodging of every price and degree of luxury is available. At this writing the town map available from the Tourist Office on the ground floor of the Palacio Municipal lists sixteen hotels and posadas, and this doesn't include some big ones on the outskirts of town.

Connections between town and the ruins are excellent. Throughout the day, about every ten minutes, *cumbes* travel back and forth; the map of Palenque shows the *cumbe*-leaving places on Calle Allende. One-way passage costs about 33¢. One of the most pleasant things about the Palenque area is that there's more to do here than just visit the ruin. In fact, some people spend weeks within a couple of kilometers of the ruins, without even visiting them. Many of these folks hang out at the **Maya Bell**.

Anyplace along the Ruta Maya, if you ask a youngish backpacking veteran if he or she has been to Palenque yet, there's a chance that the reply will be, "You mean, have I been among the mushroom eaters at Maya Bell?" This is one of those code-conversations that people sometimes have to establish understandings quantum-leapishly.

Maya Bell is a campground near the Palenque ruins. In town just take a ruin-bound *cumbe* and after passing the customs check between town and the ruins say "Maya Bell" to the driver; then when you're let out, prepare yourself to walk into the grounds looking *cool*. For Maya Bell is a *happening*. When you enter, maybe you'll hear bongo drums, and people will be running around looking as if they're trying out for parts in a 60s hippie movie. Dig? Mary Jo who's an accountant in LA 335 days of the year, now lounges in a hammock, dangling a leg adorned with Maya-style ankle-bracelets, and blowing smoke-rings. (Alriiiight! Wow!) At first every visitor at Maya Bell is an outsider, but if you stay a couple of days and squish enough mud between your toes you become a member and when you leave someone smelling of wood smoke and garlic will probably hug you real good.

On the other hand, Maya Bell also has its share of straight-laced RV'ers not taking part in any of this. In fact, the big influx of young hippy types in the Palenque area has provoked at least a small conservative backlash. The federal police are known occasionally to manifest their authority by being very strict about such things as the law that you must keep your tourist card in your possession at all times. Moreover, it's just good eco-tourism never to look or behave too far-out. Small-town Mexico's store owners and housewives deserve the same respect we afford the San Cristóbal highland's Tzotzil speakers.

Anyway, one delightful thing about Maya Bell, besides the fact that it costs only US$1.35 to pitch a tent, is that it's right next to a forest; you can sit on a bank at the edge of the sloping campground and spot bird-species typically considered to be denizens of rather

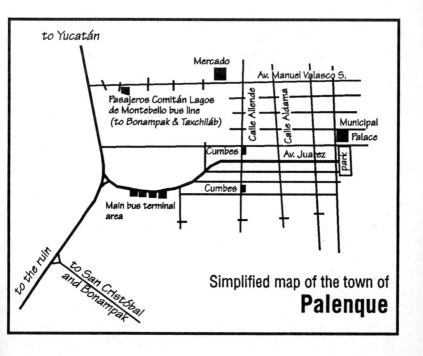

Simplified map of the town of
Palenque

The Mushroom Eaters at Maya Bell

Take a walk down some of the back roads around the Maya Bell and little kids will run out offering plastic bags of blackish, desiccated specimens of a mushroom they've collected from drying pads of cow dung in the area's pastures; selling "magic mushrooms" has been a lucrative business around Palenque since the 70's when hordes of hippies invaded the area looking for various kinds of "high."

The fungus of interest belongs to the genus *Psilocibe* — probably it's *P. cubensis*. *Psilocibe* mushrooms are hallucinogenic because they contain the toxin psilocybin, a member of the lysergic acid (LSD) family of hallucinogenic compounds, which are known to produce visions, smothering sensations and optical distortions. As little as 5mg (1.2 oz) of certain *Psilocibe* species have been known to cause visual hallucinations in 15 minutes, so it's assumed that eating large quantities would be fatal. Lacandón Indians have been documented using *P. cubensis* in their rituals; Mixtec, Zapotec and Mixe populations in Oaxaca are known to eat hallucinogenic mushrooms.

Why do mushrooms have hallucinogenic compounds in them? General wisdom is that such toxins are part of a plant's arsenal of weapons used in chemical warfare against animals that want to eat them. Maybe the mushroom's strategy is simply to scramble nerve impulses in an animal so that it will stop eating it. In the broad scheme of things, probably the fact that humans hallucinate on small quantities of *Psilocibe* is simply incidental — rather like the fact that we glimpse "stars" when we're hit over the head with a blunt object.

Discussing the effects of eating psilocybin, Orson K. Miller, Jr. in *Mushrooms of North America* (E. P. Dutton, New York, 1978) writes, "Perhaps the most important factor is the presence of other toxic compounds *in addition* (his italics) to the hallucinogenic agent in a given species." In other words, the mushroom eaters at Maya Bell are playing with fire, for who knows what poisons other than the hallucinogenic agent are attacking the body? In Andean communities where people eat peanuts contaminated with mould (which is fungus, like mushrooms), a high incidence of liver cancer exists.

For more information on the Maya use of hallucinogens, see "The Influence of Psychotropic Flora and Fauna on Maya Religion" by Marlene Dobkin de Rios in *Current Anthropology*, Vol 15, No. 2, June 1974, pp. 147 to 164.

---

undisturbed rain forest. Sometimes at dawn and dusk howler monkeys roar in the distance.

About 750 meters (half a mile) up the road from Maya Bell (toward the ruin and about 50 meters past the little hotel on the right) as you walk along the road, on the left you'll hear rushing water; next to the stream some well-worn footpaths lead into the forest. Following these trails up the hill about 50 meters brings you to some beautiful little pools of remarkably clear, cool water. Each pool is contained behind a dike-like mineral rim; the mineral is travertine, one of the many varieties of Calcite, $CaCO_3$.

Just think of the eons required for these travertine rims to grow the way they have. Because of their proximity to the main ruins (only about 200 meters!) I can imagine that to the ancient Maya they must have been very important, for in nature such lovely and strange pools are rare; if they're found at all, they're usually in caves. By the way, once you're at the pools, don't wander up the steep trails leading to the right; they lead right into the ruin's main grounds, and entering this area without a ticket is strictly forbidden. Of course guards circulate all the time.

An excellent hike is the one to the village of **Naranjo**. After buying a ticket and entering the ruin grounds, face the Temple of Inscriptions. On its left side you should see some steep stone steps leading up the densely forested hill. Climb the steps and continue ascending away from the plaza area and the temple, keeping parallel with the small stream on your left. About 50 meters up the path you'll encounter a small temple with a good view of the stream, and therefore constituting a nice spot at which to sit and bird-watch.

If you continue on this path — well worn from centuries of foot traffic — after six kilometers (four miles) you'll have crossed a sizable hill and come to a stream called the Río Chacamás and the small settlement of Adolfo López Mateo. Ford the stream and soon you'll reach the town of Naranjo, which is large enough to support a store.

The first part of this trail climbs quite steeply for a surprisingly long while; when it's wet, the stones are dangerously slick. However, during the climb several spots provide excellent views into surrounding treetops, so it's easy to add species to your bird list. You may even be lucky enough to spot some howler monkeys.

The main "problem" for bird watchers on this route is that so many native walkers from Naranjo pause to talk. They're so friendly that you feel ashamed to remain taciturn and evasive! Besides, it's fun and interesting to talk to them. During my last trip I was surprised to find that most people walking this trail believe that the keel-billed toucan and the collared araçari (both common here) are the same species; they say that the colorful keel-billed is the male and the plainer araçari is the female! Both birds are members of the toucan family, but they're in entirely different genera; the keel-billed toucan sports a rainbow-colored beak and yellow cheeks while the collared araçari's beak is black and white, and its cheeks are black. Actually, local people, even Indians, very often have false notions about the plants and animals around them; they'll tell you that every snake you see is poisonous! Sometimes I get the impression that they consider general nature lore the exclusive domain of healers and "backward" farmers.

When you're ready to end your day at Naranjo, either you can hike back on the route you came, or else take a roundabout, hill-avoiding gravel road that for ten kilometers (six miles) courses among pastures. Eventually this road connects with the paved highway between the ruins and town; you meet the road across from the footpaths leading up the hill to the travertine-dike pools. Before embarking on the ten-kilometer gravel road you might inquire as to whether the streams you must ford are low enough to be waded across: *"Caminando, es posible vadear el agua que cubre el camino entre aquí y la carretera?"*

Keel-Billed Toucan
Collared Araçari
Emerald Toucanet

The Northern Lowlands

Bonampak

Archeological orientation

Though Bonampak originally was just an insignificant Late Classic center dominated politically and cultural by nearby Yaxchilán, today it's a favorite destination for those who can afford to fly there, or else endure the strenuous overland trip. The outside world learned about Bonampak in 1946 when Lacandón Indians led some US adventurers and a photographer there. The main find was "the Bonampak murals" — well preserved paintings on the walls of one of the structures. The murals, dated soon after 800 AD, narrate the story of a battle, its aftermath, and the victory celebrations afterwards. Plate 43 in Coe's *The Maya* shows a detail of this now-famous mural, and on page 101 he interprets the various scenes, which include one showing white-robed Maya women drawing blood from their tongues, and another in which a captive obviously pleads for his life, while nearby lies another captive's severed head on a bed of leaves.

Since the structure in which the murals stand was opened the paintings' colors have faded badly. Nonetheless, it's thrilling to stand just inches from these paintings left by artists who lived in times when the fantastic, blood-curdling scenes occurred. The effect is especially powerful because of the ruin's presence in "deep jungle."

Logistics

A grassy runway right next to the ruins permits a visit by air; any travel agency in the Palenque/San Cristóbal/Tuxtla Gutiérrez area will provide the details. At this time, anyone visiting the ruins overland will need to endure ample bumps, mud and/or dust, and a walk through the rain forest. During the rainy season the approximately 160-kilometer (100-mile) gravel road between Palenque and Bonampak is, in many places, an absolute quagmire. During the dry season still a few challenging spots remain, though a four-wheel drive should have few problems, other than for the interminable bumps and dust. During the dry season a bus needs 7½ hours from Palenque to the access road leading to Bonampak; *cumbes* and four-wheel drives need four or five, depending on how fast the driver is willing to hit the bumps.

With the *cumbe* cooperative on Palenque's Calle Allende between Avenida Miguel Hidalgo and Avenida Juárez (see Palenque map) you can make a one-day trip to Bonampak (up early, a lot of hard, bumpy riding, and home late); the cost depends on how many people go. The cooperative expects approximately US$200 to make the trip; if you go with six other people, then, it costs about US$30.00. Even if you're not a member of a party of six and want to go, you can usually find a travel agency with a handwritten sign on its door reading something like,

"We need two more passengers for Bonampak tomorrow." The cooperative also offers two-day trips, which include a voyage down the Usumacinta to the ruin of Yaxchilán. All food and sleeping arrangements are taken care of; this costs about US$85.00 per person, as long as at least five people go. These prices vary a bit, depending on lots of things, not the least of which is road conditions.

Even if you go in a *cumbe* or a tourist bus, you'll still have to walk about ten kilometers (six miles) along a trail that in places can be inordinately muddy. During the wet season when *chiclero* horses packing out chicle chop up the trail the mud becomes knee-deep and can suck off boots and socks. The best I have ever seen the trail was in early March, well into the dry season, when mud in the worst places was still ankle deep.

It's possible to get to Bonampak for even less than the cost of a *cumbe* ticket; my last visit cost US$8.00, round-trip from Palenque. This was by patronizing the second-class bus-line called "Linea de Pasajeros Comitán Lagos de Montebello" on Avenida Manuel Velasco S. about three blocks west of the *mercado* (see Palenque map). Here's how:

Since Bonampak is in a frontier region into which services gradually, erratically and painfully are being expanded, bus schedules change frequently. Thus the day before you plan to leave for Bonampak you should visit the bus office, note the posted schedule, and verbally confirm that on the next day they do indeed intend to leave at the posted time. At this writing, the "Bonampak bus" is the one leaving at 0900 for Frontera Corozal, also known as Echeverría. After about 7½ hours of being shaken quite adequately you'll be deposited at an intersection about 15 kilometers (nine miles) from Bonampak, next to a small community of Lacandón Indians.

From this intersection, walk in a generally southwest direction for about an hour — four kilometers. When the road bends to the right, and on the left a footpath leads into the jungle... that footpath is the trail to Bonampak, as unmarked as you please. At this writing the Lacandóns are clearing a patch of forest to the right of the trail, planning to build a store there, so there's no telling what you'll find at the trail head by the time you get there; maybe nothing. If you continue on the gravel road past the cut-off to Bonampak, in about ten minutes you come to a small stream spanned by a log bridge, signaling that you've walked too far.

If you arrive at the trail head in a car and balk at leaving your vehicle unattended beside the road, speak to the Lacandón folk in Bethel, the community about 500 meters back up the road on which you've just come; go to the first hut on the left. If you offer a proper *gratificación* you may park your vehicle right in front of this hut. Read more about the Lacandón community of Bethel in the section on Lacanhá.

I understand the hesitation one might experience about plunging into the jungle on an unmarked trail, so here are some more remarks about the trail, just to bolster your confidence. At the trail head, right where it meets the gravel road, you'll find black charcoal on the ground, from past campfires. If you pass down the trail for 30 or 50 meters, you'll pass two areas that have been cleared with machetes. *Cumbe* drivers from Palenque park in these shady spots waiting for their passengers to hike to the ruins and back. More than a few campers have pegged tents in these clearings, too. After walking on the footpath for about two hours and fifteen minutes (about 10km) you'll come to a spacious grassy area in which stand permanent barracks and huts, and a tower with no antenna on it. This is the archeologist camp, where Bonampak's custodians stay.

You can peg a tent in this grassy area if you wish — even sleep in the bunkhouse beneath mosquito netting. The custodians won't say what an appropriate *gratificación* might be for permitting such luxury. "*Hasta las gracias son buenas*," one custodian insists — "Even nothing but a thank-you is good." However, in this isolated spot generous *gratificaciones* are particularly appropriate.

If you've been looking for a spot "deep in the jungle" that you can comfortably use as a base as you bird-watch and generally wander around exploring the forest... this is it! If your *gratificaciones* generously reflect an understanding of how difficult it is to maintain such a camp so far from any regular town or paved road, and what an effort it takes to keep the camp attractive for visitors and bring in necessities from the outside, you'll certainly be welcome to stay for several days. On an unofficial, friend-to-friend basis, the custodians and their families will even provide food and other services. Of course, all it will take is a few freeloading visitors to ruin this situation for us all.

Trails course all through the forest around Bonampak; in fact, one of the most interesting possibilities here is to hike all the way to Lagunas de Montebello (see page 238), about 100 air-kilometers (62 miles) to the southwest. Some of the trails lead to unexcavated ruins; if you want to explore them with a guide, talk to Bonampak's custodians, suggest a *gratificación* you're willing to pay, and see what kind of deal you can strike.

One very fine "jungle walk" is to the nearby Río Lacanhá. It's about 45 minutes down a trail so frequently used that even the hiker with only average experience probably won't get lost. Of course, if you do get lost in this area, it'll be a deadly mistake. If you hike the trail to the Río Lacanhá, don't take a single step unless you know beyond all doubt that the trail you're leaving behind is so obvious that, when you return, you'll have no trouble at all following it back. As you're going in, follow your general progress with a compass.

To find where the trail to the Río Lacanhá leaves the ruins, just ask any of the custodians to point it out; it's between the camp and the ruin. Ask, "*¿Puede usted indicarme donde está el camino que va al Río Lacanhá, por favor?*" By the way, probably your Spanish/English dictionary insists that the word *camino* translates to "road" or "highway," and you'll see that the trail to the Río Lacanhá hardly is that. However, in this area where traveling is so strenuous, most folks dignify even a muddy footpath with the word *camino*.

If you'd like guide service to the Lacanhá, you can say, "*Mañana queremos caminar al Río Lacanhá, donde quedamos tres o cuatro horas. ¿Hay alguien aquí para guiarnos? Con mucho gusto regalamos ___ pesos por su servicio.*" — "Tomorrow we want to hike to the Río Lacanhá, where we'll stay for three or four hours. Is there someone to guide us? We'll be happy to offer a gift of ___ pesos for guide service.

The Río Lacanhá is worth the walk because it's a medium-sized river with water so clean and clear that it causes the soul to ache with pleasure. In all my life's travels I've never seen such a large river that looked so perfectly clean! If you submerge yourself in its waters, tropical fish come right up to your nose and peck. You feel like you're in a vast tropical-fish aquarium. For me, visiting the Río Lacanhá has become even more of an attraction than seeing Bonampak's murals.

To arrange a stay in the bunkhouse for a few days, and have meals provided for you, you can say something like, "*¿Está bien si quedamos aquí ___ días y noches? Necesitamos ___ comidas cada día, como de frijoles, arroz, tortillas y a veces huevos. Claro que no queremos incomodarle. ¿Cree usted que basta si le regalamos ___ pesos para cada noche, y ___ pesos para cada ___ comida? Es decir, ___ pesos cada día?*" ("Is it OK if we stay here ___ days and nights? We'll need ___ meals every day; like, beans, rice, tortillas and sometimes eggs. Of course we don't want to inconvenience you. Do you think it'd be satisfactory if we offered as a gift ___ pesos for every day, and ___ pesos for every meal? In other words, ___ pesos every day?") Note that when dealing with ruin custodians you should never use the verb *pagar* — to "pay." The appropriate verb is *regalar*, which means "to offer as a gift."

Another interesting trip to make in this region is to the ruin of Lacanhá. However, instead of crossing the river to get to it from Bonampak, probably the most interesting approach is to hire a Lacandón Indian to guide you...

Lacanhá

Archeological orientation

Lacanhá is a modest classical ruin at which some interesting stelae have been found. The real reason for going there is for the adventure of making the trip.

Logistics

Some years ago when I was writing a book about a Seventh-Day-Adventist hospital serving Chiapas's Indians I met an Adventist Lacandón who caused quite a sensation by arriving at the hospital wearing his traditional long, black hair and white robe. He told me that he lived in the town of Bethel near the entrance to the trail to Bonampak. During my last trip to Bonampak I looked up my old friend and asked if he or any of his friends would be interested in serving as guides for this book's readers.

Now, many travelers think of the Lacandóns as "the most primitive Indian tribe anyplace in Mexico and Central America," and they are rightly concerned about visitors from the outside world "contaminating" these isolated people. Travelers who visit Trudy Blom's Na Bolom in San Cristóbal will be especially sensitive to this issue.

However, for years the Lacandóns more or less have been split into two camps — those who continue to live in fair isolation, and those who already have plunged headlong into mainstream Mexican culture. The Lacandóns around the entrance to Bonampak belong to this latter group. In fact, nearly everyone in the village of Bethel is a member of the Seventh Day Adventist religion. This is an evangelical denomination based in the US; it's enjoyed remarkable success proselytizing Indians all through Chiapas.

Despite the fact that Bethel's Lacandóns continue to wear traditional white gowns and the men keep their hair long, they know all about radio and TV and most of the men have traveled around; some drive cars, and nearly everyone in this community considers his or her membership in the Adventist Church to be as important, or more important, as membership in the Lacandón community. (By the way, I'm not in any way affiliated with the Adventist Church.)

On the day I entered Bethel, I found my friend, broached the subject of a Lacandón serving as a guide, and immediately was taken to the community's elder or chief. By the time we reached the chief's hut nearly the entire community had gathered around us. Effectively I was able to propose the idea at a "town meeting" where the idea was debated from one side to the other. In the end, the chief's son said that if the readers of this book come to Bethel looking for a guide, they should ask him; later, my friend said he'd like to be a guide, too. Therefore, here's how to arrange for a Lacandón guide:

Bethel is the last tiny settlement you passed before arriving at the bend from which the trail to Bonampak departs. When you return to Bethel, you'll see a footpath passing between the two huts nearest the road. At the hut on the left, for the proper *gratificación*, you can leave your vehicle parked, if you have one. In the hut on the right you may spot another of my friends, Sr Antonio Navarro, a near-albino

Bird jaguar, ruler of Yaxchilán, dancing during a ritual suicide; detail from a vase

Lacandón. This man will be your friend forever if you give him some vitamin pills! In fact, the whole community places a high value on vitamins, worm medicine, wound dressings and the like, so you'll be particularly well received if you *regalar* a few such items. The chief's son is Sr José Mallorca, and he should be the person you ask for first. After him, you may ask for me friend, Sr Hidalgo González Chankín, or anyone else.

Bethel is a community of about 37 adults; most of its huts lie away from the road; the large, log building you can just spot from the road, and which you may pass as you go looking for your guides, is the Adventist Temple. *¿Puede usted decirnos donde podemos encontrar a Sr José Mallorca? Buscamos un guía y nos han dicho que él puede ayudarnos,*' you can say when you enter Bethel — 'Can you tell us where we can find Mr José Mallorca? We're looking for a guide and they've told us that he can help us... '

José says that for a day of guiding he needs between twenty and twenty-five dollars. But before you make any proposals you need to understand that quite possibly your idea of what "guiding" is and what his is may be completely different. Fact is, I doubt that during our talk José understood how this tourist-guiding works, other than that he is supposed to go with you someplace. I explained about peoples' interest in medicinal herbs, birds, caves, etc., but I'm not sure he could relate to such concerns.

If you agree to pay José, Hidalgo or any other Lacandón for "guide service," you must keep in mind that possibly all you are paying for is the unique experience of being accompanied to an exotic place by an interesting-looking member of the tribe of Indians internationally recognized as "the most primitive of Mexico and Central America." Also, you'll be paying for the opportunity to be a kind of pioneer in eco-tourism.

Once your experience with a Lacandón guide is ended, perhaps you could give him a to-whom-it-may-concern written recommendation so that later travelers can benefit from knowing how your trip turned out. If you had problems, don't hesitate to at least obliquely refer to them. Let me know how things turn out, too.

At this writing, on the main road between Palenque and Corozal, each morning two or three northwest-bound buses pass the entrance to the gravel road to Bethel and the trailhead to Bonampak, heading back to Palenque; each afternoon two or three buses pass traveling south toward Corozal (the port serving Yaxchilán), and beyond.

Yaxchilán
Archeological orientation
Yaxchilán is a magnificent Classic archeological site that because of

its isolation doesn't see as many visitors as you'd expect. Here stand temples complete with finely carved roof-combs, and doorways with exquisitely carved stone lintels (most Maya cities in the Central Area employed wooden lintels). Though their hieroglyphic texts are highly repetitious, with the same phrases appearing again and again, Yaxchilán's carvings are considered among the finest extant examples of Maya sculpture.

In Thompson's *The Rise and Fall of Maya Civilization*, Plates 12-14 show some of these sculptures; Figure 21 portrays a scene from Yaxchilán's Stela 11, depicting three persons kneeling, probably about to be sacrificed by a richly clad individual wearing the mask of the long-nosed god. According to the famous Russian mayanist Tatiana Proskouriakoff, Stela 11 was erected to mark the accession to power of 43-year-old Bird-Jaguar as ruler of Yaxchilán in 752 AD. A ceremonial court here is 300 meters (1000 feet) long.

Logistics
In the Guatemalan section it's explained how Yaxchilán can be reached via routes originating in Guatemala. From the Chiapas side, it's possible to fly, or use the *cumbe* folks in Palenque who will take you on a two-day trip combining visits to Bonampak and Yaxchilán, for approximately US$85.00 per person (see page 261). However, probably the most interesting way to visit Yaxchilán from Mexico is by *lancha*, from the port of Corozal (also called Echeverría). Here's how:

Arriving in Corozal, the broad gravel road wanders through town quite a bit before aiming at the river. About a kilometer before the river there's a custom's check; you must present all documents, even if you have no intention of entering Guatemala, which forms the Usumacinta's eastern bank. At this custom station you'll need to say whether you're just going to Yaxchilán, and soon returning, or whether you intend to proceed into Guatemala. "*Estamos en Yaxchilán solamente unas horas. Regresamos hoy por la tarde,*" you can say to explain that you're only going to stay for a few hours, and that you'll be returning in the afternoon.

At the river men approach visitors offering *lancha* service to Yaxchilán. They ask about US$65.00 per boatload, but the usual fee after some discussion, if you leave early in the morning and return the same day, is about US$55.00. If you arrive in Corozal too late to leave for Yaxchilán, you can check out the hotel downtown costing about US$10.00, or a cheaper, no-star one near the checkpoint, costing about US$1.65. Corozal's buildings are so dispersed that surely you can arrange to pitch a tent in one of the many open areas.

OTHER BOOKS ON LATIN AMERICA FROM BRADT PUBLICATIONS

No Frills Hiking Guide to Mexico by Jim Conrad with Steven Vale
A handy pocket-sized guide to 33 hikes in six regions.

Backpacking and Trekking in Peru and Bolivia by Hilary Bradt
The classic guide for walkers and nature lovers.

Backpacking in Chile and Argentina (second edition)
Spectacular mountain scenery, well-run national parks, excellent food and wine, good transportation and safe cities. A hiker's and traveller's paradise.

Guide to Venezuela by Hilary Dunsterville Branch
Venezuela offers uncrowded beaches and good snorkelling, splendid mountain walks and a variety of national parks. A guide for eco-tourists.

Climbing and Hiking in Ecuador by Rob Rachowiecki and Betsy Wagenhauser
A thoroughly researched second edition of this highly-regarded guide.

Backcountry Brazil by Alex Bradbury
Three areas are covered in depth: Amazonia, the Pantanal, the north-east coast.

South American River Trips by Tanis and Martin Jordan
How to explore the rivers of South America in your own boat. Full of anecdote and humour, as well as information.

South America Ski Guide by Chris Lizza
Where to ski throughout South America, with the emphasis on the excellent resorts in Chile and Argentina.

Plus maps of every Latin American country.

This is just a selection of the books and maps for adventurous travellers that we stock. Send for our latest catalogue.

Bradt Publications, 41 Nortoft Rd, Chalfont St Peter, Bucks SL9 0LA, England. Tel: 0494 873478.

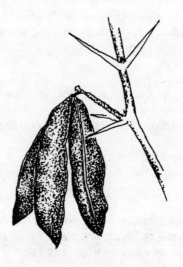

Acacia farnesiana

BIBLIOGRAPHY

BOOKS ON MAYA ARCHEOLOGY

Incidents of Travel in Central America, Chiapas, and Yucatan by John L. Stephens. Originally published in 1841; reprinted 1969, Dover Publications, New York.
Incidents of Travel in Yucatan was published in New York in 1843.

The Maya by Michael D. Coe; 1966, Praeger Publishers, Inc.; New York.

Mexico by Michael D. Coe; 1962, Frederick A. Praeger, Inc., Publishers; New York.

An Outline Dictionary of Maya Glyphs by William Gates; unabridged 1978 republication of 1931 classic; Dover Publications, Inc.; New York.

The Rise and Fall of Maya Civilization by J. Eric S. Thompson; 1954, University of Oklahoma Press; Norman, Oklahoma.

World of the Maya by Victor W. von Hagen; 1960, Mentor Books; New York.

NATIONAL GEOGRAPHIC MAGAZINE
ARTICLES ON MAYA ARCHEOLOGY
(Chronological Order)

"Yucatán, Home of the Gifted Maya" by Sylvanus Griswold Morley. November 1936.

"Into the Well of Sacrifice" by Eusebio Dávalos Hurtado. October 1961.

"Guatemala, Maya and Modern" by Louis de la Haba. November 1974.

"The Maya: Children of Time" by Howard La Fay. December 1975.

"The Maya: Riddle of the Glyphs" by George E. Stuart. December 1975.

"The Maya: Resurrecting the Grandeur of Tikal" by William R. Coe. December 1975.

"The Maya: A Traveler's Tale of Ancient Tikal" by Alice J. Hall. December 1975.

"Río Azul: Lost City of the Maya" by Richard E. W. Adams. April 1986.

"El Mirador: An Early Maya Metropolis Uncovered" by Ray T. Matheny. September 1987.

"The Search for Modern Humans" by John J. Putman. October 1988.

"La Ruta Maya" by Wilbur E. Garrett. October 1989.

"Copán: A Royal Maya Tomb Discovered" by Riccardo Agurcia Fasquelle and William L. Fash, Jr. October 1989.

"City of Kings and Commoners: Copán" by George E. Stuart. October 1989.

"Maya Artistry Unearthed" by Ricardo Agurcia Fasquelle and Wm. L. Fash, Jr. September 1991.

NOTE: In North America, during early 1991, *Natural History* magazine published a series of important articles under the heading of "The Maya Rediscovered".

BOOKS DEALING WITH RUTA MAYA NATURAL HISTORY

Wildlife of Mexico by A. Starker Leopold; 1959, University of California. Available in a softback Spanish edition as *Fauna Silvestre de Mexico* published by Editorial Pax-México, Librería Carlos Césarman, Mexico City, under the auspices of the Instituto Mexicano de Recursos Naturales Renovables.

A Field Guide to the Birds of Mexico by R. T. Peterson and E. L. Chalif; 1973, Houghton Mifflin Co., Boston, Massachusetts.

Finding Birds in Mexico by Ernest P. Edwards; 1968. Published and distributed by the author in Sweet Briar, Virginia.

The Birds of Tikal by Frank B. Smithe; 1966, The Natural History Press; Garden City, New York.

Grzimek's Animal Life Encyclopedia; 1976. This and similar encyclopedias edited by Bernhard Grzimek, and published by Van Nostrand Reinhold Company, New York.

GUIDE BOOKS FOR THE RUTA MAYA AREA

Guide to Belize, by Alex Bradbury; 1993; Hunter Publishing, USA and Bradt Publications, UK.

Bicycling Mexico, by Ericka Weisbroth & Eric Ellman; 1990; Hunter Publishing, Inc., Edison, New Jersey. Distributed by Bradt Publications in the UK.

Guatemala for You, by Barbara Balchin de Koose; 1989; Editorial Piedra Santa; Guatemala City, Guatemala, and Bradt Publications, UK.

La Ruta Maya: Yucatán, Guatemala & Belize, by Tom Brosnahan; 1991; Lonely Planet, Australia.

A Guide to Ancient Maya Ruins, revised ed., by C. Bruce Hunter; 1986; University of Oklahoma Press; Norman, Oklahoma.

Let's Go Mexico, by Harvard Student Agnecy, Inc; updated yearly; St. Martin's Press; New York.

Mexico & Central American Handbook, edited by Ben Box; Trade & Travel Publications; Bath, England. Distributed in the U.S. by Rand McNally. Updated yearly.

MISCELLANEOUS TECHNICAL PUBLICATIONS

Beard, J.S., 1955. "The classification of tropical American vegetation types. *Ecology* 36(1):89-100.

Berlin, B., *et al*, 1974. *Principles of Tzeltal Plant Classification: An Introduction to the Botanical Ethnography of a Mayan-Speaking People of Highland Chiapas*. Academic Press, New York.

Breedlove, D., 1981. *Introduction to The Flora of Chiapas*. Cambridge University Press.

Duellman, W.E., 1966. "The Central American herpetofauna: An ecological perspective." *Copeia* (4):700-719.

Folan, William J., *et al*. 1983. "Paleoclimatological Patterning in Mesoamerica." *Journal of Field Archeology*, vol. 10, pp. 453-468.

Gunn, Joel, and Richard E. W. Adams. 1981. "Climatic Change,

Culture and Civilization in North America." *WA*, vol 13, pp. 87-100.

Standley, P.C., 1930. "Flora of Yucatán." *Field Mus. Nat. Hist., Botany Series* 3: 157-492. (Taxonomy frequently outdated)

Standley, P. C. *et al*, 1946-77. "Flora of Guatemala," 13 parts, illustrated. *Fieldiana, Botany*, 24. (Taxonomy frequently outdated)

Stoddart, D.R. *et al.*, 1963. "A Checklist of the herpetofauna of Guatemala." *Univ. Michigan Mus. Zool. Misc. Publ. #22*, Ann Arbor.

Stolze, R. G., 1976-81. "Ferns and fern allies of Guatemala." *Fieldiana, Botany*, 39, N.S. 6.

Suarez, Jorge A., 1983. *The Mesoamerican Indian Languages*. Cambridge University Press.

Wasserstrom, R., 1983. *Class and Society in Central Chiapas*. University of California Press.

INDEX

Acapulquito 107
acorn woodpeckers 167
agriculture, Maya 79
Agua Azul 251
Aguateca 201
Aguilar, Gerónimo de 75, 134
Altar de Sacrificios 201
Altun Ha 164
Alvarado, Pedro de 75, 227, 228
Amatenango del Valle 248
Ambergris Caye 170
Antigua (Guatemala) 212, 223
archeology, amateur 51
army ants 8
army checkpoints 194
Atitlán grebe 227
automobile travel 13
Aztecs 82

"baboons" 171
"baboon sanctuary" 170
Bacalar 146
backpacks 21
Balankanche Cave 130
ball courts 85
banana plantation 215
Banco Chinchorro 147
Barrier Reef 152, 169
Becan 100
bee stings 42
Belize 151
Belize Audubon Society 177
Belize City 169
Belize Zoo 175
Benque Viejo 182
Bermudian Landing 170
Bethel (Chiapas) 262
bicycle travel 14
bird watching 52
birds, Uxmal area 119
Blom, Trudy 243

Bolonchén Cave 113
Bonampak 238, 258
books, finding Ruta Maya topics 57
books written by the Maya 72
Books of Chilam Balam 72
bots 43
bromeliads 63
bus travel 17

Cahal Pech 180
Cakchiquel Maya 227-229
Calakmul 105
Calakmul Biosphere Reserve 103, 105
Campeche (town) 107
Cancún 132
campsites, choosing 35
car travel 13
Caracol 180
Carib villages 153
Cascades of Agua Azul 251
Caste War 146
Castillo de San Felipe 214
Catherwod, Frederick 75
causeways 86
Cave of the Inscriptions 207
Caye Caulker 170
Ceibal 201
Celestún 122
Cenote Azul 147
Center for Disease Control 39
Cerro Cahui Biotope 205
Cerro de Huitepec 241
Cerros 158
chachalaca 8
Chacón-Machaca Biotope 214
Chalchihuitán 248
Champotón 106, 128
Chamula 247
chayote 30

Chenalhó 248
Chenes style 108
Chetumal 145
Chiapas 233
Chicaná 102
Chichén Itzá 60, 127
Chichicastenango 212
chicle 190
chicleros 190, 193, 196
chicozapote 196
chiggers 44
Chilam Balam 72
Chinkultic 239
Chiquimula 218
cholera 38
Ciudad Cuauhtémoc 236
clothing 23
cloud forests 210
Clovis people 78
coati 163
Cobá 143
Cobán (Guatemala) 224
coconut palm 55
codices 72
Coe, Michael D. 75
cohune palm 149
Columbus, Christopher 65
Comitán 236
commensalism 222
Community Baboon Sanctuary (Belize) 170
continental drift 59
Copán (ruins) 216
Copán Ruinas (town) 219
corbelled vault 85, 253
corn 80
Corozal (Belize) 156
Corozal (Chiapas) 265
Cortés, Hernán 75, 228
Cotzumalhuapan style 215
Coxcomb Range 152
Cozumel Island 134
Cozumel vireo 135
Creole language 154
Creole people 153

Crooked Tree Wildlife Sanctuary (Belize) 163
Cruzob cult 146
Cuello 159

diarrhea 37
Díaz del Castillo, Bernal 65, 75, 134
Dos Pilas 200
Dresden Codex 72
dysentery 38
Dzibalchén 110
Dzibilchaltún 121
Dzibilnocac 112

ear fungus 46
eco-tourism, definition 1
ecology, tropical 55, 63
Edzna 107
ejidos 74, 97
El Ceibal 201
El Cruce (Petén) 205
El Mirador 81, 82
El Rancho 225
El Relleno 214
El Tajín 86
elotes 30
encomienda system 70
epiphytes 63
Escárcega 106

Finca Ixobel 206
flamingos 123
Flores 128, 195
food 27
forest zones 210
Fray Bartolomé Library 243
fruit biology 64

garifuna 153
gastroenteritis 37
geological history 59
gifts 4
goals 51
grebe, Atitlán 227

Grijalva, Juan de 75
Gringo Perdido (campsite) 205
Grutas de San Cristóbal 248
Guanacaste Park 174
guanacaste tree 34
Guatemala 209
Guatemala/Chiapas border 230
Guatemala City 212
Guatemalan uplands 212
Guerrero, Gonzalo 75
gumtree 95

heat stroke 42
henequen 121
hepatitis A 41
Hernández de Córdoba, Francisco 65, 75
Hochob 111
Honduras 218
Hopelchén 110
Hormiguero 102
howler monkey 171, 173, 184, 255
Huehuetenango 212, 229
huisquil 30

ice age 77, 217
iguana 164
incense 217
intestinal worms 46
Isthmus of Tehuantepec 234
Itzá 84, 128, 197
Iximché 227
Izamal 121

jade 209
jadeite 209
jocote 219
"jungles" 183

Kabáh 118
Kaminaljuyú 82, 225
kinkajou 177
Kohunlich 147
Kukulcan 83

La Bastille, Anne 227
Labná 116
Lacandón forest 72, 234
Lacandón people 197, 259, 262
Lacanhá 261
Lago Atitlán 212, 227
Lago Petén Itzá 84, 128, 205
Laguna de Bacalar 147
Laguna de Silvituc 94
Laguna Petexbatún 200
Lagunas de Montebello National Park 236
Lamanai 161
Landa, Fray Diego de 76, 121
language schools 223
La Venta 81
leaf-cutter ants 58
leaves, deciduous vs persistent 63
lichens 222
Lívingston (Guatemala) 214
logwood 152
Loltún Cave 117
Loma Bonita cascades 239
long count calendar 81, 83, 214

mace 48
Madrid Codex 72
malaria 39
Malinche 134
Mam Maya 229
manioc 30
mango trees 219
mangrove 94
maps 11
Mario Dary Rivera Quetzal Reserve 221
Maudslay, Alfred 76
Maya agriculture 79
Maya archaic culture 78
Maya architecture 85
Maya art 87
Maya ball game 85
Maya Bell campground 253

Maya Classic Period 81
Maya empire extinction theories
   66
Maya first European contact 65
Maya languages 73, 74
Maya Mountains 152, 174
Maya Postclassic Period 83
Maya postconquest history 70
Maya Preclassic Period 80
Maya prehistory 77
Maya timescale chart 69
Mayapán 84, 128
Melchor de Mencos 185
mercados 29
Mérida 120
Mesoamerican culture 78
mestizos 153
Misol-Ha 252
Mitla 235
Mitontic 248
monkeys 171, 255
Monte Albán 235
Montes Azules Biosphere
   Reserve 234, 239
Montezuma's revenge 37
mosses 224
Montagua Valley 60, 209
murals 89
mutualism 222
mutualistic symbiosis 222

Na-Bolom 243
Naj Tunich 207
Nakum 192
Naranjo (Chiapas) 256
Naranjo (Guatemala) 187
nephrite 209
Nohcacab 113
Nohmul 161
Northern Lowlands 62

obsidian 210
Ocosingo 249
okra 219
Olmecs 81

Orange Walk 159
orchids 63

paca 176
Palenque 252
paleoclimatology 60, 61
Panajachel 212, 227
Panti Trail 179
parasitism 222
Parque Nacional de El Rosario
   202
Parques en Peligro 124
Payucan 107
peonage 71
peperomias 63
Petén 183
Petén roads 188
Petexbatún 200
photographing 52, 245
plant succession 56
Playa del Carmen 133
Pleistocene hunters 78
pollination biology 63
Popol Vuh 72
Poptún 206
Programme for Belize 153
PRONATURA 124, 125
PRONATURA Nature Reserve
   241, 242
Proyecto Flamencos 124
Punta Allen 142
Punta Laguna 132
Puuc style 108
pyramids 85

quetzal 221
quetzal reserve 221
Quetzalcóatl 83
Quezaltenango 212
Quiché Maya 227
Quintana Roo 132
Quiriguá 214

rabies 40
rain forests 63, 64, 210

rehydration solution 37
repartimiento system 71
Reserva Ecológica PRONATURA 241, 242
Ría Celestún Special Biosphere Reserve 122
Río Azul 82
Río Bec 104
Río Bec style 108
Río Dulce 214
Río Lacanhá 260
Río Lagartos 124
Río Motagua 209
Río Pasión 199
robbery 48
Ruta Maya, geography 62

sacbe 86
salt collecting 123
San Andrés 247
San Cristóbal, caves 248
San Cristóbal de las Casas 239
San Gervasio 138
San Ignacio 178
San Juan Chamula 247
Santa Elena (border) 155
Santa Elena (by Flores) 198
Santa Elena (by San Ignacio) 178
Santa Rita 157
savannahs 183
Sayaxché 199
Sayil 116
scorpions 45
Seibal 201
Seyba Playa 107
shate 224
Sian Ka'an Biosphere Reserve 142
Sierra de los Cuchumatanes 229
Sierra de las Minas 60, 209
slash-and-burn 56, 67, 79
sleeping bags 22
sleeping strategies 33
snakes 44
Southern Uplands 62

Spanish, handy sentences 55
Spanish, handy words 5
Spanish, learning 54, 222
starchy staples 30
stelae 83
Stephens, John L. 76
strangler figs 95
stucco 85, 89
Subteniente Lopez 147
succession, plant 56
sugar cane harvest 156
sweetcorn 30
sweetgum trees 217
sweet potatoes 30
sugar cane, how to eat 2
sunburn 42
symbiosis 222

Tabasqueño 113
Tahcob 113
Tajumulco Volcano 62
tarantulas 46
Taysal 84, 197
Tecpán 228
temple façades 85
temple-pyramids 85
teosinte 80
Teotihucan 81, 82
tepescuintle 176
Thompson, J.Eric S. 76
ticks 43
Tikal 203
tipping 33
tobacco cultivation 219
Toltecs 83
Toniná 250
Topoxte 192
tortillas 28
toucans 257
train travel 16
tree ferns 223
trogons 221
Tula 83
Tulum 140
Tulum National Park 141

turtles 125
Tuxtla Gutiérrez 240
Tzeltal Maya 234
Tzotzil Maya 234, 242, 243

Uaxactún 204
Usumacinta river trip 200
Uxmal 119

Valladolid 125
vegetation zones 62
veneer masonry 116
Victoria Peak 152
vines 63
Volcán de Fuego 62

water-lily motif 88
weather, ancient 60

"X," pronunciation 96
Xcaret 139
Xela 212
Xelha 139
Xlapak 116, 118
Xpuhil 99
Xtacambilxunan Cave 113
Xunantunich 181

Yaxchilán 201, 263
Yaxhá 191
yuca 30
Yucatán, discovery 65

Zaculeu 229
Zapotec 234
Zinacantán 245
ziricote tree 158
zoomorphs 215